RACE, CULTURE AND MEDIA

SAGE was founded in 1965 by Sara Miller McCune to support the dissemination of usable knowledge by publishing innovative and high-quality research and teaching content. Today, we publish over 900 journals, including those of more than 400 learned societies, more than 800 new books per year, and a growing range of library products including archives, data, case studies, reports, and video. SAGE remains majority-owned by our founder, and after Sara's lifetime will become owned by a charitable trust that secures our continued independence.

Los Angeles | London | New Delhi | Singapore | Washington DC | Melbourne

RACE, CULTURE AND MEDIA

ANAMIK SAHA

Los Angeles | London | New Delhi
Singapore | Washington DC | Melbourne

Los Angeles | London | New Delhi
Singapore | Washington DC | Melbourne

SAGE Publications Ltd
1 Oliver's Yard
55 City Road
London EC1Y 1SP

SAGE Publications Inc.
2455 Teller Road
Thousand Oaks, California 91320

SAGE Publications India Pvt Ltd
B 1/I 1 Mohan Cooperative Industrial Area
Mathura Road
New Delhi 110 044

SAGE Publications Asia-Pacific Pte Ltd
3 Church Street
#10-04 Samsung Hub
Singapore 049483

Editor: Michael Ainsley
Assistant editor: Ozlem Merakli
Production editor: Martin Fox
Copyeditor: Sarah Bury
Proofreader: Audrey Scriven
Indexer: Silvia Benvenuto
Marketing manager: Lucia Sweet
Cover design: Lisa Harper-Wells
Typeset by: KnowledgeWorks Global Ltd.
Printed in the UK

Library of Congress Control Number: 2020942888

British Library Cataloguing in Publication data

A catalogue record for this book is available from the
British Library

ISBN 978-1-5264-1918-7
ISBN 978-1-5264-1919-4 (pbk)

At SAGE we take sustainability seriously. Most of our products are printed in the UK using responsibly
sourced papers and boards. When we print overseas we ensure sustainable papers are used as measured
by the PREPS grading system. We undertake an annual audit to monitor our sustainability.

For Latika and Uma

PRAISE FOR *RACE, CULTURE AND MEDIA*

'With the publication of *Race, Culture and Media*, Anamik Saha has established himself as one of the leading critical theorists of race and the media. The book is at once both an original contribution to the fields of race, culture and media and also a comprehensive summation of the current debates. In short, there is no clearer introduction to the complex interrelations between race, culture and media available today. *Race, Culture and Media*, guides the reader through the contested and, at times, contradictory role of the media in "race-making", as Saha expertly summarizes key debates from postcolonial theory, to the political and cultural economy of the media. With carefully chosen case studies, up-to-date examples, and clear summaries of key concepts, as well as guides to further reading, *Race, Culture and Media* will be an invaluable resource for both teachers and students, interested in the latest research in media and communication studies.'

Ben Carrington, Associate Professor of Sociology and Journalism, University of Southern California

CONTENTS

ABOUT THE AUTHOR

Dr Anamik Saha is Senior Lecturer in Media and Communications at Goldsmiths, University of London, where he convenes the MA Race, Media and Social Justice. After completing his PhD in Sociology at Goldsmiths, Anamik worked in the Institute of Communication Studies at the University of Leeds, firstly as an ESRC Post-Doctoral Research Fellow, then as a Lecturer in Communications. He has held visiting fellowships at Massachusetts Institute of Technology and Trinity College, Connecticut.

Anamik's research interests are in race and the media, with a particular focus on cultural production and the cultural industries in relation to broader issues of commodification and racial capitalism. His work has been published in journals including *Media, Culture and Society*, *Ethnic and Racial Studies*, and *Ethnicities*. With David Hesmondhalgh (2013) he co-edited a special issue of *Popular Communication* on race and ethnicity in cultural production, and with Dave O'Brien, Kim Allen and Sam Friedman (2017) he co-edited a special issue of *Cultural Sociology* on inequalities in the cultural industries. In 2019 he became an editor of the *European Journal of Cultural Studies*.

Anamik's first book *Race and the Cultural Industries* (Polity) was published in 2018. In 2019 he received an Arts and Humanities Research Council Leadership Fellow grant for a project entitled 'Rethinking Diversity in Publishing', which led to a report published by Goldsmiths Press in June 2020. His research has featured across a range of media, including *BBC Radio*, *The Guardian*, *TES* and *New Statesman*.

PREFACE

I finished this book half-way through 2020, a turbulent and era-defining year. Both the Covid-19 pandemic, resulting in a disproportionate number of 'BAME' deaths, and the #BlackLivesMatter protests, reignited by the murder of George Floyd at the hands of the Minneapolis Police Department, highlight how dispensable black and brown lives remain. It has also produced a profound reckoning with race in Western societies in particular, a process that such societies have tried their best to deny.

While the question of media might feel trivial when we are literally talking about life and death, media are absolutely central to the way that these two moments are made sense of and understood, and as a consequence, our responses to them. Corporate news media continue to set, or indeed limit, the agendas and frames within which we discuss these issues. But audiences – especially those on the margins – can influence these agendas in unprecedented ways thanks to social media. Indeed, both the Covid pandemic and #BlackLivesMatter highlight media's contradictory tendencies. For instance, the accessibility of new digital technologies exposes the brutalisation of racialised people at the hands of the police or white supremacists, which are first circulated online and then broadcast on national and global media, leading to the perpetrators to meet a measure of – if not full – justice. But the mediated nature of the racial tragedy that unfolds leads to the further *spectacularisation* of black death, reduced to media content that becomes normalised as well as commodified as it circulates through media. As another example, media and cultural institutions, whether public or corporate, were quick to release statements that demonstrated their support for the #BlackLivesMatter movement. But to what extent does this represent genuine solidarity and understanding? The apparent consensus around racism as a real material force that structures life experience as articulated through these branded messages certainly feels novel, especially in this supposed *postrace* era. Yet the same actions have been read as performative, disingenuous at best, ideological at worst, that hides the way such institutions continue to exclude and exploit those racialised as Other. It remains to be seen whether this moment leads to meaningful change. Such a contradiction is arguably a mere fact of racial capitalism.

The very utterance of *Black Lives Matter* demonstrates how black lives in particular are undervalued. But media texts – especially when authored by racialised Others – can help restore humanity precisely to those who have been denied it. This is why media, and culture, matter for our understanding of race. Moreover, centralising issues of race and culture can produce valuable, or indeed, *undervalued* knowledges about the very role and operation of media in capitalist societies in particular. The study of these issues is in fact incredibly revealing about the current conjuncture and modern society in general, beyond the question of race alone. The aim of the book is to pull out these strands and deepen our understanding of the interrelations between race, culture and media. The stress is on complexity, contestation and contradiction, but in a way that does not pull its punches with regard to how racialised groups are treated by and experience media.

Anamik Saha
London, July 2020

ACKNOWLEDGEMENTS

Thank you to Sage for inviting me to write this book in the first place. I was not sure I had the capability to write such a book but I am glad I was given the opportunity to do so. I want to especially thank my editor Michael Ainsley for his encouragement and enthusiasm for the project, and for his patience when the writing would invariably slow down. I hope Arsenal can bring us both some happiness again soon!

All the people who have shaped my work – and continue to do so – were acknowledged in my first book *Race and the Cultural Industries*. But I need to thank those who contributed directly to this book, either through reading drafts, recommending readings, or helping me hone my arguments. This includes Daniel Burdsey, Angela McRobbie, David Morley, Dhiraj Murthy, Clive Nwonka, Gavan Titley, Priya Sharma and Francesca Sobande. I want to acknowledge also my colleagues at Goldsmiths, including in the Department of Media, Communication and Cultural Studies where I work, who are resisting the marketisation of higher education and are fighting institutional racism in all its forms.

I want to thank all the students on the MA Race, Media and Social Justice programme – past and present – who I have learnt so much from and who keep me on my toes! Special thanks also to my co-convenor Brett St Louis for being such a brilliant colleague.

Finally, all the love in the world to my family for their unwavering unconditional love and support. This book would not have been possible without them.

Part I
Introduction

1

Race, Culture and Media

What is the relationship between race and culture, and what is media's role in this relation?

Why 'race' and not 'ethnicity'?

Why does it matter how racialised groups are represented in media?

Why 'how media make race' instead of 'how media represent race'?

1.1 Introduction

How we live with difference remains a key issue of our time. While societies become more complex and heterogenous in character, Western nations continue to be stratified along the lines of race – economically, politically, socially. What role does media play in maintaining these racial hierarchies? The fact remains that minorities have received and continue to receive negative media treatment: the demonisation of black youth and Muslims (veiled or otherwise), the sexualisation of women of colour, the dehumanisation of migrants/refugees, and the exoticisation and simultaneous denigration of East and South Asian culture. Alongside the ongoing *silencing and stereotyping* of those racialised as Other in 'traditional' media, we see rampant forms of racism on the new, relatively unregulated digital platforms in both content and commentary. Yet is this the whole picture? On the other side of the coin media undeniably play a vital role for racial and ethnic groups, creating a sense of community and togetherness (in the face of marginalisation and exclusion) within a diaspora, over space and time. Moreover, and perhaps most crucially, media can produce forms of commonality across difference, offering new models of cultural interaction, providing images, words and sounds – and indeed feelings, emotions and *affects* – that point us towards how we can better live together.

The purpose of this book is to explore this apparent contradiction of media that both oppresses and enables those regarded as racial Others. To stress, this is more than simply stating that Western media's treatment of migrant and post-migrant populations is either negative or positive. Rather, it understands media as a site of ideological struggle – where race, or rather ideas of race, are constantly being made and remade. Capturing the full complexity of this process entails an analysis of the dynamics of culture itself. Influenced by the British cultural studies tradition (that I unpack in more detail shortly) in addition to critical political economy approaches to culture (see the next chapter), this book conceptualises culture as the sphere through which power is secured and where the racial hierarchies that characterise the nation state are maintained. But that is not to say that media as part of the cultural sphere is nothing more than a mere instrument of the dominant culture – that is, the group that has the most power in society (in Western contexts this usually means white and middle-class) – to maintain its status and privilege. As suggested, media is also the space where alternative discourses around difference can emerge that challenge common-sense understandings of race, in the process unsettling and destabilising the dominant culture. The challenge for any scholar of race and media therefore is how to develop a nuanced analysis of media that recognises complexity and ambivalence without softening the critique of media's role in reinforcing racial ideologies.

With this book I provide an in-depth analysis of the complex relations between race, culture and media, which takes each of these dimensions – and their interconnections – equally seriously. This entails a detailed discussion of the cultural forms of racism(s), and the making of race and culture more generally in their institutional and everyday contexts. It also requires an exploration of the dynamics of media and the cultural industries at the levels of production, distribution and consumption, and an examination of media's relation to the state, capitalism and empire. To think through the complexity, contestedness and ambivalence of media (Hesmondhalgh, 2018) in its treatment of race, my approach is framed around the question of how *media make race*. As I will show, the conceptualisation of race, culture and media in this way stresses how the representation of race in media is a form of power/knowledge that maintains the dominance of whiteness, albeit based on a hierarchy that is always under contestation.

The purpose of this first chapter is to introduce the subject of race, culture and media, the meaning of these concepts, and why this topic is such an important one to study. While I focus more directly on the question of media in Chapter 2, in this first chapter I want to think through what a focus on culture brings to our understanding of race and racism. I begin by defining what I mean by 'race' – ethnicity – and culture, and how these concepts are interlinked, and media's role in these interrelations. The chapter then takes a slight detour and argues for why the study of media in relation to race and culture is so important, not just in the context of media studies, but for wider academic discussions (as well as activism) around race and racism. I then return to the issue of race and culture and think it through more explicitly in relation to the question of power, introducing the idea of media as 'race-making', which better captures the operation of power in relation to race and media.

1.2 Race (ethnicity) and culture

How to define 'race' and culture, how are they related and what role do media play in their making and being? The usual place to begin is with the notion that 'race' is a social construct rather than a biological fact (hence putting 'race' in scare quotes). While certain regions of the earth produce particular types of physical traits in particular groups of humans, there is in fact no scientific basis for the idea that there are different 'races'. Nevertheless, exposing the biological spuriousness of race has clearly not been enough to eradicate racism. Race-thinking has taken such a hold in Western society that even in these globalised times where societies become increasingly complex, heterogenous and mixed, common-sense understandings of race that place people into seemingly coherent, bounded groups based on supposedly shared physical or cultural traits are still difficult to shift. During the Covid-19 pandemic in the UK it was found that 'BAME' (that is, 'Black Asian Minority Ethnic') communities are at a greater risk of dying from the disease. But rather than leading to a close examination of the complex social factors at play in this tragic scenario, it has led to the further reinforcement the idea of biological differences between racial groups (Lentin, 2020). What I am referring to here is the *essentialist* version of race; that different racial groups have certain essential – biologically determined – qualities. Essentialist ideas of race are entrenched in society and, as I shall show in Chapter 5, embedded in the very idea of nation. Thus, if race has such dubious roots, why do we continue to use it as a unit of analysis? In other words, why frame this book in terms of race? Might ethnicity offer a more fruitful alternative?

1.2.1 Race 'versus' ethnicity

The modern conception of race – that is, how we understand race today – has its roots in the Enlightenment period in the eighteenth century. The Enlightenment was an intellectual and philosophical movement that emphasised reason and rationality (over superstition/religion) in understanding humanity and the world at large. As Enlightenment thinkers began ordering the natural world according to scientific methods, they applied the same approach to humankind itself. 'Race' became a category to arrange 'mankind' into groups who share biological features but also certain qualities (temperament, intelligence, physical attributes) that are handed down through descent. But in the context of the birth of capitalism and its expansion into the rest of the world through colonialism and empire, the idea of race became a justification to colonise, enslave and then segregate/stratify non-Western peoples. Different 'races' were placed in a hierarchy of superiority, topped by white European men who regarded themselves as the epitome of evolution and civilisation (and who happened to be the authors of these new systems of classification). This conception of race became embedded in the foundation of the modern nation state itself; as sociologist Ali Rattansi (2005: 284) puts it 'conceptions of race, and especially whiteness ... have in the modern period been central to the formation of Western states and even of the ideologies of liberalism that have underpinned the formation of the liberal democratic parliamentary polity'. In other words, Western liberal democracies – founded on the idea that *all 'men' are created equally* – have the idea of race (and by extension, whiteness) embedded into their very being (after all, without the idea of there being different races there would be no need to stress that all 'men' are equal). The point to underscore here is that while the urge to classify according to race has a social-psychological dimension, in that this is how humans make sense of the world (Downing and Husband, 2005), it was central also to the spread of capitalism and colonial conquest.

Bearing in mind the ideological basis of race and its lack of any scientific foundation why not just do away with race as a concept? As an alternative many academics have turned to 'ethnicity'. If race is based on untenable biological claims, ethnicity appears to be at least rooted in the material; ethnic groups are defined not in terms of shared genes, but in terms of a common language, religion, customs, geographical root. Thus, while race refers to biological traits, then ethnicity refers to the cultural. Indeed, 'ethnicity' has generally taken on positive (if not exoticised) connotations, for instance when we speak of *ethnic cuisine* or *ethnic clothing* (Cohen, 1999; Downing and Husband, 2005).[1] Yet advocating ethnicity on the grounds of its apparent materiality is too simplistic. Ethnicity, like race, is a social construct; that is, ways of seeing people as ethnic groups is a social process. As Downing and Husband (2005: 14) state, 'Ethnicity is a social construction that is readily and routinely politicised'. For Stuart Hall (2017b: 108), one of the most influential theorists of race, ethnicity and culture (see Box 1.1), ethnicity functions in the same 'discursive chain as race' and operates, like race, as a 'sliding signifier', that is the meaning of ethnicity slides between essentialist and anti-essentialist poles. The essentialist version of ethnicity is closed, and nationalistic in character, rooted in a discourse of *blood and soil* that is exclusionary – it attempts to define itself but is better at defining who does not belong. The anti-essentialist – or 'new ethnicities' (Hall, 1988) – version of ethnicity, on the other hand, is based on a conception of culture as hybrid, fluid, plural, that is constantly being made and remade. An important concept here is how meanings around race and ethnicity are contingent, that is, shaped by their social, economic and historical context.

In its 'new ethnicities' incarnation, ethnicity has value when it is conceptualised as fluid and mutable, which undermines the essentialist versions of ethnicity that underpins nationalist discourse. But the problem with ethnicity, or rather with how it is deployed, is in how it frequently – and unwittingly – slips into an essentialist understanding of culture, that is, the idea that people can be conveniently and neatly placed into homogeneous, ethnically determined groups. For the sociologist Claire Alexander (2018), ethnicity, particularly in social anthropological studies of minorities, too often becomes a marker of essential cultural difference (rather than a social category). When deployed uncritically ethnicity reproduces the notion that cultural differences are natural and fixed (Harindranath, 2005).[2] For critical race scholars Omi and Winant (2002), the turn to ethnicity in policy reconceptualises racism and racial injustice as the natural consequence of competing ethnic groups, rather than as built into social structures through which oppression along racial lines occurs.

Thus, ethnicity does not necessarily solve the problems encountered in using race. This does not mean we should outright reject ethnicity, however, and I will still refer to ethnicity throughout. Indeed, my approach to race and culture is underpinned by Stuart Hall's notion of 'new ethnicities' – as will be unpacked further in the following chapter. Nonetheless, I have chosen to frame this book as a critical approach to *race*. This understands that while race itself is an empty signifier, in that it contains no intrinsic meaning, it nonetheless contributes to the unequal stratification of society, alongside and intersected by dimensions of class, gender, sexuality and so on. Put more simply, while a social construct, 'race' still produces very real, material effects. Another key concept in this regard is 'racialisation', referring to the ways that ideas of race are inscribed onto certain groups, but also ideas, objects or cultural practices (for instance, think of the way that rap and grime are *racialised* as 'black' music genres). The racialisation of certain groups is what shapes their experiences and life chances, often for the worse.

Thus, race is not merely the way in which different groups are made distinguishable; in the West those who are racialised as Other are seen as inferior. Racialised groups are exploited in order to further expand capitalism and reinforce the dominant position of whiteness in the world. This was most evident during colonial times, but even now empire is formally over legacies of colonialism still structure the present and shape modern formations of race (the topic of Chapter 3). In other words, ideas of race are produced through power. But in order to fully understand exactly how this power operates – and media's implication within this – we need to address the issue of culture, as it is through culture that the floating signifier of race (after all, it is a social construct with no actual material basis) is fixed. This is the main argument of the cultural approach to race and racism, the contribution of which I map in the following section.

1.2.2 The cultural approach to race

Before the emergence of cultural studies, culture was seen as an object possessed only by the most privileged in society – think of opera, 'good' literature, and 'fine' wine.

Thus, the work of the early pioneers of British cultural studies represented an important intervention in drawing attention to how culture belongs to everyone, taking culture seriously in its ordinary, everyday (and essentially, working-class) forms (Hoggart, 1957; Williams, 2011 [1958]). In addition, following the influence of French structuralist thinkers such as Ferdinand de Saussure and Claude Lévi-Strauss, culture came to be understood as essentially the language through which we under-stand the world around us (drawing from French post-structuralists such as Roland Barthes and Louis Althusser, cultural studies scholars came to understand this as a historical process that is shaped by social change and the development of capitalism in particular). Yet it took a while for these insights from cultural studies to have an impact upon the study of race and racism.

The influential collection *The Empire Strikes Back* (1982) – featuring contribu-tions from students at the Birmingham Centre for Contemporary Cultural Studies (CCCS) including Hazel Carby, Paul Gilroy, Errol Lawrence, Pratibha Parmar and John Solomos – was one of the first texts to foreground race within a cultural stud-ies framework in a concerted way. It rejected the notion of 'racism as a unitary fixed principle' (Solomos et al., 1982: 10), as well as the assumption of 'races' as fixed, whole, bounded groups, which characterised the early sociological approaches to 'race relations'.[3] The contributors to the volume stressed that the meaning of race as a social construction is 'contested and fought over' (Back and Solomos, 2000: 8) and that racial identity, rather than leading only to a worsening of an individ-ual's life chances, can also act as a source of collectivity and resistance. *The Empire Strikes Back* was published during the cultural turn in the social sciences, the field of which was being transformed by the impact of feminism, postcolonial theory and post-structuralism and the new emphasis on culture and identity (Back and Solomos, 2000; Alexander 2018). It is from this moment that we see the emergence of what can be referred to as a critical cultural approach to race (see Back and Solo-mos, 2000: 19–22). In thinking through the changing forms of racism, scholars in this new tradition began to focus on the cultural dimension of racial discourse, including questions of cultural production and cultural consumption, and indeed, media. Again, this entailed challenging homogenous, uniform conceptualisations of racism and essentialist categorisations of race (and ethnicity), stressing cultural identity as fluid, hybrid and plural. But in addition, the new cultural approach to race established the representation of race in media and the arts as a key object of study in order to understand how meaning is attached to race and ethnicity and how such meanings change during over time (Hall, 1988). In other words, in the turn towards culture the question of media begins to feature more frequently in race research.

As stated, this book is broadly shaped by this critical cultural approach to race. It conceptualises the relations between race and culture (and media) in the follow-ing ways. As a starting point, race needs to be understood as an unstable entity that consists of multiple meanings that are constantly being made and remade through cultural and political struggle (Omi and Winant, 2002). In this sense, the construction of race – that is, what certain racial qualities are said to mean – is a historical process in that they change over time as a consequence of transformation through and within the political-economic and socio-cultural spheres. Unpacking the meanings attached to race necessitates a focus on culture – as culture is the language through which meaning is constructed – and by extension, representation. Representations (and our shared understanding of them) make up culture and how we create meaning. In other words, language works through representation (Hall, 1997a). Thus, representation – for instance, what we see in media – is crucial to the construction of meanings around race, and consequently our understanding of race. Representation, however, is never a mere mirror of society. Rather, shaped through discourse (and in turn, power and knowledge), representation constructs our sense of reality. This line of enquiry will be explored in more detail in the following chapter where I look at the emphasis on representation in media studies of race. But in a nutshell, the critical cultural approach to race, rather than striving to attain the real essence of what race is, instead focuses upon how race becomes a 'knowledge' that structures the world and lived experience. It entails a focus on how racial discourse creates a 'regime of truth' (Hall, 2017b: 81) around race. As Hall (ibid.: 52) says, our knowledge of race 'is itself discursively organised and produced', and this always entails a question of power. It follows that media, which is the major source for the production of representations in society, consequently plays a crucial role in constructing meanings around race. But before I unpack this further, I want to make a case for why this emphasis on culture and meaning-making in the study of race matters, especially for racism and social justice.

1.3 Race, media and social justice

To reiterate, the cultural representation of race *always* entails a question of power. The meanings attached to race through how particular groups are represented helps maintains racial hierarchies. This in the process reinforces the position of the dominant (that is, white, middle-class) culture who happen to own the means of cultural production, or *the cultural industries* (by which I mean the industries that make books, film, music, television and online cultural content) (Saha, 2018). But as Stuart Hall (1981) argues, and as I shall unpack further in the following section, the terrain of popular culture needs to be understood as a site of ideological struggle where counter-discourses of race can emerge that destabilise, undermine and work against dominant conceptions of race. The logic follows that the field of cultural production – within which media are the biggest institution – should be understood as a key arena in the struggle for racial equality. As I shall explore shortly, Hall (1981) himself uses Gramsci's notion of a 'politics of position' to define cultural political action in this way.

However, for some activists and academics of race and racism an emphasis on media and representation (and especially popular culture) is regarded as a somewhat trivial matter in the fight against racial oppression. Is this fair? As I shall demonstrate in Chapter 2, cultural and media studies of race that work exclusively at the level of text can unwittingly neglect the power structures and material contexts within which culture is made, and in the process ignore the actual realities of the communities being represented. But equally as problematic is a certain elitist attitude towards media and its products, where discussions of culture in relation to issues of race, gender, sexuality, ableism is dismissed as a form of 'identity politics' – even from the political Left. Cultural theorist Andrew Ross (1998: 191), for instance, scorns the social Left's 'knee-jerk disdain for the "cretinizing" effect of popular culture' and its 'dogmatic repudiation of identity politics'. I would add that this is not unique to the (white) Left but also to sections of the anti-racist movement, who believe that a focus on media and popular culture in relation to race is at best inconsequential, and at worst frivolous and a distraction from the very real forms of economic exploitation and racial subjugation that define people's experience (see anti-racist activist and theorist Ambalavaner Sivanandan (1990) for the best example of the critique of *culturalist* approaches to race). While I sympathise with this argument (especially in relation to the weaker forms of media/cultural studies of race that I just alluded to), I nonetheless want to make a case for why the way that racialised groups are treated in media matters, explicitly in relation to social justice – an issue that media and communications scholars of race could engage with more directly.

Social justice has been generally understood in terms of policies and strategies that facilitate economic redistribution, where social justice is defined in terms of wealth and income and ensuring economic equality (Young, 2011). This is a particular Leftist approach to social justice. However, for feminists, anti-racists, and queer activists, while economic need is of course important, actions based solely on class politics do not necessarily attend to the very specific types of oppressions that women, people of colour and sexual minorities face that entail forms of cultural stigmatisation. As such, discussions of social justice, especially since the cultural turn, have increasingly turned into what critical theorist Nancy Fraser (2008) describes as a stand-off between the 'politics of redistribution' (of goods and resources and wealth) and the 'politics of recognition' (which respects difference, where minorities are no longer expected to assimilate to dominant/majority culture/norms).

But for Fraser this is a false dichotomy (see also Ross, 1998) for two main reasons. First, matters of social justice are much more complex than a crude opposition between class politics and identity politics, not least since each side can contain differing positions within it. For instance, the politics of recognition can encompass antipodal political positions based on either 'essentialist' (e.g. black nationalist) and 'anti-essentialist' (e.g. 'queer') conceptions of culture, while the politics of redistribution cannot always be reduced to just class (for instance, addressing the gender pay gap). Secondly, as long as there exist different social groups, different forms of justice are required to fix the specific oppressions and marginalisations that these groups face (Young, 2011). The fact is, in modern times, society is stratified in complex ways, by class and social identities, and as a consequence social justice is never just attained by attending to purely distributive or purely social forms justice. There are multiple forms of oppressions, with their own dynamics, which are separate from, but also interact with class oppression. Thus, an effective social justice programme is *intersectional* and entails dealing with the specific ways that social groups experience different forms of oppressions, using the appropriate economic and cultural remedies as necessary.

What role does media then play then for social justice in relation to race? Iris Marion Young (2011: 20) conveniently for our purposes, uses a case of media and race in her argument for the need to broaden conceptions of social justice:

> Black critics claim that the television industry is guilty of gross injustice in its depiction of Blacks. More often than not, Blacks are represented as criminals, hookers, maids, scheming dealers, or jiving connivers. Blacks, rarely appear in roles of authority, glamour or virtue. Arab Americans are outraged at the degree to which television and film present recognisable Arabs only as sinister terrorists or gaudy princes, and conversely that terrorists are nearly always Arab. Such outrage at media stereotyping issues in claims about the injustice not of material distribution, but of cultural imagery and symbols.

Thus for Young (2011: 26), the demand for non-stereotypical media representation of racial and ethnic groups represents 'nondistributive forms of justice' that includes 'the symbols, images, meanings, habitual comportments, stories and so on through which people express their experience and communicate with each other' (ibid.: 23). This points clearly to the role of media. But while Young is referring to the symbolic, the question of social justice in relation to media and race must also necessitate addressing the racial inequalities *within* the cultural industries (Saha, 2018). Echoing Young, Mark Banks' (2017: 4) conception of '*creative* justice' similarly argues that distributive justice has a cultural aspect. In the context of cultural and creative industries, Banks argues that 'people should have similar opportunities to obtain recognition, and to express or represent themselves and their world-views and interests'. He adds that creative justice entails a 'parity of participation' – that is, the right to political participation. Framed in this way, creative justice is based on ensuring that everyone has access to media, in order to develop 'the cultural industries as democratic arenas where minority and marginalised groups can advance their own fair representation and secure a more equal share of the public communicative space'. For Banks, the monopolisation of the key gatekeeper roles in media by a privileged (white) elite, who have 'the most prestigious cultural education and training, the highest pay and the best (or indeed any) kind of cultural industry job' is a form of injustice. To sum up, following Young and Banks, a social justice programme for race and media entails non-distributive forms of justice that work at the level of the symbolic and at the level of production. While I have not in this section explored consumption, as the book unfolds it will become apparent how inequalities in access to certain types of creative goods (O'Brien et al., 2017) is also a form of injustice that needs tackling.

By framing my discussion of the cultural representation of race in media in terms of social justice I am effectively making a case for why this is an important *political* issue – a notion that I have suggested is difficult to swallow for some activists. But on the other hand, this is an argument that is somewhat taken for granted by members of the so-called 'Woke' generation. Just a cursory glance of Twitter (if you dare) sees the 'negative' portrayal of racial and ethnic minorities in popular culture and the news called out as a matter of gross injustice. From social media campaigns that expose 'white-washing' (using white actors to play non-white characters) to the lack of diversity in media (e.g. #oscarssowhite, #baftassowhite), to the air-brushing of black women on magazine covers to meet the beauty standards of white editors/audiences (in the year I write this, the musical artist Solange and actress Lupita N'yongo have both been on the receiving end of such treatment), how racialised groups are represented clearly matters, especially for a generation where media plays such a central role in their lives.

However, I am concerned by the way that the discourse around race and representation often plays out in these settings. Too often it overburdens popular culture with having to get representation 'right', whether its ensuring that everyone is represented (which can feel little more than a tick-boxing exercise) or that the representation of a particular racial group is 'authentic'. For Herman Gray (2013a: 772), discussion around the politics of representation is often problematically reduced to a question of visibility, where the 'cultural politics of diversity seeks recognition and visibility as the end itself'. Moreover, in this move to 'seek correctives to images and increased visibility for communities of colour' (ibid.), there is a danger that we simplify the politics of representation to a matter of redress. For instance, if we return to Young's quote above regarding the stereotyping of black people and Arabs, the logic follows that addressing this in the name of justice (in its non-distributive form) would entail reversing these stereotypes. But, as I will demonstrate, representational politics are so much complex than replacing 'negative' representations with 'positive' ones. On a personal note, I find it slightly troubling how critics on social media (including academics!) can so easily throw around assertions that a particular media representation of race in incorrect/inaccurate/stereotypical/false, including bold pronouncements around cultural appropriation or racial commodification/exploitation. My unease is around how the politics of 'hot-takes', which characterises so much online discussion through which our ideas of race are formed, does not do *justice* to the way that race actually is made to work in media.

With this book I encourage the reader to challenge these normative, common-sense assumptions about race and media, to reject simplistic black/white assertions around the representation of those racialised as Other, or calls for greater diversity/ visibility in media that appears to entail nothing more than ticking off boxes on a racial bingo card. Instead, I call for a critical account of race and media that is adequately attuned to the complexity of both the politics of race and the dynamics of media. In the final section I unpack this complexity through introducing the notion of how media 'makes race'.

1.4 From how media represent race to how media make race

In this chapter so far I have explored two issues: (1) What a focus on culture means for our understanding of race (and vice versa), and (2) why race, culture and media is such an important topic to study, that is, why it is a matter of social justice. To conclude this chapter, I want to introduce the notion of 'race-making' – which I borrow from Herman Gray (2016) – that I will argue best describes the dynamics/relations between race, media and culture. The notion of how media make race subsequently frames my analysis of race and media. Mirroring the approaches of Stuart Hall and Edward Said, I work with both the concepts of discourse and hegemony to explore the operations of power in relation to culture. As I will demonstrate, how media make race is a form of governmentality that allows the dominant culture to secure power hegemonically, through being able to effectively decide what ideas around race take hold – and become common sense – in society. These important concepts and theories will be unpacked in much more detail in Chapters 2 and 3, but I introduce the foundational ideas here.

Hegemony, following Italian Marxist Antonio Gramsci, describes how the rule of the powerful is maintained in industrial, capitalist society. Power is no longer secured through physical force but though gaining consent. This is not just purely based on the legitimation of the authority, but by, at times, incorporating the interests of subordinated groups even if this is detrimental to the rulers themselves. In this way, hegemony can be described as a system of ideas and practices which has to be maintained and constantly updated – and this is where media plays a key role. Through hegemonic power, these ideas and practices become 'common sense', disguising the fact that they are deeply ideological and work in favour of the dominant culture. However, as Stuart Hall (1981, 1996) stresses, hegemony is never fixed, and is always subject to struggle. It is fought over by a number of interests through a 'war of position', which is more strategic, protracted and tactical (in contrast to a 'war of manoeuvre' which is a full-frontal battle). As Hall (1996: 471) is eager to stress: 'cultural hegemony is never about pure victory or pure domination (that's not what the term means); it is never a zero-sum cultural game; it is always about shifting the balance of power in the relations of culture; it is always about changing the dispositions and the configurations of cultural power, not getting out of it'. In this way, media – and the field of culture more generally – are, as I have stated, a site of ideological struggle where hegemony is fought over by opposing sides. For Hall, this is a battle that we can never escape and that can never be won.

Alongside the concept of hegemony, my notion of media as race-making is underpinned by a discursive model of cultural power, and in particular what critical race scholar Barnor Hesse (2000: 29) calls 'racialised governmentalities'. Drawing from Michel Foucault's important concept of governmentality, Hesse coins the term 'racialised governmentalities' to describe how the racialised distinction between European and non-European is maintained through discourse, that is, power and knowledge. Put another way, racialised governmentalities refers to how ideas of race are managed and manipulated by the dominant culture to maintain their position of power. For Edward Said (1991 [1978]), also drawing from Foucault's notion of discourse, to constitute an object (for instance, 'the Orient' or 'the Muslim') is to have power over it. Thus, racialised governmentalities highlights how race is a discourse – a form of knowledge, a way of understanding. It in turn reveals how the West produces a body or archive of knowledges whereby the Other is constructed and made sense of 'politically, sociologically, ideologically, militarily and imaginatively' (ibid.: 3), that is, in all spheres of life. It follows that media play a key role in the construction of a knowledge around the racialised Other.

What I am arguing here is that how race appears/is portrayed/represented in media needs to be treated as an operation of power/knowledge for the advantage of the dominant culture (both economically and symbolically). The crucial point, however, is that this power is always under contestation through the very presence of the Other (this is an important argument of postcolonial theory that I explore in Chapter 3). While, for theoretical purists, 'hegemony' and 'discourse' are incompatible concepts – Gramsci is referring to direct, fully-frontal antagonisms between classes, whereas Foucault refuses to name the sides of opposition and describes a struggle that is much more tactical, local and horizontal – as Hall (1997c: 261) contends, these theoretical positions can go together, based on their shared interest in how power operates in terms of 'knowledge, representation, ideas, cultural leadership and authority, as well as economic constraint and physical coercion'. Moreover, the concepts of hegemony and governmentality/discourse understands that power does not operate as a simplistic top-down monopoly; the dominant culture is positioned within power just as much as the dominated. As such, as Hall once again emphasises, power is never fixed; rather it is productive and circulates. It is such a model of power that we need to apply to our analysis of race and media.

This model of power also stresses that cultural representation is complex, and ambivalent. For Omi and Winant (2002: 75), the contemporary racial formation is made up of a series of racial projects which are contradictory, different in scale – and they are not all racist; as they state, 'Today, racial hegemony is "messy"'. Indeed, the case studies that feature in Part III of this book will show precisely how different racial and ethnic groups are represented in different media contexts that do not always make up a coherent racial formation. The ideological construction of race in media is complex and at times contradictory. Goldberg (2009b) argues that there are multiple *racisms* (that is, different forms of racist expressions), stressing how discourses of race exist within a particular political framework and that such discourses are never fixed, and are located in specific times and contexts, albeit inter-related. Racialised discourse sets the social conditions for different forms of racisms to emerge. As such he wants to focus on how different versions of 'racism' have been used at different times and in what ways and what meanings have been attached to it. But if this stresses too much mess, too much contingency, we need to remind ourselves of Hall's (1985, 1997c) argument that despite the broadening in the regime of representation, there is still a very narrow ideological frame within which race appears. This is why hegemony is such a key concept as it grounds our discussion within the struggle between the powerful and the less powerful (including those racialised as Other).

In light of these critiques, rather than talk about how race is 'represented', we need to reframe our focus in terms of how race *is made* in media. This better captures the complexity of the cultural politics of race, without losing sight of power and the ideological role of the cultural industries. Thinking through how media make race prevents the discussion of representation from slipping into a simplistic politics of redress – based on problematic binaries of positive/negative, authentic/stereotypical, truthful/false – as it does not assume that there is a 'right' way to represent minorities. Moreover, it emphasises how race consists of multiple meanings that are contested and fought over, and can in fact be mobilised for progressive means, or indeed for a radical programme in the name of social justice – as the contributors to *Empire Strikes Back* (Centre for Contemporary Cultural Studies, 1982) once argued. I will unpack this notion of how race is made by media further in the next chapter.

But to finish this final section I want to underline that designing studies of race and media in relation to this notion of media as race-making entails an approach that tackles together political economy, representation and audiences, and the technologies through which these dimensions are shaped and linked in order to better understand how and why media discourses of race circulate in the way that they do. We need to understand how texts work together to produce particular different types of discursive formations around race that emphasise certain (racist) meanings. We also need to take seriously how audiences interpret texts and use them in the everyday, and how they can create meanings that potentially contradict the ones they were encoded with in the first place. This notion of encoding leads us onto a third issue: the relatively neglected area of cultural production, and how cultural industries quite literally make representations of race as embodied in cultural commodities like television sitcoms, films, podcasts, music videos, web series and so on, and how these are shaped both by legacies of empire and the logics of capitalistic production. There is also the question of the digital, which has radically transformed how media is produced and consumed, but also how race is made through an assemblage of hardware and software technologies. What I am arguing is that we need to treat 'race-making' and how media make race as a form of power/knowledge (Gray, 2016: 249), which is the way the dominant culture maintains control, but is also the means through which the dominated can contest this power.

1.5 Conclusion

In this chapter I have introduced the concepts of race and culture and how they are related. I have outlined the cultural approach to race that understands culture as the sphere where ideas about race are made and circulate that reinforce the racial hierarchies that characterise Western society, but is also the sphere where such ideas are challenged/transformed. In this way I outlined why the study of race, culture and media needs to be framed as an issue of social justice. How racial and ethnic minorities appear in media, even in the seemingly most benign forms of popular culture, nonetheless shape and contribute to our understandings of particular racial and ethnic groups and the society we live in, as well as their lived experience. But the politics that emerge from this are so much more complex than we sometimes allow for, and the purpose of this book is to underline the complexity, contradiction and ambivalence at the core of representational politics. For this reason we need a shift from how race is *represented*, which too easily slips into conceptualising representation in terms of simplistic notions of positive/negative or a presence/lack, to a notion of how race *is made* by media, which underscores how the making of ideas of race is a historical, ongoing and contingent process, a form of power/knowledge, shaped by capitalism and legacies of empire.

In this first of two chapters that makes up Part I, I have outlined a cultural approach to race and explained the rationale for why a new critical approach to studying race, culture and media is needed. In Part II of this book I will flesh out in more detail what this approach will look like. But to conclude Part I, in the following chapter I will provide a critical review of how race has been tackled in media studies, highlighting the strengths of particular strands of research that I will draw from, as well as the gaps that this book will attempt to fill. Specifically, it will make a more sustained case for understanding the relations between race, culture and media as a process of race-making.

BOX 1.1 Key Thinker

Introducing Stuart Hall

In any book on race, culture and media the work of cultural theorist of Stuart Hall (1932–2014) is going to feature predominantly, and his legacy deserves reflecting upon. Stuart Hall is recognised as one of the founding figures of cultural studies (he was director of the Birmingham Centre for Contemporary Cultural Studies (CCCS)). Moreover, he was one of the first British scholars to take both the question of media *and* race seriously – at a time when both topics were of marginal interest.

Born in Jamaica to a middle-class black family, Hall came to the UK to study at Oxford. While he encountered colourism in Jamaican society (his mother looked down on him for the fact he was darker than this siblings), it was in England that he first encountered the experience of being 'black', or rather, having black bestowed upon him. This would shape his intellectual interests and work.

As a theorist and activist Hall was deeply involved in the politics of the New Left and he wrote many important texts on culture and capitalism. Indeed, Hall was a key figure in the birth of British media studies, with his interest in the ideological role of media in sustaining the position of the dominant culture through the control of cultural hegemony. It was in the 1980s that Hall starts tackling the issue of race in a more concerted way (though in his biography *Familiar Stranger* (Hall, 2017a) he describes how race was always the lens through he would critically examine and unpack a given social formation). While his initial writing on race (1980, 1985) was framed by his interest in post-Marxist theory, including the work of Antonio Gramsci and Louis Althusser (exemplified in *Policing the Crisis*, which he wrote with colleagues from the CCCS; Hall et al., 2013 [1978]), in the 1990s, under the increasing influence of post-structuralism, and inspired by the emergence of a new generation of black and Asian filmmakers and visual artists, Hall starts exploring the politics of culture, identity and diaspora. His 'New Ethnicities' (1988) essay in particular marked a critical intervention in the study of race and racism – which until then had been dominated by the sociologically-oriented race-relations paradigm – as it drew attention to culture in the making of race. For Hall, race, far from a natural category, is a signifier that produces very real, material effects, but is always ongoing, always under contestation, and manifests in society, to use a famous Hall phrase, without guarantees.

Stuart Hall's work effectively spawned the critical cultural approach to race, and made media a key site of enquiry. But more than that, he demonstrated how studying race, culture and media does not just deepen our understanding of racial dynamics in society, but the very nature of the current conjuncture as whole. Even after his death Hall's work remains a vital source of understanding for what is unfolding in the world.

Discussion

A recurrent theme in Hall's work on cultural identity is the idea of race as a 'floating signifier'. What is the significance of this notion?

Notes

1 Ethnicity is often the unit of choice in media studies, as we shall see in Chapter 2, especially in relation to the topic of how increasingly globalised communication networks form diasporic identities, bringing a 'convergence of transnational and transracial geographies of identification' (Cohen, 1999: 5).
2 Downing and Husband (2005) expose the problematic assumptions that underlie simplistic advocations of ethnicity, for instance in the way it produces a minority ethnic group-good/majority ethnic group-bad discourse which can be infantilising towards minorities (or those treated as minority), and in its inability to distinguish between assertions of ethnic pride and xenophobic nationalism.
3 This emerging area within cultural studies, which was the first to foreground issues of race and multiculture, shines a light on the ethnocentric and nationalist beginnings of British cultural studies in the 1970s (Huq, 2003). Paul Gilroy (1993: 5), in particular, exposes a reactive quality to early cultural studies attitudes to racial identity, highlighting how attempts to define notions of ethnicity were 'mobilised often by default rather than design'.

2

Race in Media Studies

What is meant by the 'politics of representation'?
What effects do media representations of race have on the audience?
What are the limitations of a sole focus on representation?
What does it mean that racial identities are made by or through media?

2.1 Introduction

In the previous chapter I outlined the critical cultural approach to race upon which this book is based. While culture is a notoriously difficult world to define, with multiple meanings (as Stuart Hall once put it, it is 'slippery, vague, and amorphous' (2016 [1983]: 4), the emphasis here is on culture as language that, through representation, is how we come to make sense of race. It follows that media – operating in the business of making cultural representations in commodity form – plays a key role in how we understand race; as was stressed, media provide the space where ideas about race form, coalesce, circulate. Simply put, how racialised groups appear in media matters. Not just because their negative portrayal can ruin our pleasure in the consumption of certain media texts. But because such representations shape society's broader understandings of race and difference, which at the very least will influence society's treatment of those groups in 'real life'.

While the question of media arose in the discussion of race and culture in the previous chapter, in this chapter I focus more closely on how race features in media research. While the field of media studies is wide and diverse, it can be characterised, albeit crudely, by two traditions: a social scientific approach to the media that characterises the field of 'communication studies', and a relatively more recent tradition of media studies shaped by British cultural studies with roots in literary studies (see Downing and Husband, 2005: x). For the way that it attends to the full complexity of culture, it is this latter tradition that is the subject here, although it should be stressed that the distinction between these two approaches is actually quite blurry (and many of the cultural studies that I refer to are also sociological in terms of theory and method). In this chapter I track the way that race has been explored in cultural studies of media, which has largely been in relation to issues of representation and, to a lesser extent, audiences (that turned the focus away from culture as representation/language to culture as lived experience). Within these broad approaches there have been influential studies that have shaped how we understand the relation between race, culture and media, particularly in relation to the question of ideology. However, the focus on representation in race and media, involving analyses of media texts, has stalled in recent times and is in desperate need of reinvigoration. It is here that I unpack in more detail what I mean by *media make race*. I draw upon two relatively new developments in race and media research, namely production studies of race, and digital studies in order to offer a more concrete understanding of media as 'race-making'.

2.2 Representation and audiences

Across the fields of media and communication studies, research into race encompasses a wide and diverse range of topics from a number of theoretical and empirical positions. However, research that follows the critical cultural perspective can be characterised as having twin core interests: (a) on how media reinforces/spreads racist ideologies/discourses, and/or (b) how audiences (and producers) resist/are shaped by these ideologies/discourses. Saying that, within this tradition, researchers have been mostly preoccupied with the question of representation, influenced largely by the work of Stuart Hall. Indeed, while the objects of enquiry are varied – from news to popular culture, from television to music, from video games to YouTube, from Twitter to film – textual studies of representation (whether semiotic analysis or post-structuralist techniques of deconstruction) is the dominant method in the study of race and media from a cultural perspective.

As explored in the previous chapter, representation is key to how we make meaning in culture, and society more generally – it is the language through which we make sense of the world and articulate our own understanding of it. Thus, how minorities are represented in media will, to varying degrees, shape how society makes sense of those minority groups. It is tempting to read the 'negative' representations of racial minorities as straightforwardly a product of racist ideology. However, such a formulation underestimates the complexity of media representation. A more nuanced way of understanding the dynamics of culture and ideology is to say that it is through representation[1] that particular ideological constructions of race become dominant – a notion I shall explore in more detail in the discussion of the 'politics of representation' that follows. In recent times the concept of 'discourse' features more in race and media studies, highlighting how representations produce different effects and consequences in relation to power. Discourse points to the complexity in the operation of power, and how certain knowledges around race take hold and become dominant. The discursive approach to race and media is particularly interested in how particular discourses come together (what Hall, drawing from Michel Foucault, calls 'discursive formations') to produce meanings in a given time (pointing to the importance of historical specificity and contextualisation in the analysis of representations of race). As shall be explored in much more detail in Chapter 3, this has been the basis for postcolonial theory, which draws attention to how representations of the Other are (a) historical, shaped by Empire and its legacies, and (b) not actually rooted in the real. For instance, Edward Said (1991 [1978]) refers to how the construction of the 'Orient' – by which he essentially means the non-West – is based on 'imaginative geography', that is, an analysis of people and place that quite literally has no basis in actual reality. For Said, the 'ideological' function of the discourse of Orientalism is in sustaining not just the superiority, but *the very idea* of the Occident or 'West' itself. So rather than media as merely misrepresenting or distorting the realities of minorities, the representation of race is better understood as a form of power/knowledge that constitutes what we understand as real. Homi Bhabha stresses this in his critical analysis of 'stereotype'; as he states, 'The stereotype is not a simplification because it is a false representation of a given reality. It is a simplification because it is an arrested, fixated form of representation' (Bhabha, 1994: 75). Essentially, the critical cultural approach to race understands that (a) all representations are socially constructed (that is, they are never a 'mirror' of society), and (b) that all meaning relating to representation is constructed within history and culture and shaped by power.

Increasingly influenced by post-structuralist theory, Stuart Hall introduces the notion of the 'politics of representation'. Stressing the *politics* at the core of representational practices emphasises how power, rather than a case of the top-down transmission of ideology onto/into a passive audience, is always contested. In his famous essay 'New Ethnicities', Hall (1988: 27) coins the 'politics of representation' in response to a new artistic and cultural movement in Britain that was emerging in the 1980s and that was articulating new ideas of what it meant to be black, Asian and, indeed, British. A response not just to an exclusionary British (white) nationalism, but also the essentialism of other nationalisms, whether Muslim, Black and so on (Gilroy, 1993; Mercer, 1994), this new creative movement depicted a diverse array of racialised experience – black and brown, gendered, queer, working-class – stressing the hybridity of black and Asian culture and British national identity itself. As Kobena Mercer (1994: 4–5) put it, 'in a world in which everyone's identity has been thrown into question, the mixing and fusion of disparate elements to create new, hybridized identities point to ways of surviving, and thriving, in conditions of crisis and transition'. This spawned a new critical approach to race and representation that was as keen to highlight and recognise the radical, destabilising and productive forms of black and Asian expressive culture (particularly in their queer and gendered forms) (hooks, 1992; Rose, 1994; Back, 1996; Huq, 1996; Malik, 2002). While weaker forms of this approach slipped into an over-celebration of popular culture, the intention of Hall through his notion of the politics of representation was to stress how representations are contested (where marginalised groups challenge dominant, hegemonic representations of race), complex (characterised by different 'regimes of representation') and ambivalent/contradictory (a text can contain both radical and reactionary elements, sometimes at the same time).

The critical cultural approach to race and media provides the most nuanced understanding of representation, but it's not without its limitations. First, it is concerned solely with the level of signification and can ignore feeling, emotion and affect (that is, our visceral bodily responses to something), which are an important component of how representation works. For instance, in her study of Muslims in American television drama post-9/11, Evelyn Alsultany (2012) finds that what appear to be sympathetic portrayals of Muslims/Arabs produce powerful *affects* and feelings of empathy, but in the process serve to hide the effects of US domestic policy towards its Muslim populations (in fact, Alsultany shows how such affects are themselves a product of racist ideology). Critical media scholar Kaarina Nikunen (2018) focuses on the role of emotions and affect in her study of 'media solidarities' and how particular representations of suffering or injustice – not least racial injustices such as the Grenfell Tower tragedy - evoke different types of solidarity amongst producers and audiences. Indeed, for Gray (2013b: 253), a focus on affect, feelings and emotions potentially liberates us away from reductive arguments over whether a particular representation is correct or not, in favour of 'critically rethinking the work of representation and its role in mobilizing sentiments and circulating feelings of attachment, belonging, and identification'. It should be said, that such a discussion is still in its relative infancy. Secondly, a preoccupation with media representation can distract from the everyday economic and social realities of minorities, where there is a lack of understanding of how exactly representation leads to racial imbalances in terms of 'economics and social value', as communication scholar Oscar Gandy (1998) puts it. For Gandy, this is particularly pronounced when we consider the propensity of cultural studies of media in particular to make generalisations about how racist ideologies/discourses circulate in society based on the analysis of just a single text, whether a film or an episode of a television sitcom. Thirdly, as stated, it can slip into an uncritical celebration of popular culture where black and brown cultural production is seen by itself as evidence of the resilience of those cultures. Fourthly, for many purely textual studies of race there is often a lack of engagement with the audience. Authors will assert their interpretation of a text even though they understand fully that a single text can mean different things to different audiences. Indeed, the emergence of audience studies was a response to the lack of care paid to the complexity of media consumption.

Audience studies has had a huge impact in complicating simplistic models of the transmission of ideology that weaker textual accounts produce. Another influential essay by Stuart Hall (1972), entitled 'Encoding/Decoding', was transformative in that regard, demonstrating how audiences are not just active, but can make meanings in multiple ways. A viewer can accept and follow the dominant/hegemonic meaning that is encoded in a text, but they can also obtain a radically oppositional position, or indeed something inbetween (what Hall calls the negotiated position). The work of feminist audience studies researchers was particularly influential in drawing attention to how the pleasure that those treated as Other (women, minorities, working classes) gain from particular popular cultural texts (which are often the most denigrated/ridiculed/patronised by the dominant culture in society) can in fact act as forms of resistance. Jacqueline Bobo's (1988) study of a group of African American women's interpretation of films on gender and race produces a valuable insight into how black women, when faced with a media that belittles/disavows their experience, learn to filter media and take pleasure from the small bits they can relate to. While Bobo and similar studies (see Sobande, 2017) have explicitly looked for forms of resistance in media consumption, other audience researchers have explored media's role in constituting diasporic and migrant experience and subjectivity (Bailey et al., 2007) and how media consumption contributes to the maintenance of a collective identity in those ethnic groups. A particularly influential piece of research is Marie Gillespie's (1995) study of the media consumption of a Punjabi community in the London suburb of Southall. Gillespie demonstrates how diasporic groups use media texts as divergent as Australian soap operas and Hindi cinema to negotiate Britishness and their own sense of Asianness, articulating new forms of *British Asian* identity.[2] More recently, digital studies have looked at networking across national borders and how they can advance or restrict participation in 'political and cultural affairs' (Georgiou, 2007: 15), often conceptualised in terms of the emergence of alternative public spheres and cosmopolitanism (ibid.: 21). Indeed, the most interesting work here looks at media consumption as part of the everyday fabric of the urban experience in particular as constituted by and constitutive of the new digital landscape – making the important point that attempting to separate all these different elements is an impossible and unproductive task (Georgiou, 2013; Christensen and Jansson, 2015).

Despite the vital contributions of audience studies, especially to our understanding of the workings of ideology, it has received a number of challenges. As David Morley (2006), a key figure in audience studies, describes, audience studies was victim to a heavy-handed political economy critique that took issue with the tendency to interpret audience pleasure as resistance, which serves to distract from the real goal of challenging structures of domination (see also Parameswaran, 2006). Other criticisms raise concerns around issues of research methods and the process of segmenting complex audiences into discrete units of analysis. For audience researchers interested in racialised communities in particular, there is a danger of slipping into essentialism that reinforces the idea that racial/ethnic groups are rigid, fixed and bounded from others (Harindranath, 2005)[3] – though it has to be said that this is a fundamental challenge for all social research into race and ethnicity (Alexander, 2006). The main critique of audience studies from a critical cultural perspective is how it can downplay the role of ideology by overplaying the agency of the audience. But as Morley (2006) again points out, audience studies was never about challenging the idea that media has power over audiences; rather it attempts to conceptualise media power in a more nuanced, complex way. In fact, a key part of Hall's (1997b) model of representation is how subjects are positioned in discourse, which encourages the dominant form of decoding. An individual has the power to step out of this position and interpret the text in an alternative way, but often it's just easier to occupy the position given rather than take the effort to step out of it.

Despite these challenges, what I take from the critical analyses of media texts and audience research that I have covered is that power, ideology and discourse produce powerful effects when it comes to race, but more crucially, this power operates in complex ways. To develop the sharpest critique of media power as it pertains to race entails an equally sharp understanding of the complexity of its operation, even if it means acknowledging awkward contradictions. A way to unpack this complexity further is to visit a famous exchange between Sut Jhally and Justin Lewis (1992), the authors of *Enlightened Racism: The Cosby Show, Audiences, and the Myth of the American Dream* and Herman Gray. In their audience study of hugely popular American sitcom *The Cosby Show* (this was sometime before Bill Cosby's conviction for sexual assault), Jhally and Lewis coin the term 'enlightened racism' that they claim reproduces a myth of mobility. Their argument is that *The Cosby Show* normalised middle-class desire such that race was eliminated in the context of a society that actually is profoundly stratified by race. Jhally and Lewis were attempting to address what they considered the apolitical nature of audience studies with its emphasis on pluralism and polysemy of meaning by placing the issue of ideology and determination squarely in the centre of their study. But for Gray, one of the most erudite scholars of the politics of representation, the authors produce a far too simplistic top-down, account of ideology and media power 'where television is politically constructed as a totalizing discourse that inevitably serves the ideological interests of the powerful' (Gray, 1993: 470). Gray also takes issue with how the study evaluates media in terms of its ability to capture the reality of black life, 'the expectation that the show measure up to "reality" constitutes a "burden of representation" that must be interrogated rather than assumed' (ibid.). Gray argues that we need to understand media consumption as much more ambivalent – describing how black audiences can 'both read with and against' the show at the same time. Rather than a system of ideological closure, television is better understood as an open system, as a 'discursive representational system' (ibid.: 471) which has enabling properties as well as constraining ones. Televisual signs of blackness are represented in a variety of ways (including gestures, bodies, plots, settings, character, language) and serve a variety of ends. As Gray continues, 'In some instances these are hegemonic, in others they are contradictory, and in yet others they are contested' (ibid.: 471). For Gray, Jhally and Lewis fail to see reception as a site of struggle over meaning, as always contested. Lewis and Jhally (1994) counter that the ambiguity and contradiction that Gray wants to underscore does not mean that ideology is being contested – rather, it is an example of the workings of ideology in action 'as television's ambiguity can be the fibrous tissue of its ideological muscle' (ibid.: 116). Nonetheless, Gray (1994: 121) argues that the authors needed to demonstrate more fully 'how the show laboured socially and culturally to produce meanings and social positions that, for different audiences, represented a new racism and heightened suspicions about it'. Gray is suggesting that the mistake that Lewis and Jhally make is in trying to find the *true meaning* or ideological content of *The Cosby Show*. In this exchange, Herman Gray is underscoring the complexity of representational politics. As Hall himself put it, as early as his 'New Ethnicities' essay, 'once you enter the politics of the end of the essential black subject you are plunged headlong into the maelstrom of a continuously continent, unguaranteed political argument and debate' (Hall, 1988: 28). When there is no fixed meaning, meaning is always up for grabs.

As I have suggested, the critical cultural approach to media representation, including audience studies, has lost momentum in recent times; as Gray (2013a: 771) argues, in racial political discourse more widely, 'there has been a waning in what a politics of representation can yield'. Despite Hall's assertion from the very beginning, that the meanings produced by a single text are never a given, that they arrive *without guarantees*, media representation today still gets discussed in the limited terms of visibility, that is, who is present and who is not, or a politics of redress that simplistically states that we need to replace negative/stereotypical/biased representations of race with more positive/authentic/truthful ones without really engaging with what actually constitutes these terms. Perhaps one reason for its decline in influence is that textual studies of race have never been able to reconcile asserting a particular reading of the text (often in terms of ideology) while acknowledging that different audiences can read the same text in multiple ways in different contexts.

As a way out of this theoretical/political conundrum and in order to reinvigorate race and media research, we need reframe the question from *how is race being represented in this particular text* to *how is race being made in a particular moment*. This entails taking an equal consideration of texts, technology, producers and audiences and their interrelations. The conclusions reached might actually not be that different, as the emphasis is still on media in relation to power, but it is the latter's more discursive, radically contextual foundation that offers a more nuanced take on representational politics, highlighting contestation, complexity and contradiction. In the remainder of the chapter I want to unpack this notion of media as race-making in more detail, by focusing on two relatively new developments in race and media research.

2.3 Cultural production and the digital

While many scholars in the critical cultural (that is constructivist) tradition have worked with the idea of race as something that is made[4], my notion of *media make race* is adopted from Herman Gray (2016: 249) when he refers to 'race-making practices' in media 'as power/knowledge that operates as a logic of production'. While that is the extent to which Gray discusses media as race-making in that particular essay, I nonetheless believe there is much scope in developing this concept further. In order to start unpacking *media make race*, a suitable starting point is the relatively new field of research that Gray is referring to in that piece, what we can broadly call production studies of race (Hesmondhalgh and Saha, 2013; Saha, 2018). This is part of a growing concern with studies of media/cultural production in relation to racial identities, which in turn is a reaction to both the preoccupation with texts and representation in cultural studies on the one hand (the limitations of which are described in the previous section) and the functionalism of certain forms of political economy on the other, which cannot account for the contradiction and contestation that characterises cultural production. Production studies of race includes studies of creative labour (Banks et al., 2014; O'Brien et al., 2016) and cultural policy (Malik, 2013a; Nwonka, 2015; Malik and Nwonka, 2017) that together explore how cultural production reproduces racial inequalities in production and consumption (see O'Brien et al., 2017). In such studies we see critiques of the whiteness and middle-classness of industry gatekeepers (O'Brien et al., 2016), the implications of cuts in the funding of black arts (Ross, 1995; Nwonka, 2015), and neoliberal advocations of diversity (Nwonka, 2015; Saha, 2018). A branch of production studies of race explores the dynamics of industrial cultural production itself (what Martin (2015) calls the moment of 'transcoding') and how they contain racialising logics. For instance, Tim Havens uses the concept of 'industry lore' to describe racialised *myths* that become the common-sense understandings that (white) executives use in the production of black television (for instance, one 'lore' that endures despite multiple examples to the contrary is that a film with a black lead will not sell in overseas markets). In my own work I refer to the 'rationalising/racialising logic of capital' (Saha, 2016) to describe how racialising dynamics are embedded in the processes of rationalisation that constitutes industrial cultural production such that they steer the work of minorities themselves into reproducing the very tropes of race that they set out to challenge in the first place.

This latter strand of production studies of race that focuses directly on the process of industrial cultural production quite literally demonstrates how race (that is, a particular representation of race) is made in the cultural industries. In doing so, it implies that a textual analysis of representation of race is not enough by itself to fully appreciate the politics of representation. The film/tv show/book/music track that features in cultural and media studies of race is fundamentally a cultural commodity and a product of the cultural industries, which in the West is in turn a product of capitalism (and the contradictions therein) and the legacies of empire (which are equally ambivalent) (Saha, 2018). In this way, as Gray states, media as race-making in the context of production acts as a form of power/knowledge that shapes how the text appears and is received at the point of consumption. As we shall see, production studies of race provide a more nuanced analysis of the 'commodification of race', as will be explored in Chapter 4. This approach, concerned as it is with how media make race, additionally highlights how cultural political interventions cannot just happen at the level of the text, that is, through purely aesthetic strategies. Rather, intervening in how race gets made entails a 'politics of production' (Saha, 2018) that deals with the underlying material structures through which representations of race are produced. The argument here is that the politics of representation is not just about refining the stories that we want to tell about minority experience, but focusing on how those stories *get made* in the context of the cultural industries.

Within digital media/Internet studies we also encounter a notion of how race is made, albeit in a slightly different way. This shall be explored in much more detail in Chapter 10, but reflecting the field of media studies and race more generally, we find two approaches to race in digital media studies: one on race as lived experience, the other on race as hegemonic mode of representation (Sharma, 2013: 47). The former in the context of the digital is an extension of audience/diaspora studies, exploring how 'people use the Internet to both form and reaffirm individual racial identity and seek out communities based on race and racial understandings of the world' (Daniels, 2013: 699). This is often framed in terms of globalisation, ethnicity and migration, which extends beyond banal pronouncements on how the internet has intensified connections across national borders, but highlights instead how new digital technologies have led to novel forms of diasporic networks that act as resources that help sustain (imagined) communities across and within national borders (Leurs, 2012; Madianou and Miller, 2013; Ponzanesi and Leurs, 2014). Moreover, the new digital worlds open up intimate spaces for discursive interaction – 'a kind of third space' (Daniels, 2013: 699) that is also available to non-members of the group. Stressing ambivalence, this process can contain both radical and reactionary forms (Cabanes, 2014).

An alternative approach in digital media studies is more focused on race and racism, or more precisely, the construction of racial identities and communities on the one hand, and the proliferation of racist discourse on the other. The starting point for this research is a critique of the original conception of the internet (in its early text-based incarnation) as a post-racial space, where individuals would no longer be defined by race, not least because their racial identities were hidden or masked by avatars and other digital forms of identification. Such a conception was utopian in its belief that people were now free to create their own online identities (for an early critique of this paradigm see Nakamura, 2013 [2002]). But as the internet became more visual this has become less the case, and consequently the emphasis now is on how the internet is a space where, as stated, racism flourishes unfettered or where minorities form communities of resistance (Mitra and Gajjala, 2008; Brock, 2012; Florini, 2014, 2015; Christian, 2018). Articulating a critical cultural approach to the Internet, Daniels (2013: 709) critiques mainstream Internet studies that, when not marginalising the issue of race, reproduces an uncritical, essentialist approach to race and racism on the internet, based on 'doing surveys on racist attitudes within a population – or where race is seen as causal variable'. For Daniels, the problem of such an approach is in its implication that people access the internet as fully realised racialised subjects (where the question then is to consider how they are represented online). But what if we think of the internet as not just constituted by, but constitutive of racial identities? Sanjay Sharma (2013) in his study of 'Black Twitter' (the significant network of African American users within the Twitter-sphere) and 'Blacktags' (defined as 'racialised hashtags' (ibid.: 47) created and used by Black Twitter and beyond) shifts the emphasis beyond the usual dual conception of race in terms of representation/ signification or embodied experience. Rather, Sharma sees race as 'discovered in its emergence through connections between bodies, and other entities and processes' (ibid.: 54). Such a notion, for Sharma, better captures the way that race works online; as he states, 'user identities, representations and meanings in online spaces are produced by material processes *vis-à-vis* complex technological assemblages' (ibid.). In relation to 'Blacktags', Sharma argues that rather than the question of the extent to which they can be read as the authentic representation of a particular African American community, the focus instead should be on what makes them 'contagious digital objects' (ibid.: 62), that is, what makes them spread and proliferate. As he demonstrates, Blacktags arise from an array of machinic networked relations, algorithmic operations and differential information flows of Twitter; in other words, they are enabled by and become part of the machinery of social media – what Sharma calls a 'digital race assemblage' (ibid.: 49) (see Chapter 10 for a more detailed case study on Black Twitter). To put it more simply, it is not just the case that new media offers a digital platform through which we represent our already established racial identities. Rather, new media in relation to race is better understood in terms of how our racial identities are made through these new technologies. To put it another way, the new digital technologies do not merely mediate racial identities, but instead make race itself. Sharma (2013: 53) echoes Herman Gray when he describes the implication of a focus on digital media as race-making in how it encourages a new, alternative account of race on the internet that 'goes beyond simply attempting to evade valorising Black users, or resist ascribing racialized cultural characteristics to their online behaviour'. Sharma is in effect arguing for a 'materialist approach' to race and (digital) media, not unlike the researchers of production studies of race who similarly want to go beyond questions of representation and purely textual approaches that too easily slip into a politics based on representational redress, either in terms of visibility or portrayal.

2.4 **Conclusion**

Shifting the emphasis to how media make race is not to say that we should disavow critical analyses of representations of race. Rather, textual approaches to race and media need further embellishment and historical contextualisation. How particular racial and ethnic groups are represented in media not only matters but is a question of social justice, as explored in Chapter 1. The problem is that after an explosion of critical cultural studies that explored the politics of representation following Stuart Hall's paradigm-shifting 'New Ethnicities' essay, the textual approach to media, race and representation has stalled in recent times. It is not the case that we no longer have anything new to say about the way that race is represented in media. In fact, within the current conjuncture, characterised by the deeply disturbing rise of far right and populist right-wing movements across the globe, critically analysing the constitution and effects/affects of racialised media discourses that have been shaped and instrumentalised by reactionary currents takes on an even greater urgency. Instead, what I have wanted to stress in both chapters thus far is that contemporary discussions of representation, despite Hall's emphasis on complexity and ambivalence, continue to critique media representations in terms of a lack, whether simplistic notions of visibility/presence or accuracy/authenticity, and with such certainty without interrogating the terms being used to make these judgements. The problem with general accounts of race and media is that they rest upon an assumption that individuals exist as fully realised racial subjects in real life who are then misrepresented by media. But the purpose of the concluding section of this chapter on production studies of race and digital media studies is to demonstrate how ideas of race, and race itself, are produced *through* media, whether as a product of power/knowledge (shaped by capitalism and legacies of empire) that are embedded within the production logics of the cultural industries, or constituted physically through a digital racial assemblage. Thus, the idea that media make race is intended to provide a more discursive account of the structural, regulatory, cultural and technological forces that shape how race is made and made sense of in the context of media. It is in this way that the notion of *media make race* is intended as an intervention. It is designed to offer a more complex account of the dynamics of race and racism within the cultural sphere, where media is a key institution.

As stated, *media make race* is adopted from Herman Gray, who offers the most productive, sophisticated and nuanced approach to understanding the new cultural politics of race. However, if I have one criticism of Gray it is that his radically contextual approach can lead to a lack of a normative framework from which to interrogate the cultural politics of race in relation to media. If everything is contingent, as Stuart Hall also argues, then how to critique and evaluate a particular representation of race as embodied in a media text? Who is to say what the correct interpretation is? Perhaps one reason for the demise in textual studies of representation is that researchers have never fully dealt with the problem of validity with this type of method. There is no correct answer to what a representation really means, not least since representations can mean different things to different people, while meanings can change over time as well as across space. However, Hall's (1997a: 9) own response to this dilemma was to stress how the researcher's aim should be to reach the most plausible answer, attempting to 'justify one's reading in detail in relation to the factual practices and forms of signification used, and what meanings they seem to be producing'. Indeed, the fact is that while the meaning produced through representation is polysemic, representations work – like language – precisely because we generally understand them in the same way, even if we have a competing or contested view of those meanings. For this reason, I want to retain the notion of ideology. While race-making practices in media shape representation in complex ways, the fact remains that the ideological frame for how race is represented remains incredibly narrow. As we shall see in the case study chapters that constitute Part III, in the current conjuncture we broadly have a situation where race is either over-determined, or racial minorities are *de-racialised* according to a neoliberal version of diversity. The aim of the book is to help explain this apparent contradiction.

Thus, the critical cultural approach to race and media that I put forward in this book stresses contestation, complexity and contradiction, in terms of how representations of race are produced within the cultural industries, and how they work in society at large. The purpose is to develop a nuanced and complex account of race and media, while maintaining a sharp critique of how media contributes to the governance of race (that is, how ideas of race are managed, circulated and intended to be received by the dominant culture). There is a strong emphasis on contestation too – as stated, media is the space where racist ideologies are reinforced, but also the space where they can be challenged. It is in this way that media's treatment of racial minorities is a matter of social justice. Our normative position is to think through how race can be made in media that *contributes to its undoing* (Saha, 2018: 23) – whether unravelling spurious biological logics or demolishing ethnic absolutism. Such a notion will be unpacked further in Part II of this book.

2.5 Introducing Part II

The aim of the book is to offer an in-depth account of the relations between race, culture and media, framed in terms of how media make race. Thinking through this notion of media as race-making necessitates a new approach that incorporates an analysis of the political-economic and socio-cultural, production, audiences and texts together. For this purpose, I conceptualise a theoretical framework called 'postcolonial cultural economy', which is an interdisciplinary, multifaceted and holistic approach that incorporates an analysis of the different dynamics that shape race-making practices in media today. These include: (1) legacies of empire, (2) neoliberalism and 'racial capitalism', (3) the politics of multiculturalism and nationalism, and (4) media industries themselves. While I have touched on each of these issues in the previous two chapters, the aim of Part II is to flesh out in much more detail the operations of race, culture and media (or indeed, how race is made) in each of these different contexts.

Chapter 3 explores postcolonial approaches to race, culture and identity. It unpacks further how the social construction of race is a historical process and how legacies of empire and colonialism shape contemporary understandings of race and gender in the West, through ideology and discourse (Said, 1991 [1978]; Spivak, 1999). It examines how the (postcolonial) nation state is based upon an ideology of ethnic absolutism, and in addition how the inherent 'hybrid' nature of the postcolonial subject – as embodied in black and Asian vernacular culture – is a challenge to the essentialist notions of race and ethnicity that the nation state relies upon. The chapter also explores the role of media in postcolonial studies, and what postcolonial perspectives bring to our understanding of global media culture. It also highlights the limitations of such approaches, particularly for a lack of engagement with the political economy of media and the complexity of media power.

In Chapter 4 I ground the discussion of race and empire more squarely within the question of capitalism. The chapter argues that rather than an epiphenomenon of capitalism, race and racism contributed to the actual birth, development and expansion of capitalism. This understanding feeds into a discussion of the current neoliberal conjuncture and the concept of 'postrace' which sustains race hierarchies as it denies the existence of racism (Goldberg, 2009a: Kapoor, 2013). It also demonstrates how under the conditions of neoliberalism, racialised groups are on the one hand oppressed, but on the other hand, their identity becomes a quality used to distinguish goods in a competitive market. This last point is key to understanding race in contemporary media culture. Once again, the focus is on contestation and ambivalence, where I demonstrate how capitalism attempts to hegemonise culture but in the process leaves spaces for contestation and resistance. This provides the framework to discuss media/cultural interventions of race in Part III of the book.

Chapter 5 builds on Chapter 3 and focuses on race and media in relation to the politics of nationalism and multiculturalism. It provides a critical examination of multiculturalism as an approach or set of policies that governs racial and ethnic minorities within a national population. It returns us to the question of how national identity is racialised, and the role media plays in constructing ideas of nationalism and by extension, the nation's inherent *multiculture*. The task of the chapter is to encourage a critical approach to multiculturalism that sees it as constituting and constituted by discourses of nationalism. I focus particularly on the way that particular types of national media industries have attempted to tackle the 'problem' of diversity and multiculturalism, whether in public service broadcasting or commercial contexts.

Chapter 6 tackles more directly the question of media power. Its focus is on the role of media as an independent structuring force upon the making of race. The emphasis will be on media texts – their production, distribution and consumption – and how ideas about race circulate through them. It provides an overview of cultural studies and political economy approaches to media (and race) in order to flesh out the macro and micro dimensions of race-making practices. The aim is to develop the ideas discussed in Chapter 2 and produce a more detailed account of the complexity of media power that recognises its complexity and contradictions, not least in taking seriously the role of audiences and the question of agency. In the conclusion of the chapter I outline the 'postcolonial cultural economy' framework in detail, which incorporates insights, theories and methods from each of the chapters that constitute Part II. In Part III of the book I then apply this framework to a range of case studies that cover the most pressing issues in relation to race, culture and media.

BOX 2.1 Key Theme

De-Westernising media studies and the geographical focus of this book

Any study of race and media needs to be clear on its context.

The question is should we focus on one particular national context or try to adopt a more global approach? The latter angle constitutes part of a shift to *de-Westernise* the discipline of media studies more broadly, which is dominated by studies based on the global north (Park and Curran, 2000). Such a move challenges two troubling tendencies in media studies where (1) theories and perspectives from very particular (and relatively small) Western contexts are taken as universal and applicable to the globe as a whole, and (2) where it is assumed that the Western world is the most developed, with the rest of the world playing catch-up. De-Westernising media studies is also an attempt to centralise research from non-Western contexts that have been historically placed on the periphery.

While any attempts to bring the periphery to the core is to be supported, the *De-Westernising* project raises slightly tricky issues for researchers who study race in Western contexts. Whereas Western intellectual ideas dominate not because of their inherent superiority (far from it) but because of the nature of globalisation, shaped as it is by colonialism and Western Imperialism, the study of race and racism in the context of Western academia very much remains marginal. As such there needs to be a similar movement to bring this research into the core of the discipline too (see Box 3.1).

The danger is that the study of race in the West comes to speak for the experience of race in other parts of the world. Such a notion is, needless to say, highly problematic. The experience of being black or brown in the UK is very different from being black or brown in South Africa or in Brazil (where the term 'racial minority' does not apply). There is something universal about the forms of Islamophobia that occur in the USA, China, India and Palestine, but it also takes very different forms in each of those geographic contexts.

While a global approach to race is encouraged, particularly if it foregrounds the 'global south' that tends to go ignored in Western academia, we must avoid tackling

(Continued)

race in general terms. As critical race scholar David Theo Goldberg argues (2009a), we cannot understand what race is doing unless it is situated within its very specific historical context. There is not just one idea of race. Rather, the world consists of multiple ideas of race that have their own histories specific to their geographic regions – though as Goldberg (2009b: 1273) stresses, these different histories of racism are *relational*, that is, they are interconnected. Alas, to cover multiple histories, while providing an in-depth analysis of media and culture that I aim to offer here, is too large a project for a single volume.

Thus, for the purposes of this book, I focus mostly on Anglophone contexts, specifically the UK, and work with the idea of race that emerged from the moment of European Enlightenment. Inevitably, a lot of the studies I draw upon will also come from the US, since it has produced the majority of critical race studies on media. That is absolutely not to say that the Anglo-world are the only regions worth studying or have the most value for the study of race and media, and where I am able to, I draw from examples from non-Anglo contexts, while acknowledging that they come with their own particular racial histories. My hope is that the postcolonial cultural economy framework outlined in this book provides a broad approach that can be applied to the study of race-making practices in other national contexts, although I very much expect it will produce different though no less valuable types of knowledge.

Discussion

What is the value of a plural notion of 'racisms' rather than 'racism' in the singular? Are there any limitations to such a discursive move?

Notes

1 It should be noted that when I refer to representation, I am generally referring to media representation. However, we should not ignore the role of other institutions in the making of representations of race. For instance, the political, legal and educational systems all help shape society's understanding of race through representation of sorts.
2 The fact that this was one of the first studies of a British South Asian community (certainly in media studies) demonstrates another value of audience studies, in taking seriously cultures that are ordinarily marginalised in political, policy, media *and* academic discourse.
3 Lola Young's (1996b) review of Jacqueline Bobo's and Marie Gillespie's respective studies, as mentioned earlier, provides a fair critique of both texts based on the epistemological foundations of their respective methods, and their failure to surmount the challenges around essentialism when researching race/ethnicity.
4 Ben Carrington (2010) applies this phrasing in relation to sport. His exploration of how '*sport helps to makes race make sense and sport then works to reshape race*' (original emphasis) (ibid. 66) echoes my own approach to media culture.

Part II
Framework

3

Media and the Postcolonial

What is postcolonial theory?
What does postcolonial theory bring to our understanding of race and culture?
How have postcolonial theorists tackled the question of media?
Is postcolonial theory properly attuned to issues of capitalism and political economy?

3.1 Introduction

Having introduced the key concepts of race, culture and media in Part I of the book, the purpose of the chapters that make up Part II is to look more closely at how media make race. This entails an analysis of the different structural forces that shape race-making practices in media, namely, (neo)colonialism, (racial) capitalism, the politics of nationalism/multiculturalism, and media themselves. It is through a discussion of each of these distinct though overlapping macro dimensions that I will piece together the conceptual framework that I call the 'postcolonial cultural economy'. Such a framework is intended to help better understand the dynamics of race in media, providing an in-depth, interconnected analysis that crucially can account for complexity without losing sight of power. To reaffirm, media is the space where racial ideologies are reinforced, but also challenged. Thus, this chapter, which opens Part II, will explore key ideas, theories that help us to understand the relations between media and, in this case, the postcolonial, while in the process introduce the postcolonial cultural economy framework that shapes the analysis across the book.

As stated, this chapter's concern is with the postcolonial context to race-making practices in media, where we consider how the relations between race, culture and media are shaped by legacies of empire. In doing so, this chapter considers the value of postcolonial theory for media studies of race. Postcolonial studies, for the way that it situates our analysis of contemporary race-making practices in media within the history of colonialism and its immediate and not so immediate aftermath, should form an absolutely integral part of any analysis of media, culture and race. Our understanding of the formation and circulation of contemporary racial discourses is deepened by the historical analysis that postcolonial perspectives bring. Put another way, we cannot properly evaluate modern representations of race without understanding how they are shaped by the history of empire and imperialism. However, I will also demonstrate that in postcolonial approaches to media the concern is mostly with texts and audiences, which means that important questions around the workings of media industries, including its institutional and organisational arrangements are neglected. In response, this chapter will show why and how we need to couple postcolonial analysis with a more in-depth discussion of the cultural industries and capitalism, including questions of media power and commodification. To begin, the chapter will consider postcolonial studies' broader contributions to scholarship on race and culture. I will then discuss its general strengths and limitations, before ending with a more detailed discussion of its value to media studies of race.

3.2 Postcolonial studies: A brief overview

Postcolonial studies is concerned with the relationship between culture and colonialism, and how such a relationship shapes modern formations of race, as well as gender and sexuality. While postcolonialism emerges from literary studies, the influence of postcolonial theory has spread into disciplines across the humanities and social sciences. As such, it can entail a discussion of topics as diverse as literature, migration, fine art, slavery, and indeed the question of media. Despite its breadth of interests, postcolonial studies is fundamentally concerned with nations that were formally colonised, or peoples who were formally colonised and who now live in the Imperial centre (Shome and Hedge, 2002). The other common thread that runs through the field (and what makes it particularly pertinent for this book) is the privileging of the question of culture.

Before we enter a more detailed discussion of the postcolonial, we need to define colonialism. Colonialism refers to the distant control of resources and direct settlement. It is the process of one country taking over another – often by force – in order to exploit and benefit from that country's people and resources. Colonialism took different forms in different contexts, but essentially included the taking of land, destroying indigenous peoples' land/or cultures, the enslavement of Others, and the colonisation of entire continents. As such, colonialism involves economic exploitation, but, as we shall see, cultural domination too. While examples of colonialism go back throughout history – with various empires spread across the globe – the modern world as we know it is shaped by the European imperial projects of the eighteenth and nineteenth centuries. Critical cultural studies theorists Ella Shohat and Robert Stam (2014: 15) refer to a specific phase of Imperialism – and with it, a specific type of colonialism – 'running roughly from 1870–1914, when conquest of territory became linked to a systemic search for markets and an expansionist exporting of capital'. What Stam and Shohat are referring to is how colonialism in this instance – referring specifically to the excursions of European nations in other parts of the world – was tied to (if not, *was intrinsic to*) the European project of modernity and the emergence of capitalism, based as it was on the economic quest for resources and labour to exploit.

Colonialism involves different types of power, including physical (through the military), and also economic and political/administrative power. But as we shall see, the impact of the early 'postcolonial' thinkers, such as Edward Said, Gayatri Spivak and Homi Bhabha, was in demonstrating how colonialism entailed a form of cultural power. The period of European Imperialism mentioned above was driven by economic exploitation but also historicist assumptions that the West was the pinnacle of humankind, and that all other nations and their peoples were following behind. As such, European colonial conquest was rationalised as a civilising mission based on the construction of indigenous peoples as savage and backward. It is in this moment that the modern idea of race comes into formation. As Shohat and Stam (2014) once again state, colonialism entailed racism abroad, but in turn produced racism *at home*. This is an important point to make once again: colonialism – and ideas of race and racial difference within it – was, rather than aberration, intrinsic to the European project of modernity. As postcolonial theorist Gurminder Bhambra (2007: 77) states, 'colonisation was not simply an outcome of modernity, but, rather, modernity itself, the modern world, developed out of colonial encounters'. To reiterate postcolonial theory's major contribution to the study of colonialism, was to shed light on colonialism's discursive operations, specifically the production of knowledges about 'the Other' in the context of imperialism through cultural artefacts (or indeed media). It is in this way that postcolonial theory provides vital historical context to our understanding of race. Having established colonialism, and how it produced the idea of race, I now unpack postcolonial studies in more detail.

Attempting to provide a neat description of postcolonial studies is complicated by the ambiguity bound up in the prefix 'post'. At face-value, '*post*-colonial' would imply the period of time after colonialism, though even this literal reading is a bit murky. As Stuart Hall (1995: 248) states in his essay 'When was the Post-Colonial?', while colonisation signals direct colonial occupation and rule, the transition to 'post-colonial' is characterised by independence from direct colonial rule, the formation of new nation states, forms of economic development dominated by the growth of indigenous capital and their relations of neo-colonial dependency on the developed capitalist world, and the politics which arise from emergence of powerful local elites managing the contradictory effects of under-development.

In other words, the colonial period is formally over but we should not mistake independence as representing full emancipation. Imperial power lingers, albeit in implicit form, through culture, military pressure, and economic and political dominance. The US, for many critics, acts as a modern-day imperial force, for instance through its influence over the World Bank, which can withhold loans to nations that do not conform to US economic policies, or its support for right-wing dictatorships in Latin America that help suppress popular socialist movements that represent a potential threat to US authority (Prashad, 2013). As feminist scholar Anne McClintock (1995: 13) puts it, the power of US finance capital 'can exert a coercive power as great as any colonial gunboat'. For Gaytri Spivak (1993: 157), another influential postcolonial feminist theorist, while colonial countries have been granted formal independence, imperial power has merely been reconfigured rather than displaced, 'fabricat(ing) allies by proposing a share of the centre in a seemingly new way (not a rupture but a displacement)'. Thus the 'post' in 'postcolonial' refers to the moment that colonialism is formally over but never totally. It is in this way that the term 'neocolonialism' is used to describe how colonial power still shapes contemporary geopolitics, not through direct military force, but through cultural and economic means.

The 'post' in postcolonial studies also refers to the development (though not necessarily the superseding) of theoretical paradigms. Similar to those other *post*-theories, postmodernism and post-structuralism, postcolonialism rejects foundationalism, that is, the normative use of universals to explain particular social and cultural phenomena. It seeks to undo, for instance, the notion that the development of 'Third World' nations follows a linear trajectory dictated by the history of Western nation states, or the idea that class determines everything, over everything else (Lentin, 2017). But to stress, postcolonialism does not mean a total displacement of a preceding narrative, but rather a decentering (Hall, 1995). Such a logic informed the recent Why is My Curriculum White? campaign on British university campuses that, contrary to what the right-wing press wrote, was never about removing white men from reading lists, but rather challenging the very idea of a canon (see Box 3.1). As Lentin (2017) puts it, postcolonial critique entails a 'politics of positionality' where the task is to identify where a subject is positioned in relation to power, as shaped by colonial discourse. Thus, the emphasis of postcolonial studies is on epistemology, by which I mean the production of knowledge, or put another way, how knowledge about a particular subject/object is constructed. In this way, while postcolonial studies as stated is a diverse field covering a wide range of topics, its main methodological tool is deconstruction, in this instance, deconstructing distinctly Western structures of knowledge and what they have to say about race, for example. Postcolonialism exposes the fundamentally particular Eurocentric nature of supposed universals.

To sum up, postcolonialism can be distilled into two key positions. First, postcolonial theorists understand that while colonialism is formally over it lives on in its 'after-effects' (Hall, 1995: 248). Secondly, the task of postcolonial theory is to expose and undo the Eurocentric ways that history and Other cultures are understood. As communication scholars Raka Shome and Radha Hedge (2002: 250) argue, postcolonial studies does not merely map the history of the transition from colonialism to postcolonialism, but instead seeks 'to undo (and redo) the historical structures of knowledge production' associated with modernity. As an example, postcolonial theorists in English literature produce alternative histories of the nation through the books written by diasporic subjects (Ilott, 2015). Postcolonialism is the task of deconstructing and dismantling the epistemic structures upon which colonialism and modernity are built. Very simply, this entails a cultural analysis of power.

3.3 Postcolonial studies' importance to the study of race and culture

To reiterate, postcolonial theory points to how it is through the cultural sphere that the West gained consent for its domination of the rest of the world. Before the impact of postcolonial studies, colonialism was generally understood in terms of physical dominance: military conquest and the use of violence to colonise populations. But as anti-colonial activist and philosopher Frantz Fanon (1986 [1967]) evocatively demonstrates, colonialism produced also a crippling, alienating psychosocial force upon the colonial subject that led to their simultaneous objectification (as Other) and alienation (as not fully human) – a theme that still finds expression in contemporary black popular culture in particular (*Psychodrama*, the debut album by British rapper Dave springs to mind). For Fanon, colonialism produced profound psychological and epistemological effects as much as political ones.

Colonialism as cultural power/epistemological force is mostly famously articulated by Edward Said and his book *Orientalism* (1991 [1978]), which arguably was the defining moment in the conception of postcolonial analysis (Born and Hesmondhalgh, 2000). Prior to this book, 'Orientalism' was a neutral descriptor for academic study on 'Oriental' nations and their peoples from the 'Near' to 'Far East' (including political, historical and anthropological studies). With *Orientalism*, Said instead exposed the ideological foundations of this supposedly objective scholarly field. According to Said, Orientalism is better defined as the process in which the West manipulates knowledge of and for the Orient, allowing for the West to gain ascendency; as Said (1991 [1978]: 3) puts it, Orientalism is 'a western style for dominating, restructuring and having authority over the Orient'. Orientalism is a discourse that constructs and maintains an absolute distinction between the West and the Orient, where the former represents progress, rationality and reason whereas the latter is backward, irrational and founded on unreason. For an illustration of Orientalism in contemporary times one just needs to observe the coverage of Middle Eastern nations in Western news media like Fox News (and contrast it to Aljazeera's). The point is that the construction of the Orient (as Other) actually defines the Occident (as Self); the West needs the Orient to give sense to itself and its own superiority. As Fanon famously remarked: 'Europe is literally the creation of the Third World' (2001 [1965]: 81). Without the 'Third World' there would be no 'West'.

For Said, Western dominance is secured and maintained through representation. As mentioned in Chapter 2, Said argues that the depiction of the Orient is a product of the 'imaginative geography' of Orientalists (that is, those who studied, researched, administered and imagined the 'Orient'), which serves to 'legitimate a vocabulary, a universe of representative discourse particular to the discussion and understanding of the Orient' (Said, 1991 [1978]: 71). The representations constituted through imaginative geography obscure and distort 'positive geography' or positive knowledges of actual realities (though Said is ambiguous about what 'positive geography' entails). Nonetheless, through the concept of imaginative geography Said wants to convey how we look at the Orient through certain lenses that contain and manage what we see. To reiterate, Said is highlighting the centrality of representation to Orientalist discourse, and how 'representations are put to use in the domestic economy of an imperial society' (2004: 41). It is through Orientalism as discourse that control of the (post)colonies and its peoples can be sustained.

While Said has been critiqued for basing his analysis on a simplistic binary between a monolithic 'Occident' and 'Orient', his work nonetheless spawned a whole field of postcolonial analysis that critically examines the cultural worlds of various colonial and postcolonial contexts, often based on literary analysis and poststructuralist techniques of deconstruction. This work has proved invaluable in demonstrating the ways that Imperial relations lives on in its after-effects, particularly in the way that racialised groups are still portrayed as Other, based upon binary oppositions, as evident in Western news and popular culture. The work of postcolonial feminist scholars has been particularly crucial for showing how Orientalist discourse had gendered and sexual dimensions, and how colonial hierarchies were cut through with gender (McClintock, 1995; Spivak, 1999). As McClintock (1995: 5) argues, race, gender and class are not separate experiences or identities that can be assembled together, but rather are articulated in and through each other. As she highlights, Imperial power was felt differently if you were a colonised woman (who had to negotiate the imbalances of their relationships with their own men as well as imperial men and women) or a white woman (who clearly experienced privileges over the colonised man or woman but had to contend with a particular form of colonial patriarchy)

(McClintock, 1995). Indeed, feminist postcolonial scholars and Spivak in particular emphasise the heterogeneity of the colonising process of subject formation (more so than Fanon and Said). Thus, in a nutshell, Western hegemony persists through the 'constant reiteration of the superiority of the West' (Venn, 1999: 45), which works via representation (whether 'factual' or 'fictional', if such a distinction exits), and *always* has a gendered dimension. For instance, in Chapter 8, which looks at Islamophobia and media, we will explore the supposedly 'threatening' figure of the veiled woman, who takes a central place in the anti-Muslim discourse that shapes the Western popular imaginary in news and popular culture.

While, postcolonialism shows us how the West gains dominance through culture, it also deepens our understanding of resistance towards (neo)colonial authority. A key figure here is Homi Bhabha, who, drawing from psychoanalysis, highlights how colonial rule, despite its dominance, was always in a precarious state. According to Bhabha (1994), colonial discourse depends upon fixing and maintaining the absolute distinction between the Self and the Other, that is, the separation between the coloniser and the colonised. But this fixity is immediately under threat by the very presence of the colonised subject, who on the one hand is constructed as Other, but on the other hand is made to conform to Western cultural and social norms and practices as part of colonial rule. In doing so, the colonised subject becomes *hybrid*, occupying the 'third space' in between the colonial Self and the colonised Other. All of a sudden, the distinction between Self and Other becomes blurred. Thus, according to Bhabha, the very presence of the hybrid colonised subject produces ambivalence at the heart of colonial structures, undermining the certainty of colonial authority. Mahatma Gandhi in some ways is a quintessential hybrid colonised subject, born in India under British occupation who then became a product of the Western education system (he studied law at University College London), an experience he drew upon to resist and challenge the British rule of India. In more contemporary times, black and Asian cultural producers in the UK continue to draw from their heritage and experience to create new 'hybrid' Black British and British Asian identities that challenge nationalistic discourse which asserts that to be truly English/Scottish/Welsh/Irish means to be white. Indeed, the concept of 'hybridity' becomes a key concept in cultural studies during the 1990s, in articulating the cultural politics of diaspora in particular and its anti-essentialist properties (see Hall, 1988; Gilroy, 1993; Sharma et al., 1996). In this way, resistance to empire and its legacy is founded upon destabilising the binary between the (white) Self and (racialised) Other, breaking the 'fixity', upon which the ideological construction of Otherness depends, or as Bhabha (1994: 56) puts it, eluding 'the politics of polarity'.

While providing a vital and persuasive critique of the cultural operations of colonial power and the dominance of the West, postcolonial studies has nonetheless received criticism. One critique is that it flattens complex and highly diverse colonial histories. For instance, the British colonisation of India is very different from its colonisation of Australia, notwithstanding the differences between different Imperial nations in how they administered colonial rule. It can also lead to a form of *colonial reductionism*, where complex contemporary geopolitical or national crises are simplistically explained in terms of the 'experience' of colonial domination (Back and Solomos, 2000). Indeed, media scholars of race need to be careful not to explain all representations of race as a direct product of colonialism as this ignores how representations change throughout history.

Another critique is that postcolonial analysis is so focused on the cultural that it downplays economic forces that shaped colonial domination. For Marxist scholars of colonialism, economic exploitation was the primary means of the oppression of colonised populations but this is downplayed in literary-based postcolonial studies. In other words, postcolonial studies, with its focus on culture, can appear disinterested in the economic. In this way historian Arif Dirlik (1994: 347), in a famous critique of the field, dismisses it as 'culturalism'. Similarly, Ella Shohat (1992), who provides another highly cited critique of postcolonialism, takes issue with the emphasis on the heterogeneity of colonial relations (as exemplified in the work of Bhabha and Spivak), which she argues blurs the distinction between colonisers and the colonised. For Shohat, this effectively empties postcolonial studies of its political urgency/agency for it posits no clear domination and no clear opposition. While Shohat's criticism of postcolonialism as apolitical due to its lack of clear lines of engagement can be countered by Stuart Hall's conception of the field of culture as an ever ongoing struggle for hegemonic power (a war of position rather than a war of manoeuvre), postcolonial theory can indeed lack engagement with questions related to the political economic contexts of race-making. Indeed, this is what ultimately limits postcolonial approaches to media in particular, as, to repeat, it can ignore the political-economic forces that shape the relationship between race, culture and media. However, postcolonialism nonetheless has much to give media studies of race, as I outline in the following section.

3.4 Postcolonial approaches to media

To recap, the major contribution of postcolonial studies is to challenge the idea of culture as an 'autonomous and politically innocent domain of social life' (Born and Hesmondhalgh, 2000: 5). Cultural relations were crucial to the maintenance and administration of colonial rule, as much as to military or economic power. Moreover, and particularly pertinent for this book, postcolonialism also deepens our understanding of the construction of race as a historical process. Colonial discourse is resilient, seductive, normative, in that it lures the West into a sense of its own superiority, its longevity ensured by the deep embeddedness of the idea of the Other as irredeemably backward (Venn, 1999). However, the historical contextualisation of the making of race in media is something that is often missing in communication studies and more social scientific studies of race and representation. This lack is problematic for two reasons. First, as stated, such an understanding of history is crucial to explaining why representations of the Other take the form that they do. That is, racial stereotyping is not *just* the product of capitalist logics or a matter of the dominant culture's cognitive need to simplify a complex world as some studies appear to suggest (see Gandy, 1998: 83–84). Secondly, the lack of attention to historical reproduction can downplay the entrenched nature of the West's construction the Other, leading to assumptions that representations of racial minorities can be easily fixed by greater visibility or producing the inverse of the 'negative' images that appear in media, when in reality the regime of representation, by which I mean the broad framework within which race is represented, is much more difficult to transform (though this of course should not stop us from trying). In the final section of this chapter I develop these points further, distilling the value of postcolonialism for the study of race, culture and media into four points. But I also discuss the limitations of a purely postcolonial approach to race and media research, predominantly for its neglect of the economic.

1   Postcolonial theory underlines the role of representation. The primary value of postcolonial theory for studies of media and race is its complex analysis of the politics of representation. It explains the persistence of essentialist understandings of race, ethnic absolutism – based upon a 'Manichean allegory' (Venn, 1999: 45) – a binarisation that paints the racialised Other as absolutely different and inferior. Moreover, it highlights the inextricable sexual/gendered dimensions to the construction of race (particularly the case in film studies, which has felt the influence of the tradition of postcolonial studies, especially in psychoanalyitcal inflection). The earliest colonial encounters with indigenous people produced a dialectical mix of fear *and* desire (Hall, 1992). While the savage was abhorred, there was something alluring too. This fear/desire of the Other is something that has become entrenched in contemporary popular culture, for instance in the particular sexualisations of black women as 'wild' and Asian/Arabic women as 'exotic'. East Asian women in particular are 'Orientalized' (Uchida, 1998) for their racial difference in Western popular culture, split into two types: either the 'docile doll/"Lotus Blossom" or the diabolic Dragon Lady' (ibid.: 162). (For a succinct overview of the sexualisation of East Asian women and men in Western popular culture and the way that they have been studied in Asian American studies, see Lopez (2018).) The way that the Other is constructed in opposition to the white Self, and then in turn, split into two binary opposites is an important theme in postcolonial theory and explains so much of contemporary media representations of race, as I shall explore further in Chapter 9 on the making of blackness. As Stuart Hall (1996: 467) puts it, 'there's nothing that global postmodernism loves

better than a certain kind of difference: a touch of ethnicity, a taste of the exotic, as we say in England, *"a bit of the other other"'* (my emphasis). The sexualisation of the Other will become a theme that runs through the case study chapters of Part III.

2   Postcolonial theory gives us the tools to deconstruct and interpret representations of race. Postcolonial theory provides a particularly nuanced theoretical and methodological approach for analysing media texts. While cultural studies can be criticised for focusing on just a single text (say, a film) to make wider claims about race, gender, sexuality and so on, somewhat wilfully ignoring questions of validity and generalisability (see Gandy, 1998: 16), postcolonial studies emphasises how texts work together, and create particular discursive formations, shaped through power/knowledge. Central to Said's concept of Orientalism as a discursive process is how texts, through time, draw from each other, each time slightly deviating but ultimately reproducing the same ideologies. As Said (1991 [1978]: 23) states: 'Orientalism is after all a system for citing works and authors', once again pointing to the construction of Otherness as a historical process. As such, in terms of method, postcolonial analysis entails a form of deconstruction that unravels the structures from which knowledges are produced, first, by situating the strategic location of the author and, secondly, by discovering the strategic formation of the text through analysing relationships between texts and how groupings of texts acquire referential power (ibid.) (this is the 'politics of positionality' that Lentin (2017) refers to). In contrast to content analyses of representations of race in media texts, postcolonial analysis pays meticulous attention to the textual but is always thought through in relation to broader histories of racial/ethnic marginalisation and denigration. This emphasis on the relations between texts, history and structure is crucial for the study of race and media. Edward Said's work remains exemplary of this approach, for instance his famous reading of Jane Austin's *Mansfield Park* (Said, 1993), revealing the presence and absence of empire in the canon of English literature.

3   Postcolonial theory deepens our understanding of the politics of culture. In the process of exposing the role of culture to the operations of (post)colonial power, postcolonial theory draws attention to forms of cultural political resistance, which again has great pertinence for the analysis of race-making practices in media. It follows that if colonial dominance was predicated on a constructed yet potent antithesis between the (European) Self and the Other, and that this epistemology has outlived physical decolonisation (that is, the gain or granting of formal independence for former colonies), then resistance in modern postcolonial discourse is necessitated on the dismantling of this very binary opposition. As I referred to earlier and in Chapter 2, it is in these terms that hybridity became such a popular concept at the height of critical cultural approaches to race, drawing attention

to how, for instance, the *hybrid* qualities of black British and British Asian cultural production in the 1990s challenged essentialist understandings of those particular racialised groups (as absolutely Other) while articulating new progressive and inclusive forms of national identity and Britishness itself. The collection *Dis-Orienting Rhythms: The Politics of the New Asian Dance Music* (Sharma et al., 1996) encapsulates a postcolonial studies-influenced discussion of cultural politics – including its limitations as well as potentialities – in relation to the rise of the 'Asian Underground' music scene that emerged in the 1990s (see Chapter 4 for a fuller discussion). Sociologists Helen Kim (2014) and Malcolm James (2015) update this discussion, bringing a broad postcolonial framework to bear upon the discussion of the making of contemporary youth culture and race in the context of neoliberal Britain. For instance, in her study of the London 'Desi' scene, Kim (2014) shows how it both represents an alternative public sphere where new forms of (British) Asianness are articulated, and embodies neoliberal ideals in its emphasis on self-improvement, entrepreneurialism, individualisation, self-commodification and consumer citizenship.

4   Postcolonial theory stresses the need to de-Westernise media studies. For media studies scholar Radikha Parameswaran (2006), speaking in the context of audience research specifically, postcolonialism decentres the implicit whiteness of normative critiques of audience studies and in the same stroke destabilises the authority of whiteness. Moreover, for Parameswaran, it foregrounds 'global audience hood' (ibid.: 332), in terms of how audiences consume both Western products and local, vernacular cultural productions. Postcolonial analysis thus encourages the researcher to question the *Eurocentricity* in the subjects that they pick. Communication scholars Shome and Hedge (2002) agree: postcolonial studies underlines the increasingly global nature of communication and, more importantly, highlights how globalisation itself is an outcome – among other things – of a set of motions instigated by colonialism and imperialism. In her study of middle-class Indian women's consumption of romance novels (which are looked down upon by cultural elites), Parameswaran (2006) demonstrates how it represents a gendered form of resistance against structures of domination (namely, high culture Western modernity and Indian patriarchy) that are shaped by the historical constitution of the Western text/non-Western audience relationship in colonial India. Thus, a postcolonial-centred approach to media research de-Westernises communication studies, challenging how very particular Western realities have become the universal condition.

To sum up, the value of postcolonial theory to media research is in how it demonstrates that images are the product of deep historical forces. Moreover, it emphasises the intersectionality of identity and how such identities are shaped by broader geopolitical forces (and histories). Postcolonial theory in media studies underscores the value of the critical cultural approach that I have emphasised thus far, focusing our attention on how 'cultures are constituted and contested' (Shome and Hedge, 2002: 262), adding much needed nuance, complexity and, crucially, a historical perspective to media and communication studies' analyses of race and culture.

But, as stated, a purely postcolonial approach to the study of race, culture and media has its limitations. In the previous chapter I referred to the danger of an over-emphasis on culture in terms of the textual, and this is something that can be applied to postcolonial studies. Central to Ella Shohat's and Ari Dirlik's respective critiques of postcolonialism is its overdetermining of culture at the expense of a proper analysis of the political-economic structures of oppression, which for Dirik in particular was the key feature of colonial rule. According to this argument, postcolonialism as a consequence fails to offer any political action capable of changing material conditions. But while this is an important criticism, that does not mean we must relegate any discussion of the cultural. Instead, to end the chapter, I develop this critique regarding postcolonial theory's disinterest in the question of the political-economic, but more explicitly in relation to media.

Postcolonial studies encounter two problems when it addresses the question for media. First is its lack of concern with popular culture, and its simplistic assertions around commodification. Perhaps a product of its literary roots, postcolonial studies is generally interested in 'high art', such as literature or film (though arthouse or 'Third World' cinema rather than Marvel superhero films) (Cere, 2011). As a consequence, it can be dismissive of popular culture. This is illustrated by postcolonialist Couze Venn's (1999: 46) critique of 'mass culture', which he sees as imbued with colonial ideology where the Other is disavowed, or sanitised, exoticised, 'commodified for the "tourist gaze"' (ibid.). As we shall see in Chapter 9, this is a common critique of popular culture's treatment of blackness in particular. According to this argument, commodified forms of culture are the primary vehicle through which Orientalist discourse and 'the constant reiteration of the superiority of the West' (ibid.: 45) persists in contemporary life. In postcolonial studies, high art forms are assumed to be autonomous, existing outside the commodity system. Popular culture, on the other hand, is a product of capitalist ideology and therefore neocolonial in nature. As shall be explored in Chapter 4, such a perspective is based on a conception of commodification that is highly simplistic, not least for how it ignores how even the most beloved texts of postcolonial scholars are, whether they like it or not, cultural commodities. For instance, Salman Rushdie's *Midnight's Children* is rightly regarded as one of the most important examples of postcolonial literature, but it is also a cultural commodity that, at the time of writing, is on sale on Amazon for £6.99, published by Vintage Classics, which is an imprint of Random House, which in turn is jointly owned by German media conglomerate Bertelsmann; it has made the publisher a lot of money. Postcolonial theory's refusal to tackle commodification seriously, and its tendency to dismiss any form of commercially produced culture as automatically ingrained with colonial as well as capitalist ideology, limits its understanding of the ambivalence of race under capitalism, and the counter-hegemonic potential contained within popular culture. Taking seriously the value of popular culture is a position usually associated with cultural studies, but as I will demonstrate in Chapter 6, it is a critical political economy approach that sheds the best light on the complexity and contradictions within the commodification of race.

The second key limitation of the postcolonial approach to media is its lack of interest in the cultural industries and the dynamics of industrial cultural production. Shome and Hedge (2002) and Cere (2011) each offer excellent accounts of the value of postcolonial studies to media and communication studies, but it is noticeable how in both texts little attention is paid to media itself, let alone the question of political economy. The focus instead for these authors is on culture and identity in relation to global communication. When not just focused on the text, postcolonial studies of media tend to be concerned with media culture at the level of consumption and how it shapes realities, from cultural identities to geopolitical relations. But it has less to say about the operation of media as institution. When postcolonial scholars do engage with questions relating to the political economy of media, they too often slip into *functionalist* and *determinist* reading of media (Saha, 2018).

This is particularly evident in Edward Said's own work on media, particularly his book *Covering Islam* (1981), which is a more direct postcolonial take on media culture in relation to Islam. Said here situates Islamophobia in the news within the historical context of Orientalist scholarship, and in doing so provides, as one would expect, a persuasive account of how contemporary depictions of Islam and Muslim nations in media are rooted in Europe's first engagements with Islam in the modern era (explored further in Chapter 8 on Islamophobia and media). Said questions the objectivity and neutrality of US news programmes in particular (and only fleetingly refers to popular culture throughout the whole book): '[they] do not only give us the news, they also (usually unconsciously) represent what's happening from the standpoint of U.S. interests' (ibid.: 45). Said explains the reproduction of Orientalist discourse, and rampant Islamophobia in the news media as due to how journalists internalise dominant ideology – 'a process of incorporation and introjection via an efficient ideology of inclusion' (ibid.). In this regard, Said conceptualises the media, just like Louis Althusser (2006 [1971]) before him, as '*apparatus*' (Said, 1981: 47, my emphasis), and in the process evokes the functionalist account of media, that is, media as a mere instrument of powerful political and corporate interests. But is the picture as simple as this? Said's line of argument regarding news reporting echoes the work of media activist Noam Chomsky and what Hesmondhalgh (2018) calls the 'Schiller-McChesney' school of political economy, which uses detailed archival and investigative research to expose how the media is owned by a powerful elite who use it to propagate capitalist/neocolonialist ideology. However, while appreciating its emphasis on politics and the challenging of media elites, Hesmondhalgh is critical of the Schiller-McChesney approach for its lack of interest/understanding in news dynamics and media production. Such a model of the media slips into functionalism in that it paints a picture of the dominant class wielding the media for its own ends, without accounting for the complexity, contestation and contradiction that characterises news/cultural production – not least the issue of the agency of individual journalists. While Said acknowledges the processes within the media that shape news stories on Muslims, he nonetheless employs a very top-down model of media, which is painted as a conduit for Orientalism. While the essence of his overall argument about how media reproduces Orientalist discourse is persuasive, the idea of media as an instrument or apparatus of power is far too simplistic. Instead, ideology works through media in a much more complex way - and is always being contested from below. I will explore the issue of media and Islamophobia in more detail in Chapter 8. Before then, in Chapter 6, I will demonstrate how critical media studies provides a more nuanced account of the operations of media power in relation to ideology.

3.5 Conclusion

Despite these limitations I maintain that postcolonial studies need to take a foundational role in the analysis of race, media and culture. Postcolonialism helps explain why representations of racial and ethnic minorities tend to fall into the same tropes or narratives. In doing so it emphasises the centrality of the cultural sphere to power, through concepts of hegemony and discourse. To paraphrase Born and Hesmondhalgh (2000), culture is not a purely autonomous, innocent sphere of life, but is how former colonial powers maintain dominance in a time when *overt* militaristic Imperial conquest is more difficult to get away with. It also helps us to formulate cultural forms of resistance, in terms of *representations* of race that challenge and attempt to break the binary opposition between Self and Other upon which nationalist discourse – and white superiority – relies (which I shall develop further in Chapter 5).

But as I explored, postcolonialism can neglect the industrial nature of the making of representations, which after all are a product of the cultural industries. Moreover, it lacks a more detailed discussion of media power itself that does not slip into functional accounts that see media as an apparatus of neocolonial power. Postcolonialism in its most elitist iterations can be very snobbish towards popular culture, which it argues, by its very commodified nature, embodies Orientalist ideology. However, my intention in demonstrating postcolonial theory's shortcomings is not to undermine its overall value. Instead, such a critical engagement highlights the need for an interdisciplinary approach to race, culture and media that incorporates postcolonial perspectives. To reiterate, postcolonialism needs to occupy a foundational position in analysis of race, culture and media. But in order to really do justice to the complexity of how dynamics, race and culture play out in media, we need to think through how economic relations shape the making of race. This is the subject of the next chapter, when I consider race, culture and media more explicitly in relation to capitalism.

3.6 Recommended and further reading

Postcolonial theorist Robert Young (1995: 163) refers to Edward Said, Gayatri Spivak and Homi Bhabha slightly ironically as the 'Holy Trinity of colonial-discourse analysis', but the work of these three figures – alongside the foundational work of Frantz Fanon – are central to postcolonial studies. While their writings are rich and complex, they are not always that accessible for those new to this field, in which case a blog post by critical race scholar Alana Lentin (2017) on 'Decolonising epistemologies' (found on her excellent teaching blog: www.alanalentin.net/2017/02/10/decolonising-epistemologies/) is a good entry point, providing an overview of postcolonial studies and also the new forms of 'decolonial' thinking that are gaining traction right now (see Box 3.1).

In terms of postcolonial approaches to media specifically, Rhadika Hedge and Raka Shome's (2002) special issue on postcolonial theory for the *Journal of Communication Theory* was one of the first of its kind in the field as whole and gives an important critical account of the state of communication studies and how it tackles questions of Otherness, and why postcolonial studies can make an important contribution to the study of media culture. As stated at the start of the chapter, postcolonial approaches to media tend to focus on texts or (global) audiences. The collection *Everyday Media Culture in Africa: Audiences and Users*, edited by Wendy Willems and Winston Mano (2017), uses a postcolonial frame to challenge the conceptualisation of African audiences as passive, and backward users of technology, but also the idea that Africa is a mere site to apply and test Western-derived ideas around media consumption. For an illustration of the representational approach, Isabel Molina-Guzmán's (2006) work on the construction of Latina women in US popular culture successfully fuses postcolonial theory with a critical account of capitalism, demonstrating how hybrid identities become commodified. The work of Paula Chakravartty (2006), including various pieces that she has co-authored (with Yuezhi Zhao, 2007; with Amin Alhassan, 2011; with Denise Ferreira da Silva, 2012; with Srirupa Roy, 2013), also provides an illustration of postcolonial accounts of media and communication that has the question of political economy at its core. In this vein, the open access online journal *darkmatter* (www.darkmatter101.org/site/) provides a rich archive of critical postcolonial accounts of media, and capitalism more broadly.

BOX 3.1   Key Issue

#CommunicationSoWhite and decolonising media and communication studies

As alluded to in this chapter, there has been a growing political and academic movement based around the notion of *decolonisation*. To illustrate this approach – as distinct from postcolonial theory – we can examine the recent attempts to decolonise academic disciplines.

For researchers of race and ethnicity there remains a feeling that such a topic is considered marginal by the disciplines within and across which they work. In the context of media and communication studies, an important piece of research conducted by Paula Chakravartty, Rachel Kuo, Victoria Grubbs and Charlton McIlwain (2018) in an article entitled '#CommunicationSoWhite' demonstrated starkly through statistical analysis how race and ethnic studies is marginalised. Examining the racial/ethnic make-up of editorial boards in the key journals, publication rates and citation rates (the number of times that a piece of research is referenced by other research), the study showed that researchers from ethnic/racial minority backgrounds are significantly underrepresented in comparison to their white counterparts. The authors argue that the field of media and communication studies have been shaped by colonial legacies where white masculinity becomes the discipline's normative core.

This intervention has been shaped by a broader move towards 'decolonising' the academy (Bhambra et al., 2018). The idea of decolonisation in the context of intellectual labour came out of a critique of postcolonial theory as increasingly convoluted, esoteric and elitist (Dirlik, 1994). The turn to decolonisation, then, was an attempt to inject a renewed political impetus. In a nutshell, the decolonial approach is based on the *decolonisation* of knowledge and the decentering of the telling of the world's history from the position of the West, challenging the assumption that (Western) modernity is universal, let alone an aspiration for all nations (Lentin, 2017). As such, the decolonial project entails the building of new decolonialised epistemologies – or frameworks of knowledge.

In the context of media and communication studies, this relates to the de-Westernising project described in Box 2.1. But it also has particular relevance for critical race scholars who can bring their perspectives on the marginalisation of race/ethnicity research to expose the white masculinist core of the discipline, as Chakravartty et al. show, that has shaped its history and development (see also Mukherjee, 2020). This is in terms of citational practices, but also hiring processes, and addressing the multidimensional ways that racial inequalities manifest in the academy at large (see Ng et al., 2020). Thus, the purpose of #CommunicationSoWhite is to draw attention to the white hegemony that continues to dictate the field and marginalise racialised Others. It does not entail the mere removal of white straight men from the canon, but the creation of new, more radically inclusive frameworks.

Discussion

What does the move to 'decolonise' knowledge capture that postcolonial theory does not? Is the distinction between the two approaches as clear-cut as we might assume?

4

Race, Capitalism and Media

Is capitalism inherently racist? If not, what is the relationship between racial ideology and capitalist ideology?

What is the value of the concepts of racial capitalism and racial neoliberalism? How do they apply to media?

Why is commodification such an important concept for understanding race and media?

What does it mean to apply a 'conjunctural' or historical approach to the study of race, culture and media?

4.1 Introduction

Having explored how legacies of empire shape how media make race, in this chapter we focus on capitalism as a determining force upon race-making practices. As we shall explore, media representations of race are consumed in the form of cultural commodities, and as such we must not ignore how capitalism plays a big role in *determining* (using Raymond Williams' (1973: 4) definition of determination as 'setting limits, exerting pressures' and placing constraints upon on an object) what representations of racial and ethnic minorities appear in the marketplace. Postcolonial studies of media tend to conflate the reproduction of colonial ideology with the cultural industries' drive for profit, leading to the claim that capitalist ideology is inherently racist/Orientalist. But is it as simple as that? Certainly, commercial media, with its tendency towards standardisation and homogenisation, turn to racial stereotypes in order to make profit (Gandy, 1998: 4). However, as suggested in Chapter 1 (and will be explored further in Chapter 6) it can also, even in its most corporate form, produce incredibly subversive content, or indeed representations of race that go against the grain of dominant culture. Indeed, this is precisely the reason why so many of us are invested in the politics of news and popular culture.

One way of opening up the discussion of capitalism, race and media is to ask the following question: is media in the West more interested in extracting profit, or sustaining racial hierarchies? For many scholars of race and media, the answer is an easy if not slightly glib one: both; that the two things go together. In this chapter I demonstrate how the picture is more complicated, and that 'both' by itself is not a satisfactory answer. Racial ideology and commercial imperative do align (in that racial stereotypes are profitable), perhaps most of the time, but their relation changes over time and they can occasionally in fact *contradict* each other. As such, more precision is needed in terms of understanding how economic and racial ideologies intertwine across different spatial and temporal contexts and how this shapes race-making practices in media. Racial ideology (race) and capitalist ideology (the economic) are inextricably intertwined, but should be understood as distinct forces nonetheless.

In this chapter I shine a light on the economic relations that drive race-making. It begins with an introduction to the notion of 'racial capitalism' as a way to think how race and racism contributes to the expansion of capitalism. This is followed by a critical discussion of the concept of cultural commodification – including what I identify as top-down and bottom-up perspectives – in order to unravel how the dynamics of race and capital play out in the cultural industries. To finish the chapter, I underline the importance of a historical – or *conjunctural* – approach to how media make race, illustrated with an analysis of 'diversity' in this moment of 'racial neoliberalism'. The overall purpose of the chapter is to develop an account of how capitalism shapes race-making practices in media that can account for complexity without blunting our critique of capitalism and racism in media.

4.2 Racial capitalism

What is the value of race to capitalism? According to orthodox versions of Marxism (sometimes referred to as 'vulgar Marxism'), racism is a by-product of the fundamental struggle between classes. It follows that to solve racism, you need to fix the problem of class. This has the consequence of sidelining both anti-racist politics and race-based analyses in general. But as critical race scholars show, racism (and the idea of race), rather than an epiphenomenon – or side-effect - of capitalism, has in fact been key to capitalism's growth.

Such an argument has been explored through the idea of 'racial capitalism'. Rather than a singular theory, the discussion of racial capitalism encompasses a range of different perspectives and approaches, some more in conversation with Marxist theory than others (Robinson, 2000 [1983]; Leong, 2012; Melamed, 2015; Bhattacharyya,

2018; Virdee, 2019). What they all have in common, however, is a desire to centralise the question of race in analyses of capitalism. The idea of racial capitalism subsequently provides a useful framework through which to explore the dynamics of capital and race in relation to race-making in media.

In its broadest sense, the discussion around racial capitalism is based on the argument that the oppression of racial minorities was central to Western civilisation and the birth of the modern nation state rather than an after-effect, as argued in the previous chapter. Race and racism contributed to the expansion of capitalism and the subsequent global dominance of the West in two ways. First is in terms of the economic, where, through slavery and colonialism, stratifying society in terms of race was a way to produce a class faction of cheap labour, thus decreasing low-skilled wages (Pitcher, 2012; Virdee, 2019). The second contribution is in terms of the epistemological: in order to expand globally capitalist nations relied upon hierarchies of race to justify slavery and colonial conquest and, in turn, reinforce the superiority of white European culture (Hall, 1992). Thus, one of the legacies of slavery and colonialism that still shapes the present is the very idea of 'race' itself. As made clear in the previous chapter, the epistemological value of 'race' to the West is particularly pertinent for the study of race, culture and media.

Studies of racial capitalism generally lack an interest in media and its implication in it. One exception comes from Anne McClintock (1995) in her book *Imperial Leather*. Though she does not herself use the term, McClintock nonetheless produces one of the strongest analyses of racial capitalism and media (broadly conceived) through a historical analysis of the emergence of 'commodity racism' in Victorian Britain. McClintock focuses on the burgeoning advertising industry of the time, particularly soap adverts that played on strong racial tropes, including a campaign for Pears soap that portrayed black babies as dirty, and white babies as angelic and pure. McClintock demonstrates how racial and capitalist ideologies fed into each other in particular ways at the peak moment of the British Empire. The basis of her argument is that, echoing the contributions to the idea of racial capitalism, 'imperialism and the invention of race were fundamental aspects of Western, industrial modernity' (ibid.: 5). Put another way, racism/sexism and capitalism exist in a dialectical relationship: the domination of the raced and gendered Other had an economic basis, and the economic exploitation of the Other depended on racial and gender subjection. For McClintock, it was through advertising that colonialism – and with it the idea of race – was transplanted into the imperial metropolis. She observes how soap manufacturing in particular flourished, not just because of its importance to the domestic economy, but because of how it carried with it ideas around both 'racial hygiene and imperial progress' (ibid.: 209). She labels this 'commodity racism', a new form of racism that replaces scientific racism. Developing her argument further, McClintock describes how 'commodity jingoism ... helped reinvent and maintain British national unity in the face of deepening imperial competition, and colonial resistance' (ibid.). Thus, according to McClintock's historical analysis, geopolitical developments in the Victoria era led to a particular conflation of nationalist/racial and capitalist ideologies within Great Britain. Through a discussion of the advertising of the time, McClintock shows us how the creation of race in the Imperial context had both an economic *and* ideological objective.

McClintock's analysis of racial capitalism in the Victorian era demonstrates how the idea of 'race' was central to the sustenance of British power at a time of global unrest. But more than an illustration of how economical exploitation and racial subjugation go hand in hand, I use McClintock's work to make a more subtle point: that race is an independent social category that cannot be reduced to the economic level of determination, that is, it cannot be explained by economic factors alone. Racist and capitalist ideologies are better understood as distinct but intertwined, entangled in a way that takes different forms at different moments in history; as stated, in McClintock's analysis the Victorian era sees a racism based on racial science replaced by a more cultural version in the form of commodity racism. Thus, rather than the idea that racism is intrinsic to capitalism (as opposed to an epiphenomenon), racism is better understood as a system independent of capitalism – they have different origins, timelines and histories. To reiterate, the idea of race and capitalist ideology need to be treated as two separate forces that exist in a dynamic relation. Such a notion shall be unravelled further later on in the chapter, when, influenced by McClintock's study, the case for a historical approach to race, capitalism and media is made. However, as mentioned, media features little in discussions of racial capitalism. As such, in the following section I provide a provide a critical analysis of race and capitalism more explicitly in relation to media, through the concept of *cultural commodification*.

4.3 Race, culture and the politics of commodification

Cultural commodification refers to the transformation of culture (which has no inherent exchange value) into a commodity with exchange value. The question of commodification needs to take a central role in the discussion of media and racial capitalism. After all, we consume representations of race in the form of cultural commodities – a book, a film, a television show, or a record – whether they arrive in physical or digital form. What makes cultural commodities distinct from other goods is their *primary* symbolic element – that is, their use value is in their cultural meaning and what they symbolise. As Comaroff and Comaroff (2009: 23) state, cultural commodification produces in fact an 'excess' of symbolic value.

Commodification as a concept helps us to think through the value of race to capitalism. It highlights how the representation of race, its production and consumption, has an economic element as well as a cultural one (something that postcolonial and cultural studies approaches to media can sometimes forget or ignore).

To repeat, the representation of racial minorities in media are consumed in the form of cultural commodities. Even the news media, which we think of as primarily informational (or indeed, ideological), should be regarded as a commodity, used to create audiences to sell to advertisers.[1] This will affect the form news takes; for instance, the increasingly competitive media environment has arguably led to the *tabloidisation* of news media – that is, the transformation of news into something more populist and sensationalist in order to drive mass sales – leading in turn to blunt coverage of racialised 'folk devils' (Cohen, 2002), a recurring theme in Chapters 7, 8 and 9 on migrants, Muslims and black youth, respectively.

Rather than a neutral, descriptive term, commodification in critical cultural theory has a negative connotation. Marxists critique commodification primarily in terms of the exploitation of the labour that goes into the making of the commodity (and how it is disguised by the aura of the commodity itself). Critical race scholars, on the other hand, focus on ideology in relation to commodification; that is, they are concerned with the ideological consequences when race/culture is transformed into a commodity.[2] I am referring specifically here to a particular *top-down* analysis of commodification. There is an alternative account of commodification that comes from a bottom-up perspective that attends to the complexity and ambivalence of commodification, which provides a more nuanced account of the relations between race and capitalism in the context of media culture. Nonetheless, with its stress on the ideological operations of commodification, the top-down version of commodification produces important insights that should still inform our analysis of media and racial capitalism.

4.3.1 The 'commodification of race'

Commodification as an ideological process refers to how the representation of race in commodity form helps sustain (rather than challenge) racial hierarchies and the (white) capitalist order. There is one version of this argument that describes when race is used as a quality to help distinguish commodities in an overcrowded, competitive market (Huq, 2003), repackaged through the language of 'diversity' as a marker of different lifestyles, market niches and branded goods (Mukherjee, 2011; Gilroy, 2013a; Gray, 2016). (I shall return to this topic towards the end of the chapter.) The version of the commodification of race argument that I want to focus on here, however, refers to when the culture of racialised groups is mined by capitalism, co-opted, repackaged and sold to the mainstream, diffusing any of the counter-hegemonic potential that the expressive culture in question might have held in the first place. For instance, in the previous chapter I mentioned the 'Asian Underground' dance scene from the mid-1990s, which for many exemplified the politics of 'hybridity' as it fused Western dance genres, such as drum & bass and breakbeat, with Asian musical influences, including Indian classical music and Bollywood soundtracks.

In doing so, the predominantly Asian DJs and musicians in the scene were celebrated for articulating new, exciting British Asian identities. Yet some cultural studies scholars felt that this was too generous a reading, and that in fact the hybridity in this music had become a commodity in itself – and reduced to a marketing gimmick. In other words, through commodification, the radical potential of hybridity is ironically transformed into exoticised, fetishised difference (Ash Sharma, 1996; Sanjay Sharma, 1996). A more contemporary example is grime music, which was once the underground expression of some of the most disenfranchised in society, but is now used by huge corporations to sell its products and services, whether Skepta in Nike's *Nothing Beats a Londoner* campaign, or Lady Leshurr in an HSBC advert selling student bank accounts.

Perhaps the most famous critique of the commodification of race comes from black radical feminist bell hooks, in her essay 'Eating the Other' (1992). hooks reads the commodification of the Other in the context of black popular culture as an ideological process that sustains the status quo and the marginalisation of non-white groups. For hooks, mass, commercialised culture is inscribed with 'imperialist nostalgia' (ibid.: 25) tied up with a longing for the primitive Other. hooks is stressing the sexual dimension to the commodification of difference. Through what she calls 'the seductive promise' (ibid.: 22) of the encounter with the Other, the White subject anticipates transformation, a transgression of racial boundaries, but crucially in a way that does not actually require the White Self to 'relinquish forever one's mainstream positionality' (ibid.). Thus, for hooks, *eating the Other* in the form of commodity consumption is a self-conscious engagement with difference but in a way that conveniently forgets the histories of oppression upon which such a consumption is based. It certainly provides one explanation for the white suburban American teen's obsession with gangsta rap. So the racialised Other has a value, but in a way that reinscribes the power of the dominant culture in the process.

What I have presented here can be characterised as the top-down version of the commodification of race argument for the way that they stress the ideological dimensions of commodification. According to this argument, there is more at stake than just the exploitation of the worker. I want to draw attention to hooks' argument in particular for highlighting the sexual nature of the consumption of Otherness in the form of cultural commodities – an issue that shall recur in Part III of this book. However, there are two issues with the top-down approach. First, the general rhetoric around the commodification of race can too often slip into polemics (bell hooks even goes as far as calling Beyoncé a 'terrorist' for the manner in which she commodifies herself, 'colluding in the construction of herself as a slave' (King, 2014)), without attending to the complexity, contestedness and ambivalence of the process of commodification itself (Saha, 2018: 69–74). Secondly, it offers an overly pessimistic account of intercultural exchange in media. The problem with the top-down version of commodification is that it forecloses the potential of the cultural commodity, essentially suggesting that as soon as it is commodified, culture is reduced to exchange value only; the battle has been lost as culture has become a pawn of capitalist ideology. Such a view is far too fatalistic, not least for the way in which it ignores how cultural commodities can enrich our lives as well as public culture. If we return to the example of grime, one could argue that acts like Stormzy have used their commodified status to draw attention to state racism in Britain, much more than any politician. Indeed, the top-down version of the commodification of race argument is incompatible with Hall's conception of popular culture as a war of position that better captures the politics of commodified culture. However, as mentioned, there is an alternative version of commodification that can be described as 'bottom-up'. In contrast to the top-down approaches concerned with the question of ideology alone, the bottom-up perspective explores commodification in relation to the production, circulation and consumption of culture commodities at the micro level.

4.3.2 Bottom-up accounts of cultural commodification

Despite my criticisms, the strongest versions of the top-down approach – such as the specific examples cited above – shed light on how commodification works as an ideological process. A bottom-up perspective of the commodification of race, however, understands that while the third space is a commodified space (in that it is increasingly difficult to produce culture outside capitalism), the cultural horizon is always open. I want to briefly focus on two approaches to cultural commodification that typify a bottom-up view.

The first comes from a group of cultural geographers, including Claire Dwyer, Phil Jackson and Phillip Crang, working in the cultural economy tradition. In contrast to the mostly theoretical speculations of the top-down approach to commodification, these authors produce an empirical study of the entanglements of commerce and culture in the transnational production of ethnicised commodities. I will discuss the cultural economy approach in more detail in Chapter 6, but in a nutshell, its aim is to blur the distinction made in political economy between culture and the economic, emphasising instead the economic nature of culture and the cultural nature of the economic. Using a number of case studies, from the mass manufacture of jarred Indian curry sauce in Britain (Jackson, 2002; Crang et al., 2003) to fashion designers working across Mumbai and London (Dwyer and Crang, 2002; Jackson et al., 2007), the researchers begin with an urge to deconstruct simplistic and romantic notions of 'culture' (as meaningful, creative, authentic) and disdainful versions of 'commercialism' (which is seen as vulgar and materialist, where agency is subordinated by the logic of capital). Together, they make two broad arguments that challenge the top-down version of the commodification of race and its emphasis on ideology. First, echoing the literatures on digital race culture that was covered in Chapter 2, the authors in their various case studies argue that ethnic identities do not exist in a pure state prior to commodification, but are reproduced through the social and material processes of cultural production itself. Secondly, critical of the tendency to overly celebrate or overly critique 'ethnicised commodities', Dwyer and Crang (2002: 412) would rather declare an 'open-verdict' on the political outcomes of commodity culture. As Phil Jackson (2002: 16) asserts, in a direct counter to bell hooks, 'while "eating the Other" may be an expression of power and privilege (in some circumstances), it may (in other circumstances) provide an entrée to more critical forms of multiculturalism'. Drawing from personal experience, I think of my (white) brother-in-law, and how his profound love of black music genres like hip-hop, soul and funk opened his eyes up to experiences beyond the predominantly white world within which he grew up (see Street (2012: 166) for a telling of a similar personal story based on his encounter with the song 'Shopping for Clothes' by The Coasters). Dwyer et al.'s arguments are the result of an empirical analysis of how cultural commodification is experienced on the ground and highlights the complexity of cultural production and consumption.

While the emphasis on complexity is important, this particular empirical approach to cultural commodification can paint a picture of production and consumption as a mere tangle of circuits leading to random outcomes. Such an approach, in my view, dangerously downplays structure – and ideology. The fact is, there is something about how race is fetishised and instrumentalised in commodity culture that needs to be recognised, but that avoids the economic determinism that can characterise the top-down approach to commodification. Anthropologists John Comaroff and Jean Comaroff (2009), in their book *Ethnicities Inc.*, provide a more theoretically robust bottom-up account of commodification that can explain ambivalence rather than just declare an *open verdict*. To begin, similar to Crang, Dwyer and Jackson, Comaroff and Comaroff (ibid.: 23) reject a dialectical model of commodification that places identity and culture in opposition to commerce. As the authors state, 'The intensive marketing of ethnic identity may involve a Faustian bargain of sorts [but it] also appears to (re)fashion identity, to (re)animate cultural subjectivity, to (re)charge collective self-awareness, to forge patterns of sociality, *all within the marketplace*' (ibid.: 27) (my emphasis). In other words, ethnic identities are effectively constructed within the marketplace, which in turn can be enabling for those groups in terms of forging community. Through a number of case studies, the authors demonstrate how 'indigenous' cultures of various sorts, whether the Pedi people of South Africa or the Welsh in Great Britain, have at times commodified their identities, which may involve homogenisation or exoticisation, but can also lead to material gain and/or political recognition. For instance, the way that the Maasai people in Kenya have become a tourist attraction where they perform their rituals and customs for foreigners in exchange for a fee might make some uncomfortable, but it has led to the growth of their population as well as ensured the survival of age-old customs. Comaroff and Comaroff's emphasis on ambivalence captures the politics of the commodification of culture in a more nuanced way than the cultural economy approach described above. Indeed, it is this understanding of commodification's inherently enabling/constraining dynamics (Saha, 2018) that needs to underpin our analysis of how media make race in the context of racial capitalism.

4.4 A historical approach to race, capitalism and media

To recap, this chapter asks: what is the value of race to capitalism and how does this shape how media make race? Through a discussion of racial capitalism, I began by arguing that we need to think of racial and capitalist ideologies as two distinct forces that are nonetheless wound up in each other. This prevents a slip into a simplistic argument that capitalism is inherently racist. Rather, racism is better understood as an independent force shaped by capitalism in particular ways at particular conjunctural moments (and vice versa). As sociologist Ben Pitcher (2012: 8) states, 'the relationship between racism and capitalism is contingent on the historically specific conditions of a given social formation, and not on the essential character of capitalism *per se*'. As an illustration of this dynamic we can refer back to Anne McClintock's account of racism during Victorian Britain, where she describes a shift from scientific racism to commodity racism, shaped by geopolitical developments, the growth of consumer markets, and the development of new media technologies with respect to advertising. As we shall see shortly, the shift towards neoliberalism has changed the nature of racism once again, with the ascendency of discourses of 'postrace' and 'diversity'. So again, we should avoid simplistic arguments around the claim that capitalism produces racism. Rather, capitalism, both its ideology and structural form, shapes racism and ideas about race in particular ways at particular times.

In the section that followed I demonstrated the importance of commodification as a concept to help think through how capitalism shapes race-making in media specifically. As stated, ideas or representations of race are consumed in the form of cultural commodities. I presented two arguments, the first a *top-down* account of the 'commodification of race' that stresses commodification as an ideological process that determines the production and consumption of race through commodity culture, sustaining racial hierarchies in the process, and the second, a *bottom-up* approach, that describes commodification as a complex and ambivalent process. I suggested that the latter approach better captures how media make race, not least in relation to Hall's notion of the field of popular culture as a war of position, but only if, in the move to stress complexity and contestation, we do not downplay power. After all, there is a reason why racial and ethnic minorities continue to be represented according to the same seemingly immutable tropes, despite whatever contradictions may (and do) occur. In a nutshell, I am arguing that in order to understand the relation between capitalism and race in relation to media, we need to adopt a historical approach, not in the sense of presenting historical case studies, but in the sense of how at different moments in history certain forces (whether capitalism, racism, nationalism, technological) come together in particular ways to shape the organisation of society. Stuart Hall and Doreen Massey talk about this in terms of conjuncture, 'a period during which the different social, political, economic and ideological contradictions that are at work in society come together to give it a specific and distinctive shape' (Hall and Massey, 2010). We might think of this current conjuncture as defined by (racial) neoliberalism. Thus, in relation to the topic of racism and media, the task then is to unpick what capitalism and racial ideology *are doing* at a specific conjuncture, and then apply this to media's making of race. Such a historical or conjunctural approach (see Gilbert, 2019) attends to the specific histories of race and capitalism as they develop in particular national contexts.

Exemplifying the approach to race, capitalism and media that I am calling for is Herman Gray's (2005) discussion of black cultural production and cultural politics. Gray is similarly cynical of 'polemics about the commodification of blackness' (ibid.: 25), and instead argues for an understanding of 'media, commodification and technology as social forces and circumstances, structuring the conditions of possibility within which black cultural politics are enacted, constrained and mediated' (ibid.: 3–4). Gray encourages us to think through how blackness circulates as commodity, 'disrupting and threatening, domesticating and reorganising social and cultural relations, as it touches down, is taken up, disarticulated, and redeployed in different locations' (ibid.: 4). Not unlike the cultural economy approach outlined earlier, Gray underscores the circuits and networks of black cultural production and consumption, rejecting top-down conceptualisations of cultural commodification in the process. But unlike those authors cited, this is framed explicitly in terms of the politics of representation, the potential of such a politics, but also the constraints placed upon it. Gray provides a complex account of the relations between race and capitalism in relation to media culture and technologies. But we can boil down Gray's argument to one key point: the commodification of blackness is ambivalent in that it can produce both radical and reactionary effects, and this crucially depends on context. The cultural politics of race as Stuart Hall puts it, is *contingent* (Hall, 1988: 28). Thus, to reiterate further, to answer the question '*how does capitalism shape race-making practices in media?*', we need a historical approach that seeks to unravel the particular relation between economic and ideological forces within the given social formation.

4.5 Racial neoliberalism, diversity and media

To illustrate such an approach let us take this current moment and examine the 'structuring conditions' (Gray, 2005: 20) that are shaping race-making practices in media. These are particular interesting times as far as the question of race and media is concerned, as we are seemingly presented with a paradox: a situation where race is represented according to either a colour-blind version of 'diversity', or in a way where it is *over-determined* and the source of content itself. In either case, we have gone from invisibility to *hypervisibility* (Gray, 2013a). Flicking through Netflix, the current cinema releases or indeed the channels that make up terrestrial television (if anyone still does that), it is increasingly rare to find productions that do not contain at least one black, brown or Asian face in some capacity. One might explain this as a *natural* consequence of how black, brown and Asian people have become more integrated into Western societies. However, such an assertion is hard to swallow in a period that has witnessed the rise of far-right populism, the Windrush scandal, a 'hostile environment', rampant Islamophobia, the recurrence of antisemitism that in fact never went away, and the revoking of citizenship and deportation of black and brown people, being *sent back* to somewhere that in many cases they have never actually been. Rather, the hypervisibility of difference in media can be better read in terms of the nature of contemporary racial capitalism, and specifically, the current conjuncture of neoliberalism.

Neoliberalism, very simply, dictates that the market is king and that state must be removed from all aspects of life (though it relies on the state to enact its policies). This is carried out in the name of economic growth, although such growth appears to apply to literally a handful of individuals; the gap between the wealthiest and the poorest in Western society, economist say, has never been wider. Through neoliberal policies we find the decline of public institutions and increased marketisation, not least in media, which has led to the dominance of a handful of major corporations which dominate production. Returning to the question of race, the critical race scholar David Theo Goldberg (2009a) describes a new form of racial governance under neoliberalism, that he calls *racial neoliberalism*. There are two aspects to this. First is the emergence of a discourse of 'postrace', that, it is claimed, signifies the end of racial oppression. However, as Goldberg (ibid.) states, postrace is better understood as a form of anti-racialism, that is the muting of race and racism when trying to explain structural inequalities in society in terms of race. While the Macpherson Enquiry drew attention to institutional racism in the police force and beyond, under racial neoliberalism institutions now disavow racism (Nwonka and Malik, 2018). Racism has become the problem of the individual rather than something that is in fact entrenched in the state (Kapoor, 2013). Secondly, under racial neoliberalism emerges a new form of citizenship based on consumer sovereignty (Gray, 2013a: 778); consumer rights rather than civil rights. The politics of recognition (Taylor, 1994), initially based upon ensuring representational parity for marginalised groups, has now become conflated with a logic of niche marketing. For Paul Gilroy (2013b: 557), this has placed limitations on the political imagination: 'The very best we can hope for may be that the old chestnuts of whiteness and blackness will fade away into generic, market-based identities or "life styles"'. In these terms, racial neoliberalism 'willingly concedes, even celebrates difference' (Gray, 2013a: 780), but in a way that disavows entirely the question of racial oppression and structural inequalities (according to the discourse of postrace). For Barnor Hesse, this is a new form of racialised govern-mentality, built into the very structure of Western democracies that 'promote racial equality while sustaining racial inequality' (quoted in Burtenshaw, 2012).

How has racial neoliberalism shaped how media make race? As stated, it is led to a proliferation of *postracial*, colour-blind depictions of racial and ethnic minorities, where their racial difference is a 'veneer' to look at rather than something to explore in any kind of depth (Kohnen, 2015). This is the logic of what Sarita Malik (2013a) calls 'creative diversity' discourse in the context of British public service broadcast-ing, a shift in policy from the soft anti-racism of multicultural policy to a race-less notion of 'diversity'. Diversity in this sense has led to the commodification of racial identity that dehistoricises and removes the question of race altogether (Leong, 2012; Gray, 2013a). As such, in fictional programming we see colour-blind forms of casting, which appear progressive in that characters are not reduced to their racial identity, but in fact suppresses any discussion of racism (Warner, 2015b). A similar trend is found in reality television and lifestyle programming which displays an abundance of difference, where the inclusion of black and brown faces literally adds *colour* to the line-up of contestants (Malik, 2014).

But this is not the whole picture. As stated, we also see an over-determining of race in media discourse. As media scholar Amy Hasinoff (2008: 327) argues, depictions of race are not always raceless under neoliberalism; at times it 'valorizes and commodi-fies racial self-transformation'. Hasinoff is referring to popular reality TV show *Amer-ica's Next Top Model* and the case of African American model Danielle. *America's Next Top Model* is a typical reality show from the 2000s, where a group of young women are plucked from obscurity and placed in an artificial environment to have their behav-iours judged by the viewing public – as well as the actual judges in this instance, who decide who has the qualities to become a professional model. In her critical account, Hasinoff demonstrates how the management of Danielle's particular southern (that is, racial and class) identity, and specifically her accent, becomes a key arc of the series. Hasinoff unravels how, in this instance, race, rather than something that is either ignored or airbrushed, becomes media content itself (see Titley, 2019). How-ever, while the over-determination of race, where it defines the storyline and the con-tent, might appear to go against the grain of postracial diversity discourse, the author shows how it nonetheless fulfils a neoliberal logic, where race, rather than a product of structural inequalities, is a problem of/for the individual; something that Danielle has to get over herself (while absolutely *not* drawing attention to structural racism and sexism that defines the beauty industries). In the process, the storyline reinforces the notion of what Jo Littler (2017: 151) calls 'neoliberal postracial meritocracy'; the myth of society as a level-playing field, where individuals – black and white – are equal participants in a game where those with the most talent and strongest work-ethic get the furthest.

Thus, under racial neoliberalism, racial difference and what it means has been reconfigured, such that ideas around cultural diversity go hand in hand with neoliberal principles of postracial neoliberal meritocracy and what Nisha Kapoor (2013: 4) calls the 'privatisation of race'. In the context of media, we see a proliferation of racial difference, but in a way that facilitates the opening of new audiences, and in turn, new markets and opportunities for business. Within this neoliberal conjuncture racial ideologies intertwine with capitalist/neoliberal ideologies in a particular way to produce a discourse of diversity as a 'technique of power' (Gray, 2016: 242). Crucially, diversity is enacted in a way that does not merely wilfully ignore, but is outright hostile towards any discussion of structural racial inequality (Titley, 2019). Conversely, media loves nothing more than racial conflict at the level of individuals for the reason it produces valuable content.

4.6 Conclusion

The discussion of capitalism, race and media was framed initially by the question: is media more interested in reproducing racial inequalities or making profit? I suggested that the obvious answer, 'both', while broadly true, does not attend to the complexity of how capitalism shapes how media make race. In this chapter I made four points: (1) capitalist ideology and racist ideology need to be treated as separate and distinct forces (it is not the simple case that capitalism is inherently racist); nonetheless (2) capitalist and racial ideologies are inextricably intertwined and together produce different types of racism at different points in history; (3) the way these forces come together determine the nature of cultural commodification as it takes place in media; (4) we need a historical approach designed to unpick the interrelations between ideologies of race and capitalism within a particular social formation and how this determines, though not in a straightforward way, race-making practices. The chapter ended with an illustration of such an approach in the discussion of the ascendency of 'diversity' discourse within the neoliberal conjuncture.

The discussion of how media make race in the period of neoliberalism was intended only as an opening; in the case studies that constitute the chapters of Part III we will look in much more detail how racial neoliberalism has shaped, for instance, Islamophobia in media, and the production and circulation of 'blackness'. In those chapters as well, there will be a greater emphasis on contradiction. Indeed, the issue of contradiction will be addressed more directly in Chapter 6, where I consider the specific nature of media power in relation to race and culture. But first, I want to focus on another determining force upon race-making practices in media – the politics of nationalism and multiculturalism. This acts as an extension of the previous chapter on postcolonial approaches to race, culture and media, but thinks through in more detail the relationship between the state and media, and the latter's role in the creation of national identity and community.

4.7 Recommended and further reading

Racial capitalism/neoliberalism is a vital backdrop to a better understanding of contemporary race-making practices. Key literatures that were referenced above include David Theo Goldberg's (2009a) *The Threat of Race: Reflections on Racial Neoliberalism* and an essay by Nisha Kapoor (2013) on 'The Advancement of Racial Neoliberalism in Britain', although there is little direct discussion of media in these texts. Gargi Bhattacharyya's (2018) book *Rethinking Racial Capitalism, Questions of Reproduction and Survival*, is an important contribution to the theorisation of racial capitalism, and how 'racism shapes patterns of capitalist development' (2018: 103). Moreover, in chapter 6 on 'Consumption and Indebtedness' Bhattacharyya provides a critical account of how racial identities become commodified and attached to consumer lifestyles and pleasures, which exemplifies a nuanced, 'top-down' approach to the question of the commodification of race thesis. Further elaboration on this particular issue comes from Herman Gray (2013a) in an essay entitled 'Subject (ed) to Recognition', which provides a sharp critique of the politics of recognition in the current conjuncture that, like Bhattacharyya, highlights how racial identities become brand identities under the paradigm of 'diversity'.

Ben Pitcher's (2014) book *Consuming Race* provides a highly original 'bottom-up' approach to the commodification of race argument. In this book Pitcher demonstrates how racial meaning saturates our social lives, especially in the way that we consume products – even those that appear on the surface to not have much to do with race, such as gardening, Danish furniture and children's cuddly toys. What is particularly valuable about Pitcher's book, and what makes it distinct from other studies of consumption, is the highly sophisticated theorisation of capitalism (see chapter 2), where he argues for the need to be attentive to the specific cultural and social formations within which race is made, and the way that capitalism 'informs, structures and shapes practices of race' (ibid.: 35).

BOX 4.1   Key Issue

'Bling', race and the politics of consumerism

An alternative route towards understanding racial capitalism and the ambivalence of commodification is a focus on race in consumer culture. As we shall see, an aspect of racism was denying racialised groups entry into consumer markets, which makes the emergence of 'bling' culture in black popular culture in the early 2000s such an interesting moment. Bling is the term used to describe the celebration and explicit display of material wealth and luxury brands, whether Cristal champagne or Rolex watches, in the promotion of 'urban' music genres such as rap or R&B (Mukherjee, 2011). Bling culture appears to be a clear epitomisation of racial neoliberalism, where a politics of solidarity and community has been replaced by a politics of individualism and consumerism – this is no longer about civil rights but consumer rights (Gilroy, 2010).

(Continued)

However, in the field of critical consumer studies (Banet-Weiser and Mukherjee, 2012) scholars have wanted to complicate straightforward readings of this type of racialised consumerism (albeit, without blunting their critique of neoliberalism). For instance, Roopali Mukherjee (2011) situates bling culture within the civil rights movement, which had the freedom to participate in American consumer life as a key goal, coming at a time when black people were prevented in entering white-owned shops and department stores. Moreover, while the material wealth that certain black people have attained is supposedly symbolic of the postrace era, Mukherjee demonstrates how consumer culture remains stratified along the lines of race through notions of taste and distinction, where black consumption of luxury goods is seen as crass by the media commentariat and even the brands themselves.

Critical consumer studies also critically examines the way that capitalism has adopted social justice issues as part of marketing campaigns – for instance, Nike's campaign of support for Colin Kaepernick, the American footballer who was ostracised by the football establishment for protesting the American national anthem in the name of racial justice. Banet-Weiser and Mukherjee (2012) coined the term 'commodity activism' to explore the politics of market-based activism. Again, the authors' aim is to complicate readings of these types of intervention as representing pure resistance or pure domination. For instance, Mukherjee (2011: 187) analyses rapper Kanye West's outburst on network television following the devastation of New Orleans by Hurricane Katrina, where he famously went off-script to declare that 'George Bush doesn't care about black people'. For Mukherjee, West's speech gave voice to an anti-racism that emerged 'organically – unrehearsed and impassioned – from bling cultures of mainstream hip-hop' (ibid.: 188). But she also shows how, in doing so, West evokes neoliberal ideas of individual intervention (he alludes to using his own wealth to support the aid relief) rather than placing demands on the state. Thus, the politics of activism in the space of corporate media culture are not as easy to read as we might assume. As I shall stress in the chapters that constitute Part III in particular, our question around media spectacles like the one involving West or Kaepernick is not whether they represent corporate appropriation/ exploitation or resistance. But rather, what race *is doing* or *how it is being made* in a particular moment.

Discussion

The 2020 Black Lives Matter protests sparked an unprecedented number of statements of support from media and cultural institutions, including from corporations which generally avoid any kind of political pronouncements. How might we read this response in relation to the concept of racial capitalism?

Notes

1 Obviously, this does not apply to public service news media, although some argue that under political pressure, *BBC News* in particular is becoming increasingly commercial in character if not in terms of economics.

2 This has been criticised by Marxist political economists who argue that cultural studies of the media in general tend to over-emphasise ideology, in the process deflecting attention from the real problem of economic exploitation (Mosco, 1996; Garnham, 2000). Stuart Hall, in particular, has received criticism in media studies in this way (Stevenson, 2002).

5

Nationalism, Multiculturalism and Media

What is nation? What is the relationship between nation and modernity? What does it mean that national identity/community is imagined? What is media's role here?
How are ideas of race embedded in nation?
What is media's role in creating national communities? How is race articulated in media discourses of nation?

5.1 Introduction

This chapter continues the discussion of the macro forces that shape race-making practices in media (and vice versa). The focus here is on nationalism and multiculturalism, and how the changing cultural politics of 'race' in relation to the nation and 'diaspora' shape (and unfold in) media cultures. This will continue the discussion from Chapter 3 regarding how legacies of empire affect how media make race, but situates it more directly in the context of the nation and contemporary nationalisms. As globalisation intensifies in its spread, social and political scientists have queried whether the nation state is losing its power/relevance. However, it is safe to say that the death of the nation has been greatly exaggerated. While the flow of finance and informational commodities (including media texts) may make borders appear increasingly pervious, the boundaries between nations quickly materialise when it comes to the movement of people, particularly when it involves those of a different hue. Despite government attempts to restrict who can reside within a nation's borders, societies are invariably becoming more heterogeneous in character, not least in terms of their ethnic and racial composition. In this context, media become a crucial space where nation states attempt to create – whether directly or indirectly – a coherent sense of national community out of its natural state of difference, often through playing down this fact. But as each of the chapters thus far has stressed, this is *always* under contestation. Put more simply, media is the stage where national identity – and ideas around who and who does not belong – is played out.

While we might approach the politics of nationalism in terms of citizenship and rights, the critical cultural approach focuses us on ideology, representation and cultural identity, or as media scholar Ramaswami Harindranath (2005: 5) describes it, rethinking citizenship in terms of the way that 'meaning-making, belonging and the exercise of power are linked'. National identity, like race, is a social construct rather than an identity with intrinsic essential qualities (despite politicians' attempts to convince us otherwise). Thus, in this chapter I think through how media contribute to the making of meaning around nation and belonging – and how this necessarily entails an articulation of race. The first section of the chapter focuses on nationalism, where I will demonstrate how national identity, while imagined, nonetheless contains within it racial logics that produce real exclusionary effects. In the second section I then explore diaspora and how, with its inherently anti-essentialist qualities, it is seen as a threat to nationalism but, crucially how this can be generative and productive. In the third section of the chapter I explain how the dynamic tensions between nationalism and diaspora/multiculturalism manifest in media, which entails a discussion of the formal mechanisms that the state employs to create a sense of national identity in the form of multicultural policy (for instance, state-run/public service media and community media), and the more indirect ways that community and belonging are imagined – and contested – within media. I will emphasise the complexity of racial politics at the heart of discourses around nation and belonging, no matter where they are staged. Thus, the stress is again on ambivalence and contestation; the cultural industries are deeply implicated in the construction of national identity – in both conservative/reactionary and radical ways – which has a profound effect upon how race is made and consumed.

5.2 Nationalism and race

Before we discuss nationalism, race and media in detail we need to begin with nation, what it is and how it is constituted. Communication studies scholar Eugenia Siapera (2010) provides a useful overview for how nation is analysed, distinguishing initially between 'perennial' and 'primordial' approaches. The primordial version of the nation is concerned with how nations come into being, or rather, how people coalesce around ideas of cultural or supposedly biological attachments, which leads to the creation of nations. The perennial approach understands the nation as an entity that occurs naturally, and as such is more concerned with how it produces strong forms of attachment and belonging, often in terms of how they are dependent on strong exclusionary logics that lead to antagonism and violence against those viewed as outsiders. Siapera goes on to describe a third view of nation that sees it as a distinctly modern formation – emerging at the same time as modernity, capitalism and the industrial revolution. In contrast to the perennial and primordial versions of nation, the modernist view states that what we now understand as the nation is thoroughly modern in character, based upon an 'unprecedented form of organisation' (ibid.: 17) (including forms of rationalisation, bureaucratisation and, indeed, the development of a mass media system) that we now recognise as the nation state. Therefore, what we experience as nation in contemporary times is a direct product of modernity. This is the version of nation that I work with here for the reason that, as I will show, it highlights how ideas of race become central to the idea of nation.

Historical analyses of the nation are typically framed in terms of economic and political development, but what does a critical cultural lens reveal about the emergence of the modern nation state? Quite simply it emphasises how the ascendency of nation states was and still is dependent upon the role of culture in creating a sense of national community. Following industrialisation, the now rapidly expanding cities demanded a larger, educated and technological workforce in order to grow economically. This subsequently pulled people from their rural, smaller (more homogeneous) communities. As a consequence, the challenge for the dominant class was to create social bonds between an increasingly heterogeneous group of people (in terms of cultural and regional identities) which in turn necessitated defining a shared root and shared commonality. It is in these terms that political scientist Benedict Anderson (1983), in a famous and much cited argument, defines the nation as an *imagined community* dependent on *nationalism* – that is, a set of ideas and practices that evoke the nation state[1] – that allows people to feel a bond with others, the vast majority of whom they will never in fact actually meet. According to Anderson, the purpose of nationalism then is to establish a common language (culturally as well as linguistically) and common time frame (allowing a population to share a past, a present and a future). Specifically, it relies on stories and narratives to help establish an idea of nation as a united community, albeit one that is constructed *imaginatively* and is not necessarily rooted in the real.

While Anderson's argument alludes to nationalism as an ideological project, it is in danger of painting nationalism as somewhat benign. But the critical cultural approach emphasises how nationalism reproduces social – and indeed, racial – hierarchies. Nationalism enacts this in two ways in particular. Firstly, while the purpose of nationalism is to create bonds within a population, it is underpinned by the idea that, as Siapera (2010: 18) puts it, 'the ethnic basis of the nation should always be the same as that of the political elite that governs the nation'. That is, according to nationalism, the population is to be ruled by people from within 'their' community (whether they are in the majority or minority). Secondly, nationalism defines national identity in terms of who *does not belong* more than who does. That is, national identity is created in relation to the Other. As Stuart Hall (1997d, 2017b) states, you cannot have a history without the Other. This is famously illustrated in Hall's evocative quote that as a Caribbean subject he is the 'sugar at the bottom of the English cup of tea' (Hall, 1997d: 49). In other words, English nationalism – as embodied in the quintessential *English cup of tea* – relies on its colonial history for its very sense of Self. He continues,

> there is no English history without that other history. The notion that identity has to do with people that look the same, feel the same, call themselves the same, is nonsense. As a process, as a narrative, as a discourse, it is always told from the position of the Other. (ibid.)

It is in this way that ideas of race become crucial to nationalism. Paul Gilroy, in his influential book *There Ain't No Black in the Union Jack* (1987), which remains one of the most important critiques of the essentially racialising qualities of nationalism, defines a 'new racism' that he distinguishes from the scientific racism that preceded it. New racism is less about biological inferiority and more about who belongs to the nation and who does not. For Gilroy, this is marked by racial distinction; the idea that to be English can only ever mean to be white. Gilroy's argument is that nationalism is based on ethnic absolutism – essentialist ideas about racial and ethnic Others as absolutely and irreconcilably different from the white Self.[2] Building upon Gilroy's work, Sivamohan Valluvan's (2017, 2019) analysis of contemporary ethno-nationalisms finds the same exclusionary racial logics at play. As he states, societies 'actively produce and entrench ideas of nation, conceptions of the national subject … that are necessarily exclusionary' (Valluvan, 2017: 238). In other words, the modern version of nation is *by its very design* intended to exclude by lines of race and ethnicity. Evoking the modernist account of nation, Valluvan explains how the new nationalisms that are spreading throughout the West have their roots in the very birth of the European nation that in turn coincided with the time where ideas of race began to be most strongly articulated. This is a point worth underscoring: that the emergence of the modern version of nation had ideas of race (which are also a product of modernity) hardwired into it from the very beginning.

The exclusionary logics of nationalism are enacted via state policy (for instance, in terms of immigration law), but as the critical cultural approach stresses, nationalism has a strong symbolic component, operating at the level of the imaginary, via cultural discourse such as news and popular culture. Indeed, a key component of Benedict Anderson's argument regarding nation is the centrality of media to the creation of national (imagined) communities. Returning to his point that the purpose of nationalism was to create a common-bond between ever-expanding and heterogeneous populations, Anderson (1983: 52) refers to 'print-capitalism' – specifically the mass production of newspapers – 'which made it possible for rapidly growing numbers of people to think about themselves, and to relate themselves to others, in profoundly new ways' (ibid.). To reiterate, ideas of nation are produced through narrative, myth, tradition, heritage and seemingly shared values; nationalism is effectively the stories that the nation tells itself about itself (Hall, 2017b). As Valluvan stresses (2017), it is specifically *myths of origin* that are the most powerful, simultaneously tying people to a glorious historical past and a utopian future (see also Shohat and Stam, 2003). Think of the way that British tabloids refer to Dunkirk, the Battle of Britain or *Blitz Spirit* – those iconic moments from the Second World War when plucky England came back from the brink of defeat (at the same time conveniently erasing the vital contribution of Britain's colonised subjects) – whenever the nation is faced within a national challenge (whether the football World Cup or the Covid-19 pandemic). It is in these terms that postcolonial theorist Homi Bhabha (1990) coins the notion of *nation as narration* – how the idea of nation is effectively a narrative, or is *narrativised*. And in the modern nation state, it is the mass media that stages the story of nation.

Thus, media provide the space where ideas around nation and national identity are articulated. Our (national) identities are produced through the cultural sphere, and as such, who gets to narrate the history of the nation becomes crucial to our sense of self and feelings of belonging and not-belonging (Venn, 1999). This returns us back to the question of representation, media and ideology. As Hall argues, representation is structured in dominance, and as such, representations of national identity and racial Others are produced through the ideology of the dominant culture – though this is always contested – as we shall see in the following section on diaspora and multiculture. But before we enter that discussion it is worth stressing that despite presenting itself as cohesive (or indeed *strong and stable* to use the words of former British Prime Minister Theresa May), nationalism, much like culture itself, is slippery. As Shohat and Stam (2003: 10) put it, the national is 'contradictory, the site of competing discourses' within a nation. For instance, for 'New World' nations such as Australia or Canada, nationalist discourse appears to recognise and incorporate indigenous populations within its idea of nation but does so while simultaneously enacting their marginalisation and exclusion politically, economically, socially and culturally. Moreover, as shall be explored in the final section of this chapter, different types of media produce different types of 'national selfconsciousness' (Shohat and Stam, 2003: 9). To recap: (1) media plays a crucial role in the narration of nation, (2) this always involves an articulation of race, and (3) this is complex, contingent, and always under contestation.

5.3 Diaspora and multiculture

Despite nationalism's exclusionary racial logics, multiculturalism, as critical theorist Stanley Fish (1997: 385) puts it, is 'a demographic fact'. Virtually all nations are multicultural in some way, a consequence of many factors, such as the existence of an indigenous population prior to the formation of the state itself, a reliance on immigration for economic expansion, or the intake of refugees following geopolitical tensions (of which the host nation itself is often the source). By the nature of their liberal-democratic foundations, modern Western nations in particular have had to learn to accommodate difference – or at least to appear to do so. After all, in the US Declaration of Independence 'all men [sic] are created equal'. Indeed, it should be acknowledged that running alongside nationalisms are cosmopolitan currents that have opened up ideas of citizenship (Born, 2013). There are many different approaches to cosmopolitanism, which focus on its philosophical, political, sociological and cultural dimensions. But following sociologist Ulrich Beck (2006) (one of its most famous proponents), cosmopolitanism refers to, on a very basic level, an idea of a global world society that transcends nation states, containing within it ideas of community that are in opposition to the exclusivity and parochialism that characterise nationalisms. However, while this appears to contain progressive ideas around the recognition of difference or at least the idea of there existing 'multiple modernities' (Bhambra, 2011: 323), Beck's formulation has been challenged for positing a Eurocentric version of cosmopolitanism that is in fact unable to really address the issues raised by multiculturalism (ibid.). Nonetheless, it is against this backdrop of *nationalism versus cosmopolitanism* that modern nation states have adopted forms of multicultural policy in order to 'manage' their inherent heterogeneity. Ideas around multiculturalism shape social policy (education, housing, immigration) or cultural policy (media, arts-funding). Needless to say, different nations have their own different approaches to multiculturalism, based upon different philosophical foundations (Murphy, 2012) – and their own particular histories of empire and colonialism. In this section I want to explore how the politics of multiculturalism, in relation to nationalism, have a determining effect upon race-making practices in media.

While a nation's *multiculture* is a fact, the question of multiculturalism and how to best address a nation's inherent diversity is highly contested. In recent times politicians – including national leaders – have declared a 'crisis' in multiculturalism in Europe (Lentin and Titley, 2011), that the accommodation of difference has spiralled out of control. Siapera (2010) suggests three reasons for this supposed crisis: (1) the apparent failure of multicultural policy to enact justice and equality, (2) the ascendency of neoliberalism that has produced an ideology of individualism, where community-based policies are seen as a problem/threat, and (3) religious/racial/ethnic tensions following 9/11. But more broadly, the latest crisis around multiculturalism is part of a terminal anxiety about what Hall (2000: 216) calls 'globalisation's accompanying shadow'. Modern capitalist nations facilitated globalisation in the name of economic expansion, and through various means have pressured the rest of the world to follow suit, leading to globalisation's further intensification. With this came the mass movement of people, including the arrival into Western nation states of those from what historian Vijay Prashad (2008) calls *the darker nations* – many of which were former colonies of said nations. This has threatened the unitary nature of national identity, which in turn has produced a crisis of identity throughout the West (Hall, 1997c).

Before we further expand upon why multiculturalism is such a threat to national identity, it is worth noting that multiculturalism is criticised from both the Right and the Left. These criticisms come from different perspectives but notably there is some overlap that comes from a shared nationalist foundation (Valluvan, 2019). According to conservative critics, multiculturalism is an assault on the universal values of the nation and its canons of culture, is a retreat from Enlightenment principles, is too tolerant of intolerant cultural minorities, and exacerbates community tensions rather than produces cohesion. Leftists have criticised multiculturalism for not being radical enough in terms of contributing to social transformation, for producing a false consciousness that detracts from class-based politics, for breaking up (white) working-class communities (who are supposed to be the core of the workers' movement), for being too obsessed with cultural difference, and for fulfilling the logic of capitalism that needs difference to expand (Žižek, 1997). Critical race scholars, however, have challenged these critiques, not necessarily as self-professed defenders of multiculturalism, but from an anti-essentialist position. One of the key counter-responses from a critical race perspective is that critics of multiculturalism – whether politicians or newspaper columnists – are hard pressed to define what the 'multiculturalism' they decry actually is (see Murphy, 2012). Gavan Titley (2014: 249), for instance, argues that multiculturalism as a policy has in fact hardly been enacted; surveying the literature on what multicultural policies supposedly consist of, Titley concludes that they are 'piecemeal, disjointed and enormously modest histories, and non-histories'. Indeed, as Shohat and Stam (2003: 6) argue, the concept of multiculturalism more generally is a 'contested and in some ways empty signifier', in that it can mean many things to different groups in different contexts. Like 'nationalism', like 'culture', the term 'multiculturalism' is itself slippery, and can take bottom-up resistant forms or hegemonic top-down ones. It is no surprise, then, that critics of multiculturalism struggle to define *what multiculturalism* they are attacking exactly. Thus, to repeat, criticisms of multiculturalism as expressed in public discourse tell us little about the nature of specific multicultural policies and instead reveal more about a wider nationalist anxiety around the loss of identity tied to a fear of the Other. As we shall see in each of the chapters of Part III, media are a key arena where these anxieties unfold and find expression, particularly evident in media's treatment of Muslims and migrants (Chapters 7 and 8).

Unpacking why multiculturalism – which, from this point in the chapter, I refer to in its explicitly anti-essentialist sense – is such a threat to the nationalist project returns us to the question of race, and introduces the concept of diaspora. 'Diaspora', derived from the Greek *diaspeirein* meaning *scattering of seeds*, refers to the spread of a particular group – usually defined by race, ethnicity, religion – across the globe, beyond their homeland. Diaspora often gets used in relation to the concept 'hybridity' to describe how diasporic identities, very crudely, mix cultural elements from both the 'home' and 'host' culture to create new syncretic identities. While a simplistic definition of diaspora is in danger of assuming the prior purity or authenticity of the cultures being mixed, Paul Gilroy (1993) articulates a notion of diaspora grounded in history, rejecting racial or cultural essence while acknowledging that displaced populations carry with them an imprint of the shared experiences of colonialism, racism, oppression and migrancy. In the previous section I stressed how nationalist discourse requires a (racialised) Other. Gilroy (1987, 1993, 2004) extends this by stressing how British (or English) national identity relies on preserving the supposed purity of its culture. Thus diasporic, *hybrid*, subjects are considered a threat to national identity, by virtue of their inherent syncretic nature, which dirties and sullies the purity of national identity. But to underscore again, the threat of the Other finds expression in political discourse not in terms of biological inferiority (though we are seeing a disturbing return of racial science), but in terms of the cultural racism described in the previous section. This excludes racial and ethnic minorities in terms of their perceived cultural difference, for instance, for not sharing the same core values like freedom of speech. Put another way, the cultural racism that underpins nationalist discourse is less explicitly about the (biological) inferiority of other cultures or races, and more about a racial/ethnic minority's negative influence on national culture and the nation's way of life.

But that is not to say that diaspora and the presence of diasporic populations in the context of the nation state can only ever have a destructive effect upon the nation and any sense of community. In fact, it can be incredibly generative and point us towards new possibilities of how we can better live together. Once again, the work of Paul Gilroy helps to unravel this further. In *After Empire* (2004) Gilroy explores the *dialectics* of nationalism/multiculture that I am essentially referring to, through two concepts: 'postcolonial melancholia' and 'convivial culture'. Drawing from the work of psychoanalyst Sigmund Freud, postcolonial melancholia refers to the 'neurosis' that Britain feels in relation to its former Imperial past and its loss of global power but based upon a wilful amnesia regarding the atrocities committed in the name of Empire. Rather than work these feelings through, including facing up to these traumas, national energies are spent actively denying and repressing such histories. As a consequence, the very presence of postcolonial peoples produces unease as it reminds the nation of its imperial and colonial past (ibid.: 110). A discourse of ethnic absolutism is one way that nationalism attempts to fix a distinction between those who belong and those who do not.

But if that paints a bleak future for Britain, Gilroy finds flowers in the cracks. He is referring to convivial culture and the everyday experience of 'demotic multiculturalism' (ibid.: 108), the ordinary, natural interactions that occur between different people in the quotidian. Gilroy is effectively describing a form of *multiculturalism* from the bottom-up (as opposed to that which is imposed from above). And for Gilroy, this is not merely a challenge to, but the very antidote for postcolonial melancholia. As he states (ibid.: 108):

> The pressure from below has enriched and expanded the country's public sphere. I would like to bring about a new appreciation of this unheralded multiculture, which is distinguished by some notable demands for hospitality, conviviality, tolerance, justice, and mutual care.

Gilroy stresses that conviviality is not a fetishisation of difference; it is organic, ordinary, spontaneous – a radical 'indifference to difference' (Amin, 2013: 3). It reduces 'exaggerated dimensions of racial difference to a liberating ordinaryness' (Gilroy, 2004: 131). With particular pertinence for this book, Gilroy uses examples from popular culture to illustrate convivial culture, from Ali G, a notorious British comedy character from the 1990s and 2000s created by comedian Sasha Baron Cohen, where much of the humour is derived from his racially ambiguous identity, to the particular version of *postcolonial* English nationalism evoked in the band 'The Streets' that, as Gilroy puts it, is at ease with difference. Elsewhere, Gilroy (2013b) refers to the 2012 Olympic Games and the mediated successes of non-white British athletes Mo Farah and Jessica Ennis. Gilroy (ibid.: 557) notes how the 'popular pleasure that was generated by the epiphany of these particular "golden Brits" expressed the submerged yearning for a different country, less burdened by the past and less anxious in the face of alterity'. Gilroy here speaks to the utopian possibilities of convivial cultures, providing images of how we can better live together. The question that follows, then, is to what extent does media enable convivial culture, or succumb to postcolonial melancholia? Or more broadly, how does the dialectic of nationalism/multiculture shape how media make race? These questions inform the final section of the chapter and also frame the case studies explored in Part III.

5.4 Managing multiculture in media

Nationalism and the politics of multiculturalism – that is, how a nation manages its inherent diversity – shape race-making practices in both direct and indirect ways. In terms of the direct, I am referring to how nation states formally use media in order to create a sense of national community and identity, primarily through public service media (PSM). PSM can take many forms, in terms of funding (most national PSM systems are funded publicly, although sometimes augmented by commercial income) and the extent to which they are independent of the government. The role and significance of PSM also varies between nations, which have their own distinct media systems consisting of different relations between PSM and commercial media. All these factors make it a challenge to generalise about PSM as a whole.

Nonetheless, one characteristic that all PSM share is the job of articulating national identity and creating community among a nation's (diverse) population. How PSM approaches this depends on the state's own broader approach to multiculturalism and the extent to which it recognises difference. Taking the example of Europe, the United Kingdom, the Netherlands and Sweden have proclaimed to be multicultural societies where integration should take place without the need for cultural assimilation, and as such these nations have a tradition of creating programming specifically for minority groups (Hultén, 2014). Whereas other counties, such as France, Belgium and Spain, work with a principle of individual integration, where there has been less accommodation for minorities in national media, replaced with a stronger narrative around universal ideas of national identity (Malik, 2014). Cultural policy researcher Joop de Jong (1998) has identified four different PSM approaches to multiculturalism: (1) policy aimed at assimilation, (2) policy aimed at ethnicity (that is, policy that seeks to make it possible for each group involved to hold on to a specific sense of shared cultural identity), (3) policy aimed at compensating specific social disadvantages that some groups – ethnic or otherwise – might have, and (4) transcultural policy aimed at intercultural exchange.

But increasingly, across all PSM we are seeing a shift away from multicultural policy towards 'mainstreaming' diversity as global cultural industries become increasingly commercialised and marketised (Saha, 2018: 100–108). As a consequence, policy that once focused on catering for specific minority groups is being replaced with an approach based upon integrating minorities into mainstream broadcasting. While such a shift prevents the tendency to ghettoise minority programming, for media scholar Sarita Malik (2013a) it has resulted in a *de-raced* version of multicultural programming, where the issue of racism in society – which still structures minority experience – receives less attention. As such, we have seen a shift from multicultural programming that attempted to counter-balance the poor treatment of minorities in media (and everyday) life, to a new form of mainstreaming that emphasises cross-cultural exchange. This includes a mixture of cosmopolitan styles that are most visible in urban youth culture, and subject matter that 'deals with cultural identity as an important field of both pleasure and anxiety in modern western societies' (Leurdijk, 2006: 42). The mainstreaming of diversity finds particular expression in reality television formats and lifestyle programming, which presents a diversity of different characters – though with little direct reference to their difference. (See also Chapter 9 and the discussion on colour-blind casting.) To put it simply, as explored in the discussion of racial neoliberalism in the previous chapter, the turn to diversity has resulted in either the silencing of race or its over-determination (Hasinoff, 2008), although as we shall see, this produces ambivalent effects.

If PSM represents a top-down version of multicultural policy, there's a bottom-up version in the form of independent community media. Community media is often commercially funded, but because it serves under-privileged or socially disadvantaged groups, they can receive public money as they are considered to play an important role in helping newly arrived immigrants in particular 'integrate' into society (Georgiou, 2005). However, community media can be criticised for fragmenting audiences and, by extension, national community (see Deuze, 2006). Such an argument is countered by media scholar Myria Georgiou (2005). Based on a study of Greek community radio in London, Georgiou argues that even though diasporic media in Europe appears particularistic and potentially undermining the universal European values that mainstream media seemingly represents, they are in fact better understood as embodying both. As Georgiou states (2005: 483): 'Even when their content promotes insularity and closure, they still depend for their existence on universalistic values ingrained in the modern nation-state (that supports them with money and infrastructure), on universal human rights and the freedom of communication (that protects their rights to exist)'. As such, rather than undermining mainstream national media, community media in fact contributes to the creation of national community too, much like a grassroots version of PSM. And also like PSM, the version of nationalism/multiculturalism presented is contingent, and is equally capable of reinforcing or challenging dominant narratives of nationalism.

These are the formal ways that nations operationalise their media to create a sense of national community, shaped in turn by the politics of nationalism and multiculturalism. But within a nation's media system, such forces also influence race-making practices in less direct ways, via the understandings and values around ideas of national identity and belonging that symbol creators (that is, media professionals, creative workers and artists) bring to their work. This again will have both conservative and radical elements, but in alternative media we see the latter in particular (the nationalistic elements of media will be the subject of much exploration in Part III of this book). Alternative media has provided fertile ground for cultural producers from racially and ethnically marginalised backgrounds, whether underground music scenes (Kim, 2014; Bramwell, 2015; James 2015), independent cinema (Nwonka, 2015; Malik et al., 2017; Nwonka and Malik, 2018), web series (Christian, 2018; Herbert, 2018), or indeed social media itself (Leurs, 2012; Sobande, 2017). Indeed, new digital technologies have further opened up the possibility for counter-nationalistic discourses, where racialised youth have created content that both challenges essentialist ideas of race, while creating more inclusive ideas around national identity against a nationalism that contains strong, racially exclusionary logics. But while it is not surprising that cultural producers from racialised backgrounds have turned to alternative media to create their own narratives around identity and belonging, since these spaces offer the most creative autonomy, we should not underestimate mainstream media that, even in their most commercial, standardised, formulaic forms, can nonetheless offer alternative versions of nation and national identity. For instance, throughout her work, Sarita Malik (2013b, 2014) considers the cultural politics of lifestyle programming, 'reality tv' and self-improvement shows that dominate prime-time national television. For Malik, even while part of a wider shift towards diversity that removes race and racism from the agenda, such programmes by their very nature rely on having a diverse range of social types (in order to add *colour* to a production), resulting in a 'hyper-visibility of multicultural societies'. No matter how formulaic, or indeed conservative such programmes are, they can nonetheless offer spaces 'where people of colour, of odd shapes and sizes, and of new eclectic creativities, can emerge as cultural heroes' (Jakubowicz, 2014: 238). For instance, the immensely popular British competitive baking show *The Great British Bake Off*, which in its aesthetic presents a very traditional version of British culture (see Box 5.1), in 2015 was won by hijab-wearing British Bengali Nadiya Hussain, providing an iconic moment for multicultural Britain. Paul Gilroy himself recognises the convivial culture that emerges from home-improvement shows (that inevitably feature racial and ethnic minorities for the reasons that Malik suggests) producing a 'liberating ordinariness that makes strangeness recede in a fog of paint fumes and sawdust" (Gilroy, 2004: 119).

The danger for any analysis of media, nationalism and multiculturalism is that it falls into presenting either an overly critical account of paternalistic/Eurocentric top-down approaches, for instance in the case of PSM, or over-celebratory narratives of heroic, resistant, bottom-up grassroots initiatives. Instead, I want to underline how the dialectic between nationalism and multiculture produces ambivalent effects in the context of media. The socio-political terrain of the nation can be conceptualised as an unresolved set of tensions between policies based upon a cosmopolitan/anti-racist politics shaped by a social inclusion framework that foreground human rights and the recognition of minorities, and a nationalistic discourse that is hostile towards to immigrants and opposed to a multiculturalism *that has gone too far* (Jakubowicz, 2014: 233). As Georgina Born (2005: 102) describes the state of the nation: 'The moral settlement of the nation-state is affected by both transnational migration and internal restructuring; as a consequence, cosmopolitan ideas of citizenship now coexist with new nationalisms and fundamentalisms'. And tensions between cosmopolitanism and nationalism play out in media in particular ways at particular moments within a conjuncture. As Shohat and Stam (2014: 7) state: 'Just as the media can "otherwize" cultures …, they can also promote multicultural coalitions …. And if dominant cinema has historically caricatured distant civilisations, media today are more multicentered, with the power not only to offer countervailing representations but also to open up parallel spaces for symbiotic multicultural transformation.' New digital technologies have had a profound affect in this regard, as mentioned above, and as will be explored in Chapter 10. Moreover, while I began this chapter with the assertion that the supposed decline of the nation state can be over-stated, what cannot be over-emphasised is how our media consumption is global in character, more than ever before, which in turn is transforming our sense of national identity in complex ways. Considering the prevailing dominance of US-made popular culture, we may read this as another form of cultural imperialism that is producing homogeneity (or indeed, Americanisation), or we could interpret it as a form of what anthropologist Arjun Appadurai (1990) calls *indigenisation*, that is, the transformation of global influences into something hybrid and new, and grounded in the local. I will explore Appadurai's work on what he calls 'global cultural economy' in the next chapter, but the point that I want to underscore again is that we need to reject functionalist accounts of media that see it merely as a tool of the dominant class, and instead emphasise that global media and representation are better understood, as I have stressed in the book so far, as a site of ideological struggle, in this case between nationalist and anti-essentialist multicultural forces.

But that is not to say anything goes, and we need to understand how nationalistic discourse becomes institutionalised and embedded in capitalistic logics as well as state policy that are a determining force upon race-making in media. Indeed, the dominant theme of Part III of this book is how nationalist forces are the main source of racialised Othering in media. So again, our challenge is to recognise complexity and ambivalence in media culture, but without softening our critique of how media (re)produces strong racialist discourses, especially in articulations of nation.

5.5 Conclusion

Speaking again of the ambivalence of reality television in relation to race, nation and community, Sarita Malik (2013b: 525) states that

> the social function of democracy and cultural pluralism that reality television superficially delivers requires deeper probing. The shifting rhetorical value of convivial culture means that processes of commodification, incorporation, and identification are all involved in how these ultimately racialized discourses are mobilized and subsequently become institutionalized.

What Malik is saying here is that we cannot fully understand or evaluate convivial media culture in the context of democracy and multiculturalism if we study it in a vacuum. Rather, representations of multiculturalism – and race – are produced through historical, social and political-economic determinants; or in other words, through legacies of empire, capitalism and the dialectic of nationalism/multiculture as explored in the second part of the book thus far. The question that remains, which Malik alludes to in the above quote, is how is racialised discourse or ideology institutionalised? Malik is referring to how race is made by media itself. This is the subject of the following and last chapter of Part II, where I focus on the question of media power and how ideas of race inform and find expression through media practices themselves.

5.6 Recommended and further reading

One of the most important postcolonial critiques of nationalism and media is *Unthinking Eurocentrism: Multiculturalism and the Media* by Ella Shohat and Robert Stam (2014). This book is noteworthy for its use of an explicitly multicultural frame (especially unique considering that critical race scholars can be ambivalent about the term) and also for its global frame, which draws from media from the global south as much as the West. For a general account of contemporary nationalism in the British context, Sivamohan Valluvan's (2019) *The Clamour of Nationalism: Race and Nation in Twenty-First-Century Britain* is a vital read and provides a sophisticated critique of Right-wing and Leftist nationalisms (while written in a highly readable style). Like Paul Gilroy's (2004) *After Empire*, Valluvan's book provides an important context in which to analyse media's role in the articulation of nation, race and identity. While it is slightly older, Stuart Hall's (2000) conclusion to the edited collection *Un/settled Multiculturalisms: Diasporas, Entanglements, 'Transruptions'*, edited by Banor Hesse, is a useful critical cultural account of multiculturalism, including a delineation of different approaches to multiculturalism, situated in the context of globalisation and the question of the postcolonial (see Hesse's (2000) introduction too). For an account of multiculturalism, nationalism and media, Sarita Malik's (2002) *Representing Black Britain: A History of Black and Asian Images on British Television* remains an important history of British public service media's vexed relationship to issues of race.

BOX 5.1 Key Issue

The Great British...

The dialectic between nationalism and multiculture explored in this chapter is exemplified in popular British entertainment. In this chapter I reference the 2015 edition of hugely popular competitive baking show *The Great British Bake Off* (2010–present) won by British Muslim Nadiya Hussain. While it is troubling that a British-born Muslim winning *Bake Off...* should still be regarded as *novel* in the twenty-first century, there was nonetheless something very striking about the image of a hijab-wearing woman holding the winning trophy in the context of *Bake Off's* backdrop, featuring rolling English countryside, a pristine white tent with union flag bunting and white-clothed tables with vintage cake stands. The show spawned or ran alongside other 'Great British' inscribed television series on the BBC, including *Great British Menu* (2006–present), *Great British Railway Journeys* (2010–present), *Great British Sewing Bee* (2013–present) and *The Great British Pottery Throw Down* (2015–present). It is interesting that all of these programmes shared *Bake Off's...* Victorian/war-time aesthetic, embodied also in the various *Keep Calm...* paraphernalia that had swamped Britain's gift shops throughout the mid-2010s.

How to make sense of this particular discursive formation around British national culture? Well, first, these programmes and images epitomise what Michael Billig (1995) calls

(Continued)

'banal nationalism' – not the violent expression of nationalism, but the background white noise of nationalism that makes up the everyday. More critically, the aesthetic of these shows also seems to exemplify Paul Gilroy's (2004) notion of 'postcolonial melancholia', a yearning for a mythical moment in British history – that happened to exist before post-war immigration from the former colonies. We must not ignore either the political economy of television formats and how shows are sold abroad. *Bake Off...* is particularly popular with global audiences, and no doubt its success is due to the quintessential vision of Britishness it sells.

While the range of contestants on these shows may reflect the diverse communities of the nation, the overarching aestheticisation of these programmes presents a version of Great Britain that lacks even a hint of modern multicultural Britain. It is noteworthy that the *Great British...* programmes I refer to were broadcast at a time where Britain was seeing a swell of nationalist feeling (with anti-immigrant sentiment its underbelly) that led to the electoral breakthrough for right-wing populist party UKIP in the general election of 2015, and eventually a win for the 'Brexit' campaign in 2017. While I am not suggesting a direct causal link, the media discourses embodied in these forms of British popular culture aligned with the nationalism of the political discourses at the time (anti-EU, the 'crisis of multiculturalism', David Cameron's 'muscular liberalism'). These discourses effectively came together to produce what Evelyn Alsultany (2012: 7) called a 'hegemonic field of meaning' that created the conditions within which Brexit could occur and the Conservative government could implement its 'hostile environment' policy that eventually led to the Windrush Scandal. Once again, I am not suggesting that *The Great British Bake-Off* caused Brexit! But I am making a more modest point that while competitive cookery shows can appear as trivial and benign forms of popular culture they can in fact be very revealing about the nation's sense of Self, and who really belongs and who doesn't.

Discussion

The above discussion used examples from public service media in a very particular national context. As media becomes more global, with great value attached to television formats that can be sold to international markets, is media becoming less *nationalistic*?

Notes

1   There are also versions of nationalism that are not necessarily tied to a specific state, such as black nationalism, but they are *nationalistic* in that they are based upon the same ideas of self-autonomy, self-determination and self-governance.
2   Indeed, Gilroy (1993) finds the same tendency in other nationalisms, such as black nationalism that, since it is based on the same essentialist ideas of difference, he finds equally as problematic as white nationalism.

6
Race and Media Power

Where is power located in media with regard to race?

How do we make sense of the 'contradiction' of media power? What does this mean for racialised identities?

What is the value of conceptualising media as a site of struggle in relation to the production of meanings about race?

What is postcolonial cultural economy? As a concept and as an approach?

6.1 Introduction

In this final chapter of Part II, which explores the macro forces that shape race-making practices in media, I focus on media as an independent determining force. A limitation of some accounts of media and race is that they do not do justice to the complexity of how media power operates. Sometimes the emphasis is so much upon unpacking the character of racial ideology as embodied in a particular media text that it leads to the assumption that said racist ideology simply emanates from media and into society unobstructed. Put another way, the question of *how* exactly such an ideology is transcoded into the media text and then received by audiences is ignored. That is not to undermine the argument that media propagates the ideology of the dominant culture. But the process is not as straightforward as studies of race and media sometime suggest. And as I have stressed in this book so far, in order to sharpen our critique of how media make race we need to attend to and be able to explain complexity, contestedness and contradiction, no matter how difficult or inconvenient to our arguments that might be.

As such, in this chapter, building upon Chapter 2, I draw upon media studies accounts to unpack the nature of media power. In doing so, I challenge both functionalist accounts of media as *culture industry* that render it an instrument wielded by the status quo to maintain its dominance, and simplistic notions of media effects that paint the audience as passive recipients of a dominant ideology. Presenting a more nuanced version of media power highlights the value of a critical cultural approach to race and media. This does not just entail a cultural studies approach to media; I additionally draw from political economy traditions, specifically those approaches that centre the question of culture. In the past cultural studies and political economy used to be problematically seen as two oppositional positions, but thankfully this is less the case in recent times and in this chapter I offer a case for how these approaches can work together.

In the first part of this chapter I provide a broad overview of the way that media power has been explored from both political economy and cultural studies perspectives. In the second section I then apply these approaches to the topic of race and media specifically to think through how media themselves shape race-making practices. I finish the chapter by returning to the concept of *postcolonial cultural economy*, which attempts to tie together all the strands discussed thus far. Using a relatively new field of media research called cultural economy as its base, postcolonial cultural economy as a theoretical framework brings together questions of macro and micro, structure and agency, and questions of production, representation and consumption. It also entails a historical analysis, that situates particular media/social phenomena within its conjunctural setting. Its aim is to provide a multidimensional account of race, culture and media that acknowledges the complexity of race-making practices without obscuring the ideological processes that shape the production, representation and consumption of race. The *postcolonial cultural economy* framework is then applied to the case studies that make up Part III, which explores how media make race in specific contexts.

6.2 The nature of media power

To begin this chapter, I want to focus on the broad issue of power and media. The fact is, research on media power – particularly from a political economy perspective that addresses this question most directly – very rarely tackles issues of race. But that is not to say such discussions do not hold value for our interest in race, culture and media. Indeed, the most important accounts of media power are the ones that take issues of cultural identity seriously. To reiterate, the main aim of this chapter is to demonstrate how media itself – which in the context of Western capitalist nations is relatively autonomous from the state – is a determining structural force upon race-making practices. But a secondary aim is to show what tackling the subject of media and ideology through the frame of race brings to the study of media power in general. This will become evident in the section that follows where I apply the approaches introduced in this section to the specific issue of race and culture.

We should begin by stating that there are different versions of media power. Media scholar Des Freedman (2014) distinguishes between approaches that explore media in terms of political power (including the extent to which media supports or impedes democracy), economic power or symbolic power, that is, media's power in constructing social reality. This latter version, which recognises media as a cultural as well as an economic phenomenon, is the one I work with here. Freedman also identifies different theoretical perspectives, including a Foucauldian argument that sees power as all-evading, enacted through our bodies as much as it is through institutions, postmodern perspectives that sees our lives as increasingly mediated and media as material that constructs reality itself, and post-Marxist approaches that emphasise ideology as the 'cement' of any late capitalist social formation that imbues media with tremendous definitional power (ibid.: 7). Once again, it is the last of these three versions, the post-Marxist tradition, that informs my critical cultural approach to race and media, though it additionally takes in elements from the other perspectives outlined.

As mentioned, there was a moment where media studies was blighted by a face-off between those working in cultural studies and those working in political economy. Most media researchers have moved on from this crude dichotomisation and in this book I want to provide a further demonstration of how cultural studies and political economy approaches can in fact work together – or indeed, *need* to work together – in order to provide a deeper understanding of how media work, particularly in relation to the question of power. However, as I much as I want to knit these perspectives together – the concept of the *postcolonial cultural economy* aims to do precisely just that – to start the discussion I will treat cultural studies and political economy approaches to the question of media power separately. While as stated, political economy is the field most concerned with media's relationship to powerful interests, I want to begin by exploring what cultural studies brings to this discussion.

6.2.1 Cultural studies approaches to media power

As explored in the opening chapter, cultural studies provides the most in-depth and sophisticated analyses of the nature and complexity of culture. Of particular value is its understanding of how culture relates to social power. That is, while we should not underestimate the state's capacity to use physical force to maintain control, in modern society culture is the key sphere though which power is enacted, especially in the everyday. In terms of media power, cultural studies draws attention to questions of representation and audience – and production too – that demonstrate the complexity of power dynamics. We have touched on many of these issues in Chapter 2, but they are worth recapping here.

In terms of representation, cultural studies demonstrates how media texts are important, not just in terms of what they literally communicate about the world, but also how they construct our very sense of reality. One key question for cultural studies scholars specifically interested in media is the extent to which media texts reflect the interests of the dominant culture (through patriarchal, heteronormative, ableist, classist and racist discourses/ideologies) that in turn reproduce inequalities in society. On the opposite side of the coin, cultural studies scholars are also interested in how media texts produced by marginalised groups challenge the dominant culture, either directly (through producing explicitly counter-hegemonic narratives or representations of difference) or indirectly (through the creation of texts that are less 'political' but produce pleasure for groups that mainstream media ordinarily marginalises). The strongest cultural studies emphasises the complexity of media culture, drawing attention to *polysemy* – that is, how texts produce multiple meanings – and other effects of media representation that go beyond the question of signification, such as emotion, affect and feeling.

This takes us to the question of audience. To reiterate a point made in Chapter 2, audience studies, in its stress on the agency of viewers, is seen as suggesting that audiences have more power than media owners. But apart from extreme postmodern versions, this was never the argument of audience studies researchers. Rather, audience studies sought to challenge the notion that the powerful elites that own media wield complete control over passive audiences. Researchers of media audiences working in the cultural studies tradition take seriously those forms of popular culture most denigrated by cultural elites. In foregrounding issues of subjectivity, identity, discourse and pleasure they demonstrate how judgements of cultural value might relate to the politics of social identity, especially class, gender, ethnicity and sexuality. This is in terms of what forms of consumption and pleasure are sanctioned or valued, or how the consumption of media texts creates forms of solidarity and community among marginalised groups. At times it shows how the consumption of such texts by the most patronised or decried in society can actually amount to a form of resistance. I will argue that such arguments must be taken seriously in any account of race, culture and media.

To finish my account of cultural studies of media power we need to acknowledge the strand of cultural studies that is interested in questions of production. Cultural studies is mostly associated with texts and audiences, but an interest in production was present in the very early days of the discipline (Williams, 1973) and has come back into fashion in recent times. Once again, its purpose is to complicate functionalist accounts of media production. It aims to shift the debate from an economically determinist version of the production of culture (which argues that since culture is produced by capitalism it automatically embodies capitalist ideology) to a more fluid version of 'cultures of production' (Negus, 1997) – or production as culture (Mayer et al., 2009). The emphasis once again is on complexity and contestation and cultural production as a site of struggle. This is an issue that will be pulled out further in the following account of political economy, but for now I want to underline how cultural studies of media power in general complicate simplistic models of the transmission of ideology by highlighting how cultural meaning is articulated and struggled over in each of the spheres of representation, consumption and production.

6.2.2 Political economy approaches to media

Cultural studies of media produce an important challenge to elitist conceptions of culture, and the economic reductionism that characterises more orthodox Marxist accounts of media. But as a consequence, cultural studies can leave the question of structure, or the *political economy*, out of its analysis. Referring to cultural studies of race and media specifically, there tends to be a sole focus on issues of representation that implies that media texts are created in a vacuum rather than as a product of industrial processes, shaped by the structure of media itself. Thus, developing a fuller analysis of the nature of media power entails a political economy analysis.

Political economy in its broadest sense is a form of economic analysis distinct from mainstream or neoclassical economics, in that it is less interested in markets and efficiency and places more emphasis on analysing economic systems in terms of social justice and equality. Thus, critical political economy[1] exposes the ways that media, operating under capitalistic conditions, produce inequality (social and economic) while serving wealthy elites, whether state or corporate. The most nuanced political economy accounts of media power, however, complicate the argument that cultural industries are simply an instrument of the powerful. Similar to cultural studies of production, this particular strand highlights media as a site of struggle between different groups, some more powerful than others. It is in this way that media researcher David Hesmondhalgh (2018), working in the cultural industries tradition of political economy, describes cultural production as *complex*, *contested* and *ambivalent*.

However, that is not to paint media as a free-for-all where anything goes. Like Hesmondhalgh, Des Freedman (2014) paints a theoretically-grounded analysis of media power. He argues that rather than economic interests determining media, they instead exist in a dialectical relationship. That is, media power 'is structurally tied (but not subordinated) to wider patters of privilege and control' (ibid.: 10). In making this argument Freedman places a greater emphasis on contradiction in his account of media power. Adopting a historical materialist perspective, Freedman underlines how Karl Marx recognised that capitalism was in fact a revolutionary force although its expansion depended on the exploitation of the worker. Hence media, like other forms of production, has both enabling/revolutionary as well as constraining/exploitative dynamics (see also Garnham, 1990; Hesmondhalgh, 2018). As Freedman (2014: 28) puts it, 'There have been several examples of how, in recent years, small portions of the mainstream media, despite their frequent involvement in the amplification of powerful voices and reproduction of existing relations, have also provided space to more critical or "magical" perspectives (such as in relation to class, gender or ethnicity)'. The contradiction of media power for Freedman is 'a simultaneous desire for a narrow consensus and yet a structural imperative for difference' (ibid.). In other words, media has contradictory tendencies. But Freedman is not suggesting here that media is equally as enabling for minorities as it is for the dominant culture. Instead, he is arguing that while media is mostly used by powerful elites for their own goals, it nonetheless has openings – or what Raymond Williams (1973) calls emergent tendencies – within it, formed through the logic of capitalistic production itself that minorities can harness for their own 'magical' ends. Thus drawing from both critical political economy *and* cultural studies perspectives, a more nuanced conceptualisation of media power understands media as a site of struggle, but one that is *structured in dominance* as Stuart Hall (1980) would put it, that reproduces inequalities but invariably leaves spaces where the authority of the dominant culture can be challenged by the less powerful.

6.3 A critical cultural approach to media power and race

The task now is to apply this model of media power to the study of race and media. In Chapter 1 I demonstrated how studies of race and media, while strong on the nature of racial ideology and discourse, were often less strong on the question of media itself. That is, such studies offer sophisticated, critical and in-depth accounts of how media texts embody/reproduce racist ideologies/discourse (or indeed, counter-hegemonic/counter-discursive narratives around race), but seem less interested in how (a) media texts are encoded with particular ideas of race, and (b) how these ideas are received and consumed and made sense of by audiences. So to reiterate, there is a tendency to over-emphasise ideology/discourse, with less attention paid to the distinctiveness of media power itself.

A notable exception against this tendency appears in the work of Herman Gray, and in particular his book *Cultural Moves: African Americans and the Politics of Representation* (2005) – a contribution I discussed in Chapter 4. To recap, in this work Gray examines how different ideological, institutional forces and the audience itself shape black cultural production in US media. Gray's argument is complex but can be distilled into three parts. Firstly, he highlights how media industries attempt to control cultural production and the terms and circumstances in which their products circulate and take on value, with particular pertinence for black cultural producers. Secondly, this entails differentiating audiences into niches, segments and making products of different value for audiences of different value. That is, industry processes produce different audiences as markets for different media products/cultural commodities, and when audiences start becoming defined by their race this again affects black cultural production in very particular ways. Thirdly, black audiences themselves make their own claims around blackness. These claims can contradict industry attempts to position them, but they can equally fit squarely within these media logics too. Gray's point here is that the processes of making texts for audiences, or making audiences for texts, rather than being predetermined (that is, determined by industry/economics) are mutually constitutive. Thus, Gray demonstrates how the making of blackness is subject to shifting market imperatives, competing cultural claims made by audiences, and conflicting political interests. He is, in effect, emphasising both the roles of structural and discursive influences upon race-making practices in media.

In his account, Gray is making a case for a need for more production-based analyses of race and the cultural industries that attend to industry dynamics (see also Gray, 2016). I now expand this argument, in order to tie together the strands of the previous three chapters. Drawing on Gray's account, I show why an analysis of how media itself shapes race-making processes needs to incorporate macro and micro perspectives, the structural and the discursive.

6.3.1 Macro dimensions of race-making practices

The aim of the previous three chapters was to explore the structural determinants that shape how media make race, which I revisit now. First, I focused on (post)colonial forces. According to postcolonial theorists, while the colonial period is formally over, colonial power has been reconfigured rather than displaced. They also emphasise how power is enacted through the cultural sphere, and it is through representation that racial hierarchies are maintained into the *post*-colonial period. Indeed, a key contribution of postcolonial theory to the study of race and media is how the representation of racial and ethnic minorities is historically rooted: colonial structures relied upon the creation of a binary opposition between the colonial Self and the colonised Other that reinforced the idea of the (racialised) Other as absolutely different and inferior, a signification system that still broadly shapes contemporary representations of race. Postcolonial approaches to media and culture also highlight spaces for resistance, especially the role of the hybrid subject, that by their very presence destabilises these crude binary oppositions, and by extension colonial authority itself. Therefore, media representations of race are still informed by empire, which helps keep the dominant culture in place, but while appearing resolute the status quo in fact exists in a more precarious state, or at least is always under contestation.

Second, while legacies of empire shape representations of race, they also shape contemporary nationalisms which in turn act as structural forces upon race-making practices. Nationalism produces strong forms of belonging despite being a social construct (much like 'race'). Because it is not rooted in anything real, in order to define itself national identity needs an Other (it is easier to define what we are not than what we are). Thus, following a colonial logic, nationalism depends on the construction and maintenance of binary oppositions between the Self and the Other, those who belong and those who do not, and this always entails an articulation of race/ethnicity. Saying that, nationalism is never fixed and responds to shifting geopolitical developments and movements of people that have intensified under the spread of globalisation. Media is crucial to nationalism as it is through media that a coherent sense of national community is created and maintained. This happens in direct ways (usually through some form of public service media) and indirect ways. But while top-down forms of nationalism can produce strong exclusionary forces in media, there are bottom-up forms of multiculture that contest these forces. In this regard, media is the stage where ideas of national identity, and who belongs and who does not, play out.

The third structuring force upon race-making practices that I identify is capitalism. There is a tendency, especially for anti-racists and those on the Left, to assume that capitalist ideology is inherently racist. Yet it is more accurate to understand racism and capitalism as made up of two distinct ideologies that are inextricably intertwined. For instance, the commodification of race in the context of media, by which I mean the transformation of representations of race into cultural commodities, is an ambivalent process. It *mostly* results in exoticised, reductive representations of race since stereotypes are instantly recognisable and therefore deemed sellable, but at times it can produce alternative narratives of difference that go against the grain and destabilise nationalist/neocolonial discourse (bearing in mind Des Freedman's comments that media contain within it a structural need for difference). Moreover, cultural commodities become the material through which racial minorities create their sense of Self, with both damaging and empowering effects.

I wish to make two points with regard to how capitalism shapes race-making practices. Firstly, we need to consider how legacies of empire and nationalist ideologies become institutionalised in media and embedded into media logics, as Herman Gray refers to above (see also Malik, 2013a; Nwonka and Malik, 2018; Saha, 2018), which takes us to the field of production studies of race covered in Chapter 2. Secondly, we need a historical analysis of how capitalist ideology and racial ideologies intersect in particular moments and in particular social formations to shape how media make race. In this current period of neoliberalism, for instance, we see a resurgence of white ethnonationalism that is strongly felt in news media in particular, especially in the representation of migrants and Muslims. But this is happening alongside a growing demand for *diversity* as audiences and producers alike criticise media for its institutional whiteness, reflected in the lack of minorities working both on- and off-screen. A historical approach entails examining how nationalist and capitalist ideologies are coming together within this specific geopolitical context, to produce this apparent contradiction.

The overarching theme of these chapters was to demonstrate how capitalist ideologies and racial ideologies (shaped by the remnants of empire and contemporary nationalisms) are distinct but interwoven, the relation of which takes different forms in different historical moments within different social formations; racism is shaped by capitalism/nationalism in particular ways in particular conjunctural moments. But the emphasis has also been on contestation. While these structural forces produce strong determining effects upon how media make race, this is not the entire picture, not least for the reason that these forces do not go unchallenged.

6.3.2 How race is made in consumption

While the previous three chapters have focused on the macro dimensions of race-making, we need to ensure that, as postcolonial audience studies scholar Ramaswami Harindranath (2009: 19) puts it, we avoid the 'conceptual trap of structural determinism'. A focus on neocolonial, nationalist and capitalist ideologies helps us understand why representations of race take the form that they do, but they do not explain what audiences do with this material. *All* scholars of media and culture recognise at least that audiences, rather than passive dupes, are active and can decode a text in different ways that can even go against the original intentions of the creator. But we need to avoid a simplistic reading of audiences and race – that different ethnic groups consume different types of media based on their ethnic identity, which then reinforces their ethnic identity. Hence, what does an account of media consumption focused on the question of media power that does justice to the complexity of audience reception look like?

To begin with, it needs to adopt an anti-essentialist position. We need to avoid claims around audiences that reduce all interpretation to race. Rather we need to factor in other influences, such as class, gender, education, and how these not only shape an audience's reading of media texts, but also define their relationship to their racial, class, gender identities and so on (Harindranath, 2005). As another postcolonial audience studies researcher Radhika Parameswaran (2006: 316) puts it, such an approach needs to stress the 'relational web of porous social formations' through which the identities of media viewers are formed. Thus, it should entail an analysis of media consumption that accounts for audiences' contradictory experiences of affiliation and alienation. (For instance, it is possible to love rap music but reject its lapses into misogyny.) It should also understand that media becomes the material that individuals use in novel ways, not least in how they construct their racial identities – look at how diasporic South Asians from LGBTQ backgrounds refashion and repurpose the heteronormative narratives of Bollywood cinema into an articulation of queer desi identities (Dudrah, 2006). As discussed in Chapter 2 in relation to production studies and digital race studies, and Chapter 4 in relation to commodification, racial identities are constructed through consumption rather than consumption being reflective of prior, fully formed, established racial identities. A critical cultural approach to race and consumption understands that race is a site of meaning shaped by the cultural sphere and the construction of meaning is a collaborative and collective process (Pitcher, 2014).

Secondly, a radical audience studies approach must recognise inequalities in consumption, and how the uneven distribution of cultural resources affects or impinges upon audience choices. It should also consider what different types of consumption are valued and undervalued. As such, we need to recognise agency, but also how power shapes choice as well as places different levels of value upon different types of cultural consumption (Harindranath, 2005). We need a modified Foucauldian approach that understands how subjects are produced historically through power/knowledge, and media discourses specifically, but are not just passive recipients of these dominant messages (Parameswaran, 2006). This necessitates a more nuanced, historically contextualised account of reception that accounts for power and contradiction, to explore how, once again, racial identities are made through the consumption of media texts.

To end this section, I want to sum up the discussion above by making two points with regard to media power and how media make race. First, capitalist and racist ideologies (shaped themselves by nationalist and neocolonial forces) are distinct but bound up in each other and shape media in particular ways within a particular social formation. This in turn affects the content and form of representations of race that in turn produce different types of meaning that are made sense of in pluralistic ways by audiences. So we need a historical approach to understanding how race is made in specific moments in time and space. Second we need an approach that can explain contradiction. What makes cultural industries distinct from other types of industry is how, as much as it has a natural inclination towards standardisation and homogenisation, it also has to contend with the audience's demand for originality and difference as well as familiarity. As political-economist Nicholas Garnham (1990: 160) states, the cultural commodity resists homogenisation since the 'use value is novelty or difference'. This has a critical effect upon how media make race and explains those instances when we encounter something deep, illuminating and enriching with regard to race even when so much of what we see on our screens feels like the opposite.

6.4 The postcolonial cultural economy approach

As I have shown, an account of media itself acts as a structural force upon how media make race entails insights from both political economy and cultural studies. From critical political economy we learn how media industries serve the powerful elites that own them (whether state or corporate interests) but how this is always contested within media itself. Indeed, the most theoretically grounded political economy accounts emphasise contradiction as a key characteristic of media power (backed up by close empirical accounts of media production that stress complexity and contestation in how symbolic goods are made). From cultural studies we learn how representations of race matter (in terms of how they construct our ideas of racial difference), but how these texts are never consumed in a straightforward manner by audiences. Indeed, the cultural commodities made by media become the material that help constitute racial and ethnic identities. However, while I have wanted to produce a complex picture of media power, with a particular stress on contradiction and ambivalence, I do so without wanting to downplay the ideological role of media when it comes to race. Combining this account of media power with the analysis of the structuring forces explored in the previous three chapters, the overall argument that I have made in the book thus far can be boiled down to three points: (1) capitalist and racist ideologies combine to shape race-making practices in media in particular ways, (2) media nonetheless is relatively autonomous and works according to its own distinct logics that more often than not reproduce these ideologies but can also produce counter-ideologies, and (3) the picture is complicated further by how audiences *make race* based on their own distinct patterns of consumption, which in turn are structured in dominance (see Pitcher, 2014). The challenge now is to create a new theoretical framework that can incorporate an analysis of each of these dimensions of race-making. This is the purpose of the 'postcolonial cultural economy' that I outline in more detail in the final part of the chapter.

6.4.1 The cultural economy approach to media

As the name suggests, the postcolonial cultural economy approach is based on a form of media analysis called cultural economy. Cultural economy is a relatively new approach and consists of two versions. The original version adopts an explicitly post-structuralist approach. Challenging the economic reductionism of political economy traditions, cultural economy in this iteration seeks to radically destabilise the distinction between the economic and the cultural. More precisely, it uses culture as the main analytic to study production and the economy. So it understands production as a cultural process, and the economy as a cultural entity (rather than an objective fact) produced through discourse; needless to say this is an approach strongly influenced by Michel Foucault. It is cultural economy's equal investment in the economic and the cultural (where political economy and cultural studies scholars tend to focus on one over the other), which is why it provides the initial foundation for my approach. However, this particular iteration of cultural economy tends to be descriptive rather than critical and less interested in the normative questions that political economy engages in (see Hesmondhalgh, 2018: 69-70). Given the issue of commodification, for instance, cultural economists would be more interested in deconstructing it as a process, rather than exploring its harmful effects upon society.

More recently, there has been a cultural economy approach that is directly concerned with media and culture as a realm of symbol-making. Moreover, situating itself within the tradition of political economy, its analysis is framed explicitly in terms of social justice (Hesmondhalgh, 2018: 70). Coming from a critical cultural policy perspective, cultural economy is intended as an alternative to the creative industries framework that shapes contemporary cultural policy in many capitalist nations. Like the original version of cultural economy, this approach reconceptualises the intersection between culture and economics. But it brings a particular emphasis on value, and how economic and cultural value intersect in particular ways during cultural production in its institutional and everyday contexts (O'Connor, 2016). Its key argument is that cultural industries need to be understood as producing different types of value – not just economic value – and as such, cultural production should be organised differently (via policy) instead of operating under purely capitalist conditions, which is having a destructive effect upon culture-making and who gets to do it.

This emphasis on value in the context of the cultural industries resonates with Herman Gray's analysis of black cultural production described earlier – and how race is attached to different sets of values whether economic, cultural or political. However, coming from a policy perspective, this version of cultural economy is less interested in issues of cultural identity (and by extension, race-making practices). A useful intervention then comes from De Beukelaer and Spence's (2018) notion of global cultural economy. It is grounded in O'Connor's version of cultural economy with its specific interest in cultural production and consumption. But it also draws more explicitly from Arjun Appadurai, who coined the term 'global cultural economy'. In a famous essay, Appadurai (1990) uses the notion of global cultural economy to counter a particular cultural imperialist approach to globalisation that simplistically sees it as a form of Americanisation that is homogenising local cultures around the world. Appadurai instead stresses the *unevenness* of global flows, which emanate from a variety of international metropolises (not just the US), and how they are *indigenised* within the new societies they enter. So this is a version of globalisation that conceptualises it as a profoundly complex, if not heterogenising, force. According to Appadurai, the new global cultural economy has to be understood as a complex, overlapping, disjunctive order that is producing culture in distinct ways. De Beukelaer and Spence (2018) apply Appadurai's notion of global cultural economy to explore the dynamics of global cultural industries specifically. Their focus is on how global and local forces interact to shape domestic cultural industries, and in turn, domestic cultural industries' relations to global markets. The global cultural economy approach makes two interventions that underpin the postcolonial cultural economy approach. First, it pays attention to the '*diversities* of cultural production, circulation and consumption' (De Beukelaer and Spence, 2018: 36, my emphasis) and, crucially, plays equal attention to each of these dimensions. Second, they reject a particular (Eurocentric) teleological approach that measures the development of non-Western creative industries in relation to Western nations, in favour of a postcolonial critique focused on unpacking global hierarchies (though in a way that rejects simplistic binary oppositions between the West and non-West). However, with its focus on cultural policy there is once again less interest in media texts and the politics of representation.

An analysis of how media make race takes the production of racial epistemologies as its starting point and it is for this reason that I choose to frame my version of cultural economy more explicitly in terms of the postcolonial.

6.4.2 Defining 'postcolonial cultural economy'

Thus, the postcolonial cultural economy has two components: (1) a cultural economy approach to media production/circulation/consumption, and (2) a postcolonial approach to race and culture. The purpose of the postcolonial cultural economy framework is to map the social, cultural and economic terrain within which knowledge about the Other is produced. It underlines how race is produced in the context of media through a complex interplay between economic and ideological forces. It has three key characteristics, which I outline here.

Firstly, it takes seriously the macro and micro dimensions of how media make race. It thinks through together production, representation and consumption and how each of these phases is defined by the interplay between economic and cultural dynamics. It not only focuses on how broader structural forces, both political-economic and ideological, produce determining effects upon race-making practices, but also recognises and treats seriously the agency of both cultural producers and audiences in contesting dominant narratives/ideologies and producing new claims around race (though it recognises too that as the owners of the means of cultural production the balance is still tipped massively in favour of the dominant culture).

Secondly, it is based upon a historical analysis. By historical, I do not just mean in terms of presenting historical case studies. Rather it is more akin to a conjunctural analysis (though less dogmatic than the orthodox Marxism that gave birth to this approach), which takes a specific moment and examines how capitalist ideology and racial ideology intersect within the given social formation through which race-making practices occurs. While this book is mostly engaged with the making of race in the West, the postcolonial cultural economy framework rejects a teleological approach that sees Western cultural industries as the most 'developed', with the rest of the world lagging behind. Instead, following De Beukelaer and Spence (2018), it takes seriously how different societies are defined by their own economic, social and cultural relations which shape cultural production in ways that are unique to those contexts.

Thirdly, and this brings us back to the themes of this specific chapter, postcolonial cultural economy is based upon a nuanced understanding of media power. Adopting a cultural economy approach, it rejects the economic reductionism/functionalism of certain political economy approaches and, as stated, it takes cultural production, media texts and patterns of consumption equally seriously. It also centres around the issue of the commodification of race (as in the context of Western capitalist nations, race-making practices in media occur mostly – though not totally – under capitalist conditions), but understands that this is an ambivalent process, shaped by the contradictions of media power, as outlined above. Indeed, drawing from Stuart Hall's (2000) account of globalisation, the postcolonial cultural economy framework understands that global capitalism, while attempting to totalise and control culture in its entirety (through the process of commodification), cannot achieve this, and moreover inadvertently produces emergent cultures that challenge the authority of the dominant culture. This is the dynamic through which race-making practices are shaped. Thus, to reiterate once again, the stress is on complexity, contestedness and contradiction.

The postcolonial cultural economy framework is designed to navigate and explore the topography within which race-making practices in media are situated. Our task is to get to grips with this complex terrain in order to better understand how race is being made in a particular moment within a specific context. This will allow us to evaluate exactly how race is being made and with what effects in that context. The purpose is to produce knowledge that can inform new counter-strategies of resistance which attempt to make race in a way that contributes to its undoing.

6.5 Conclusion

In this chapter I have demonstrated how media itself acts as a determining force upon race-making practices in media. I drew directly from media studies of power to demonstrate how this is the case. This involved a discussion of critical political economy that provides a nuanced account of how the *structure* of media affects media content, particularly with its emphasis on contradiction. I also drew from cultural studies accounts of media power, which complicate simplistic accounts of how media transmits ideology, with a particular emphasis on *agency* (of producers as well as audiences). How media make race is complex, but there are patterns that lead to the reproduction of historical constructions of Otherness.

At the end of the chapter I tied together the discussions from the chapters that make up Part II of the book to outline the postcolonial cultural economy framework. This entails (1) an equal focus on macro and micro, structure and agency, (2) a historical approach that situates race-making practices within its given conjunctural context, and (3) an understanding of cultural production/consumption as complex, contested and contradictory. I should stress that postcolonial cultural economy is not a prescriptive approach. Rather, it offers a broad conceptual framework that helps us to think through together all the different dimensions that shape race-making practices in media. It is grounded in social theory, fusing concepts and theories gleaned from cultural economy, critical political economy of culture and a critical cultural approach to race, in order to explain and evaluate the complexity of the operation of racial ideology in media, while being able to account for the contradiction that characterises how media make race.

6.6 Recommended and further reading

For a deeper understanding of media power from a critical political economy per-spective, *The Contradiction of Media Power* by Des Freedman (2014), *Critical Political Economy of the Media: An Introduction* by Jonathan Hardy (2014) and *Cultural Indus-tries* by David Hesmondhalgh (2018) provide excellent overviews. Hesmondhalgh's book in particular also includes a good account of cultural studies approaches to media power. While these books only have fleeting references to race (see Box 6.1), Oscar Gandy's (1998) *Communication and Race: A Structural Perspective* is one of the few analyses of race and media from, as the title suggests, a structural perspective. Another rare example of a critical political economy analysis of race and ethnicity in media comes from Vicki Mayer (2001) in her study of the historical development of 'Latino media' in San Antonio, Texas. With apologies for the shameless plug, my own book *Race and the Cultural Industries* (Saha, 2018) pulls all these approaches together to provide an account of the production of representations of race. For read-ers interested in the contradictions of media and race, I recommend Eithne Quinn's (2013b) study of the production and consumption of gangsta rap in the book *Nuthin' but a 'G' Thang: the culture and commerce of gangsta rap*, and an essay by Murali Balaji (2009) that provides an important critical account of political economy approaches to popular culture and its value to understanding the commodification of race.

6.7 Introducing Part III

In Part III of the book I operationalise the postcolonial cultural economy approach and apply the framework to four case studies related to race and media that I con-sider the most pressing in our time. The first chapter in this section – Chapter 7 – examines media's treatment of migrants. This draws in particular from Chapter 5 and theories of nationalism, race and media. Applying postcolonial cultural economy's historical approach, I frame the analysis in terms of 'crisis', which refers directly to the 'migrant crisis' that made the news in the mid-2010s, but also to how the making of migrants in this instance is shaped by a 'crisis in hegemony' reflecting European anxieties over the loss of national identity. In Chapter 8 I develop some of these same issues to examine Islamophobia in media. Once again, this draws from theories of nationalism and also the postcolonial regarding fear of the Other. In this chapter I demonstrate how Islamophobia entails a form of racialisation, but how it also rep-resents a distinct form of racism. As with Chapter 7, the chapter entails a discussion of how Muslims and allies are attempting to challenge dominant discourses through their own race-making practices. In Chapter 9 I apply theories of racial capitalism and commodification to examine the making of blackness in media. While Chapters 7 and 8 involve an explicit discussion of racism and media, this chapter focuses on the forms of fetishisation/fascination as well as denigration that characterise the commodification of black culture. Once again, though, the emphasis is on bottom-up and top-down forms of race-making, emphasising how the making of blackness in different contexts can both sustain and destabilise racial hierarchies. In this chapter as well I build on Part I of the book to complicate straightforward accounts of representational politics. Finally, in Chapter 10 I analyse the making of race in digital media contexts. While it is tempting to assume that the digital is a mere extension of the 'real' world, in this chapter I demonstrate how the very architecture of online technologies – specifically web 2.0 – is a determining force upon race-making practices. In other words, while it does reflect racial dynamics offline, it produces new racialising outputs. Like Chapter 9, the analyses are set within the context of racial neoliberalism, and how race becomes commodified in the form of branded identities in the name of 'diversity'. But once again, I emphasise contestedness and contradiction to explore the way that racialised groups have harnessed digital technologies to make race in more radical ways that challenge hegemonic conceptions of race.

BOX 6.1   Key Issue

Political economy and studies of race

A recurring theme in Part II of this book is that researchers of race and media would benefit from a greater engagement with critical political economy (including cultural economy approaches) that provides a more in-depth examination of media in relation to capitalism and power. It is deeply concerning, however, that the topic of race features so little in political economy research (see Hesmondhalgh and Saha, 2013). Perhaps this is the reason why race scholars engage so little with this field. But why is there a lack of interest in race in the field of political economy?

With social justice their normative frame, I do not doubt that critical political economists are invested in issues of racism. However, this recognition only makes this gap in the field more stark. In Chapter 1 I discussed how anti-racists from a more explicitly Marxist background are critical of culturalist approaches to race, and identity politics in general. Sharing the same foundation in Marxist thought, critical political economy contains the same reservations about culture-based politics as is evident in their lack of interest in popular culture, texts and representation. Moreover, I would suggest that political economists slip into a Marxian tendency to emphasise class politics *over* anti-racism (rather than intersecting concerns).

However, the major issue for critical political economy is that it sees race in terms of identity rather than as a determining force upon production. Researchers in critical political economy see racism as a negative outcome of a capitalistic media system, rather than a force that structures media practices and processes, even in contexts where the question of race is not apparent. Political economists see the drive for profit and economic domination as the determining force upon media output. But in doing so they fail to see the role media plays in reinforcing racial hierarchies. In addition, they fail to

(Continued)

recognise how capitalism interacts with racial ideology in ways that affect the institutional and organisational arrangements of media as well as its content. Indeed, while race and media scholarship needs to engage more with political economy approaches, the latter would similarly benefit from a close reading of racial capitalism.

Discussion

In what ways might racism structure the organisation of media industries? How does this affect media output?

Note

1 Hesmondhalgh (2018) uses 'critical political economy' (my emphasis) to distinguish between Marxist or leftist versions of political economy and the conservative version as found in the work of Adam Smith.

Part III
Case Studies

7
Media, Migration and Racism

In what ways do media's treatment of migrants entail a form of 'negativisation'?
Why do we need a 'race' frame when studying media's treatment of migrants? How are particular groups of migrants racialised – even those seen as white?
How does a historical approach shed light on the making of migrants in media?
What is the value of the concept of 'crisis' in helping us to understand contemporary representations of migrants?

7.1 Introduction

While I have argued that how media make race is a complex and ambivalent process, analysing the representation of migrants in mainstream media feels straightforwardly 'negative'. Indeed, one of the most glaring examples of media's negative portrayal of racial and ethnic minorities comes in the treatment of migrants. The popular press in Western nations in particular are notorious for headlines that express anti-immigrant sentiment. Migrants – whether asylum seekers, refugees, economic migrants, or even international students – are seen as taking 'our' jobs while somehow simultaneously 'sponging off' welfare, and as increasing the crime rate and social disorder in general. But according to the relevant social statistics, none of these assertions about black and brown migrants is substantiated. As a macro-economist at Cambridge University trying to make sense of anti-immigrant sentiment in the 2014 British Social Attitudes survey considers, '[O]ne has to ask why such perceptions are so out of kilter with the reality ... perhaps the anti-immigration rhetoric that features so prominently in much of the popular press is the answer'. The fact that an economist is suggesting that news media is a determining factor in people's feelings towards migrants demonstrates how social research into migrancy cannot avoid the question of media. Furthermore, research into migration needs to frame its analysis more explicitly in terms of race, something that is not always the case (Erel et al., 2016). As this chapter will show, it is impossible to discuss media and migrants without directly tackling the issue of racism.

We are in the middle of a crisis. This is a reference to what Western news media have labelled a 'migrant crisis' in relation to events since 2015, when a high number of people from the Middle East and Africa arrived in the European Union (EU) after crossing the Mediterranean Sea, with thousands of lives tragically lost in the process. But more broadly, we are experiencing a crisis in *hegemony* that has led to significant ruptures in national politics: 'Brexit', Trumpism and the rise of populist and far-right parties and movements across the world. (I write this in the midst of a lockdown following Covid-19 – who knows what this global pandemic will bring politically, socially, culturally.) In the UK, the victory of the 'Brexit' campaign was based on numerous factors (lack of transparency, excessive bureaucracy, the question of sovereignty), but the issue of immigration – and the belief that there's too much of it – was inarguably the most significant (Valluvan, 2019). Considering its influence upon national politics, the nature of news coverage of migrants is one the most urgent issues relating to media (see Smith and Deacon, 2018). It is certainly a matter of social justice.

This chapter explores the racialisation of migrants (and stories involving migrants) and considers what it reveals about the current 'crisis' and the nature of racism in this postrace era. As such, it is worth underlining that the chapter's focus is on 'non-white' migrants, who are seen as a problem, unlike white migrants (though the British media's *racialised* treatment of Eastern Europeans will be considered in this chapter). To begin with, it provides an overview of how media and communication studies has covered the topic of media's treatment of migrants. This predominantly involves the news media and the issue of representation, and occasionally the topic of news production. While this section will underline the contributions made by media scholars, especially in identifying the narrow range of frames within which migrants are portrayed, it will also highlight the limitations of studies that fail to situate their analysis within a historical account of media and migration. As such, the second part of the chapter provides a slightly alternative account, more explicitly framed in terms of 'crisis', that explores media's treatment of migrants in the context of capitalism and imperialism. It initially considers the particular nature of racism in society, one that is slippery enough to deflect accusations of racism, before thinking through how racism shapes how media make *migrants* in each of the spheres of production, representation and consumption. While this chapter draws from research across a number of national contexts, as with all the chapters that follow, its main focus will be on the UK.

7.2 How has the topic of migration, race and media been explored?

As stated, the treatment of migrants in media has generated a lot of research in the field of media and communication in particular. In what follows, I consider the main contributions of these studies, particularly in relation to representation and production, before highlighting the limitations of studies that do not tackle the (cultural) dynamics of racism in a more concerted way.

7.2.1 Studies on the framing of migrants

Studies of media and migration generally share three features. Firstly, the focus (either explicitly or implicitly) is on how media creates a disconnect between people's perceptions of immigration, which is generally negative, and the reality of migrants' impact upon society, which is actually positive, certainly economically (McLaren et al., 2018; Smith and Deacon, 2018). In other words, the starting point is how media *misrepresent* migrants. Secondly, the interest is nearly always in news media (with little discussion of popular culture), based upon one of the fundamentals of critical media studies: that news media is never 'neutral' and instead is driven by its own ideological and commercial/institutional imperatives. Thirdly, in terms of method, media studies of migrants – particularly those grounded in the discipline of communication studies – entail content analyses and survey analyses of newspaper articles, focused on the level of the text. Charles Husband's (1975) influential study of British newspapers' coverage of immigration remains one of the best examples of this approach, identifying how migrants are framed only ever as a 'problem', with hardly any stories on the positive contribution of minority populations to society, let alone the racial and social injustice that such communities experience.

Framing is the dominant mode of analysis in which communication research into migration and media has been conducted. Frames refer to the specific ways, *tropes* or *discourses* within which migrants are portrayed in the news. While researchers identify an array of different frames with regard to the representation of migrants, they can be reduced to the following:

1   The *prominence* of migrant stories in the news. This has two components. First is how news media inflate or exaggerate the number of migrants entering Western nations, which is actually low in comparison to non-Western states that receive the greatest number of those seeking asylum in particular (Khiabany, 2016). Put another way, the amount of column inches generated by stories about migration is disproportionate to the actual level of immigration into a country like the UK. Second is how news coverage of migrants becomes prominent at certain moments regardless of the level of immigration at the time. For instance, in their survey of research on media and migration, Smith

and Deacon (2018) describe how coverage of immigration in the UK context did not become a major news story until the 1970s, before subsiding and then spiking again in the 2000s and then the 2010s.[1]

2 Conflation of categories. This refers to the way news media conflate migrant types; terms such as 'immigrants', 'asylum seekers', 'refugees', 'economic migrants' become interchangeable. Such conflation can have dangerous implications in terms of what they *imply* about the legal status of migrants. For instance, 'refugees' and 'asylum seekers' appear substitutional terms, except *refugees* are those who have been granted a legal right to stay, while *asylum seekers* are merely in the process of applying. But technicalities aside, underlying this terminology are claims about the illegibility of migrants applying for legal status, with the assumption that they are 'bogus' until proven otherwise. Indeed, as Smith and Deacon (2018: 7) state, the issue with the conflation of categories is not just about imprecision, but how it leads to the 'public's (mis) perceptions about the scale, nature, and distinctions between types of immigration'. This in turn impacts upon policy, which, as we shall see, is formed by politicians attempting to placate public opinion.

3 Negativisation. '*Negativisation*' is a term used by critical discourse analysts to describe the negative ways that migrants are portrayed (see van Dijk, 1991: 213–214). This includes problems of reception, with migrants portrayed as a drain on resources (such as housing, education, healthcare and welfare), or as failing to integrate due to their inherent cultural difference. Migrants are also negatively associated with crime and violence, as well as driving 'illegal' immigration itself. As Smith and Deacon (2018) once again observe, even positive stories on migrants as victims of racism negativise them in terms of seeing them as passive and needy. The point here is that there is not much diversity in terms of the ways immigration gets reported, which is generally negative even when appearing sympathetic.

7.2.2 Making news on migrants

In considering why the treatment of migrants is so negative in the news, the easy answer is to blame it on the whiteness of the newspaper industry. For Husband (1975), the media is institutionally white and therefore produces *white media* based on assumptions of race that go unnoticed by either prejudiced or liberal white people, who fundamentally share the same assumptions. Journalism studies scholars have looked more closely at the dynamics of news production. They explore this from a range of angles, but once again the general findings can be reduced to two key issues.

First is the narrow range of news sources that journalists draw upon, whom Hall et al. (2013 [1978]: 61) describe as 'primary definers'. Primary definers are official institutional voices – politicians, judges, the police, immigration officers – who are interviewed for stories on immigration. Such sources are seen as more reliable, objective and trustworthy, but they also happen to represent the interests of the dominant culture and get to effectively frame the way that immigration is discussed. Conversely, studies show that sources reflecting minority perspectives, which could give greater balance to news coverage, are impeded by the institutional whiteness of the newsroom, the lack of clout that migrant advocacy groups carry, which prevents them from putting forward their own sources, and the fears of migrants themselves, who, in a *hostile environment*, are scared of speaking out. As such, the dominance of 'official' sources, compounded by the lack of minority voices, leads to news coverage reflecting the perspectives of the dominant culture, as stated. As Hall et al. (2013 [1978]: 68) state, 'the prevailing tendency in the media is towards the reproduction, amidst all their contradictions, of the definitions of the powerful, of the dominant ideology'. It is the role of primary definers that leads to the negativisation of migrants in the news.

Second is that journalism scholars point to news value itself as producing negative coverage. That is, the (mis)representation of migrant groups is because of news values that distort and objectify. So this is less about the individual values of journalists and instead about how news values and norms steer journalists into presenting stories in ways that are likely to picked up by audiences. As such, news values invariably privilege stories around migrants that provoke sensational, 'grabby' headlines rather than ones that rely upon nuance and subtlety. As Canadian media and race scholar Augie Fleras (quoted in Spoonley and Butcher, 2009: 356) describes, 'newsworthiness prefers the negative and adversarial over the positive and cooperative, the processing of news information reflects systemic bias namely, a bias that is institutional, not personal; consequential, not intentional; routine, not random; cultural, not conspiratorial; and structural, not attitudinal'. For Matthews and Brown (2012), negative framing is also a result of the particular types of news value that tabloids embody, for instance privileging 'moral values' over political ones and public opinion over empirically-grounded research. Moreover, they contain an ingrained antagonistic stance to governing elites who claim to be tough on immigration but are regarded as anything but.

7.2.3 Limitations of media and communication studies of migration

While the studies of migration referenced above have deepened our understanding of how migrants are treated in the (popular) press, there are problems with content-based accounts of news in particular, and adjoining production studies which lack the deeper cultural and historical account that this book is advocating. One of the main issues is that they can suggest a straightforward causal relationship between anti-immigrant news coverage and the public's attitudes towards immigration.

Occasionally there is an attempt to study reception of the news via social scientific methods, such as interviews, surveys and focus groups, but to what extent do they capture the complexity of media effects? Part of the problem here is the sole focus on news, without paying attention to the broader landscape of popular culture, which, rather than demonise migrants, is more likely to articulate what media scholar Bethany Klein (2011: 47) calls the 'multicultural ideal' and a more progressive (or rather colour-blind) view of living with difference (whether this is as progressive as producers think is another question that I will explore in subsequent chapters).

Underlining this question of complexity, the lack of a historical approach means that studies are unable to explain why representations of migrants take the shape that they do, other than to blame it on a racist media, or more broadly, racial ideology. But is it that simple? For instance, take the coverage of the *Windrush Scandal* of 2018. This was when migrants from the Caribbean who had lived in Britain for over fifty years – commonly referred to the Windrush Generation (named after the ship that brought over the first wave of West Indian migrants) – were either wrongly detained, denied benefits and medical care or even deported back to their country of origin based on their migrant status. These individuals were effectively the 'unintended' victims of former Home Secretary Theresa May's 'hostile environment' policy, which included a range of measures designed specifically to deter 'foreigners' from settling in Britain, for instance, the Right to Rent scheme, where landlords are required to check the immigration status of its tenants. Campaigning from affected families and activists, and investigative journalism from *The Guardian* newspaper, provoked a massive national outcry covered by the press across the political spectrum and a shared consensus that this was a grave injustice, leading to the resignation of the Home Secretary Amber Rudd. How to read such a situation in light of the research above? It is my contention that the models proposed in that research – especially around negativisation – cannot be applied so easily to this case. I am arguing that research into media and migrants needs to take the issue of contradiction more seriously, which in turn demands a historical approach – the kind precisely set out by the postcolonial cultural economy framework. The research above shows how media distorts and misrepresents migrants. Adopting a critical cultural approach, our interest turns to how race is made in the coverage of migrants in media, and what this in turn reveals about the nature of racism in the current conjuncture.

7.3 A critical cultural approach to the migrant crisis

In this section I want to explore migration and media in terms of 'crisis' as a way to (a) deepen our understanding of media's treatment of migrants as well as the nature of racism itself, and (b) in doing so, demonstrate the value of a critical cultural approach to this topic. Earlier in the chapter I referred to Smith and Deacon's

(2018) observation that news coverage around immigration comes around in cycles regardless of what is actually happening in terms of the number of immigrants entering the country. Instead, we see spikes in news coverage at moments of *crisis*.

7.3.1 Defining the crisis

As mentioned earlier, crisis here refers to the ongoing 'migrant crisis' since 2015. It also broadly refers to the 'crisis in multiculturalism' mentioned in Chapter 5, which in turn shapes how the current migrant crisis is made sense of. But on an even broader scale I am also referring to a crisis in hegemony. This is when the authority of the dominant culture is threatened, leading to conjunctural shifts, or historical rupture. A famous example is the British national crisis of the 1970s – as covered in two texts mentioned in previous chapters, *Policing the Crisis* (Hall et al., 2013 [1978]) and *The Empire Strikes Back* (Centre for Contemporary Cultural Studies, 1982) – where a story around two young black 'muggers' was amplified to produce public consensus for more law and order, in turn paving the way for Thatcherism and a more authoritarian state. With specific reference to the issue of immigration, van Dijk (1988) provides an analysis of the Tamil refugee crisis in the 1980s that produced a moral panic in the European news media, after European governments, unnerved by the incoming Tamil refugees, created policy to police the entry of 'non-European migrants'. This generated newspaper headlines that transformed a once unknown group of people into a prominent object of (negative) attention that in turn shaped public opinion 'which expectedly was easily persuaded to resent the "threatening" presence of another non-white, foreign group' (ibid.: 20). The result was further political panic around this issue and the further legitimation of anti-immigrant policy. Following Hall et al. (2013 [1978]: 41), we can describe this as an 'amplification spiral' – the intensification of a crisis via its mediation. Van Dijk's (1991: 2) own point is that 'What once was primarily a humanitarian issue, now had become an ethnic and political "problem"'.

Beyond the migrant crisis, we might think of a global crisis in hegemony in terms of the rise of ethnonationalism and right-wing populism, not just exclusive of the West (Brexit, Trump), but of non-Western nations too (I am thinking of the elections of Indian Prime Minister Modi and Brazilian President Jair Bolsonaro – both right-wing populists – in two of the world's biggest democracies). The ascendency of reactionary nationalist movements has been founded on demonisation of the Other – and the threat of migrants in particular. And this always involves an articulation of race. Van Dijk's argument in relation to the Tamil refugee crisis is that what was a humanitarian crisis became *racialised* – a term that we will explore in more detail shortly. We can say the same about the current crisis when the term 'migrant' so often becomes synonymous with 'Muslim' (as shall be explored in more detail in the following chapter). As Hall et al. (2013 [1978]: 34) once again put it, 'Race is the lens through which people come to perceive that a crisis is developing. It is the framework through which the crisis is experienced. It is the means by which the crisis is to be resolved; *send it away*' (my emphasis). Thus, in order to understand the current crisis around migrants we need to unpack the nature of racism in this specific historical moment.

7.3.2 Media and racism in the current conjuncture

According to the contributors to *Empire Strikes Back* (Centre for Contemporary Cultural Studies, 1982), the national crisis of the 1970s needs to be understood as part of a long historical process, rooted in the development of colonial societies in the context of British imperialism, which, as covered in Chapters 3 and 5, generated a particular type of nationalism that is hostile to immigrants. The same applies to what is happening in the present day. In a powerful polemical piece, media scholar and activist Gholam Khiabany (2016) argues that imperialism/capitalism is still the most important frame for understanding the migrant crisis. Khiabany is critical of migration studies that fail to frame their analysis within the broader historical context; as he puts it (ibid.: 756), 'the refugee crisis (and media coverage of it) has everything to do with place, history, class, capitalism and imperialism'. Basically, the migrant crisis has been instigated by Western exploits abroad.

This returns us to the question of nationalism and capitalism, as covered in Chapters 4 and 5. The current crisis is borne out of a contradiction of capitalism. On the one hand, capitalist nations facilitate the expansion of globalisation for the reason that they require immigration, not just in terms of providing a source of cheap labour, but also in terms of replenishing the population (immigrant populations tend to be younger and more productive). But on the other hand, immigrants are painted as a threat to the 'social integrity of the nation state' (Back et al., 2002: 4.1) – that is, the (imagined) cohesion of the nation. To unpack this further we need to turn back to Paul Gilroy's (2004: 97) important concept of 'postcolonial melancholia', and what he calls the 'perennial crisis of national identity'. As explored in Chapter 5, postcolonial melancholia describes a nationalistic longing for a mythical time – 'an imagined, homogenous, and unsullied time, before immigration' (ibid.). The point for Gilroy is that such a time never existed, but it is such a myth that binds the nation together, even though it depends on excluding the Other. In this way, the arriving immigrant is seen as 'an alien wedge cutting in to the body of an unsuspecting nation' (ibid.: 133). Vukov (2003) highlights a passage of Foucault, who sees state racism as a key form of *biopolitical* governance founded on the idea of protecting the body (population) from infection or pollution (immigration). This explains why immigration is so often described in terms of disaster metaphors – *a flood, a deluge, a swarm, a swamping*. It's not just that these metaphors are in poor taste; rather, they speak directly to the belief in the purity of the nation and the fear of contamination from the Other. The dominant culture's response to this is to practise an essentialist logic of 'ethnic absolutism' (Gilroy, 2004: 137) that seeks to maintain an absolute distinction between the

White national subject and the immigrant Other, who are marked according to their *'racialised* difference' (ibid.: 155, my emphasis). And for Gilroy, this is asserted at the level of the popular imagination – which includes in the form of media texts.

Racialisation is an important concept in a critical cultural approach to migration and media as it highlights how news stories on immigration become about race; *that race is the problem.* Racialisation refers to the process by which ideas about race are constructed, become meaningful and acted upon. As sociologists Karim Murji and John Solomos (2005: 3) put it, racialisation is the 'process by which racial meanings are attached to particular issues – often treated as social problems – and with the manner in which race appears to be a, or often the, key factor in the ways they are defined and understood'. In this regard, news reports on immigration, even when racial and ethnic identities are not mentioned, entail a form of racialisation that evokes the logic of ethnic absolutism, as Gilroy describes. As an example, Fox et al. (2012) go so far as to argue that news coverage on the arrival of (white) Eastern Europeans from nations who joined the European Union after 2007 racialised the migrants in question, specifically Romanians and Bulgarians. The authors find that despite the relatively new presence of these migrants, 'existing cultural tropes and racialized plot lines' (ibid.: 686) are used to frame the new Eastern European arrivals – whether exaggeration of their number or their alien cultural practices – that in the process places them in a racial hierarchy. (In one infamous *Daily Mail* article, the paper claimed that Eastern Europeans migrants were killing swans for food; see Malone, 2010.) As Fox et al. (2012: 691) state, categories like 'West' and 'Europe' carry unambiguous colour connotations wherein 'those to whom membership is bestowed in these categories are lightened and those to whom membership is denied are darkened'.

Another facet of the new racism that characterises the current crisis is how racism itself becomes something to be debated and contested rather than a social fact. I refer here to the technique of denying racism while saying something racist – exemplified by the adage, *'I'm not racist but…'.* Augoustinos and Every (2007) identify three ways that racism is denied in (racist) migration coverage: (1) claims to objectivity and the painting of negative traits belonging to migrants as natural and based in fact, (2) *discursive deracialisation*, referring to how speakers attempt to deracialise negative representations of groups by referring to their religious or national identities, which appears less contentious than describing them by their race or ethnicity, and (3) emphasising liberal values of equality ('*we see no colour*') as a device to ensure that any attempts at positive discrimination that address racial inequality are decried themselves as being racist. For Gavan Titley (2019), what he calls the very *debatability of racism* is a product of a perverse irony of living in a supposed postrace society: since the idea of race no longer matters, the calling out of racism is itself racist.

Based on a reading of these literatures, I want to make three points on the nature of racism in the current conjuncture with regard to media's treatment of migrants. Firstly, postcolonial melancholia produces a deep ambivalence around the arrival of migrants – despite the value to capitalism (as low-skilled migrants represent a cheap source of labour that can be exploited) – and in times of crisis this ambivalence turns into outright hostility. Secondly, the migrant is racialised (even when light skinned), and moreover is seen as a threat to the nation, to its cohesion, to its (racial) purity. And thirdly, to counter accusations of racism, the dominant culture turns racism into something to be debated and denied. This offers us an explanation of how such racism is able to persist in media despite how it is supposed to be an antithesis to the foundation of liberal democracy.

7.3.3 How media make migrants

So far this discussion has provided an explanation of the dynamics of racism within the current conjuncture, mostly in the British context, and how this shapes how the migrant crisis is represented and constructed. But what about media? Is it enough just to say that (mainstream) media are a mere conduit for racist, ethnonationalist ideology? In this section I want to return to the issue of production and the difficult issue of consumption/reception to think through the complexity of the workings of ideology in relation to media and migrants.

In the previous selection I drew from journalism scholars, who demonstrate how negative coverage of migrants is due to the elevated position of primary definers and news values themselves. But other journalism studies scholars highlight how the situation is far from straightforward. As Gemi et al. (2013: 278) state, news value can be enabling when '[i]ssues that are reported cover personalised, emotion-laden stories that can interest a wider public, stories that show the "human" and "every-day" aspect of migration' – for instance, in the case of the Windrush Scandal, or the case of Aylan Kurdi, the three year-old Syrian migrant whose dead body was found washed up on a beach in Turkey after attempting to cross the Mediterranean. In other words, news values do not always have to produce reductive outcomes. Bennett et al. (2013), in a study of over 60 journalists who cover immigrant stories, find that they do not racialise their coverage of immigrants on purpose, and in fact are quite aware of slipping into racist tropes (although this still can produce racialising effects, as discussed). The authors find that the journalists believe that professional ethics is enough to produce balanced reporting on migrant issues.

But this is not enough to defer from the fact that migrants are consistently represented along reductive, Orientalist tropes. Media researchers Olga Bailey and Ramaswami Harindranath (2005) agree that the negative framing of immigrants is not because of the racist values of individual journalists but a result of how narratives around asylum seekers, rather than being isolated, are part of a long historical discursive formation that, in effect, 'demonstrates a form of racism which has become part of a commonly held vision of nationals security and sovereignty' (ibid.: 275). So, in other words, it's not an overt racism but one that has become embedded in society in terms of its attitude to others. For the authors, 'journalism has not fully embraced the Other' (ibid.: 278) and instead slips into simplistic binary oppositions that do not to pay due attention to the complexity of geopolitical situations that force people to leave their homes. The authors effectively argue that journalists are too nationalistic in their worldview and need to adopt a more cosmopolitan outlook – in terms of the universal values of human rights – that transcends the rhetoric of nationalism. (It is worth considering whether the shift to digital is having an impact on the nationalistic coverage of migrants that Bailey and Harindranath describes, as news production and consumption becomes more global.) While I would argue that merely encouraging journalists to adopt a more cosmopolitan perspective may be too easy a solution, this account nonetheless provides a stronger explanation of how ideology is reproduced, which does justice not only to the agency of the journalist, but also to the workings of dominant ideology.

But how does ideology filter into society? How is it consumed? While *all* media scholars recognise the agency of the audience, studies focused at the level of ideology alone can implicitly suggest a straightforward model of media effects. But the situation is so much more complicated than audiences simply believing what they read. The strongest studies of racism in media tackle the complexity of ideology in terms of its reception. For instance, one of the key arguments of *Policing the Crisis* (Hall et al., 2013 [1978]) is that for news to 'work' it needs to be based on a social consensus – that is, a common understanding shared among the public. The point is what makes a social consensus is deeply ideological. In addition, ideology does not just operate at the level of meaning: for Vukov (2003), the mediation of immigration is designed precisely to produce a particular *affective* response from the public that gives the state a sense of urgency in enacting racist policies around immigration. Certainly, sensationalised headlines around migrancy produce strong visceral responses among readers.

These two examples offer a consideration at least of how publics are affected by ideology, but they lack an empirical study of audience reception. To repeat, too many studies assume a direct correlation between how migrants are portrayed in the news and the publics' attitudes towards migrants. But as I have also stated, measuring media effects is notoriously difficult, especially in the context of social scientific methods like surveys and focus groups that measure media consumption in artificial settings divorced from everyday media practices (Gray, 1993). A more productive route comes from media ethnographer Myria Georgiou (2016), who situates media consumption within everyday multicultural experience. The particular study I am referring to is not so much about immigration itself, but rather the dynamics of multiculture in relation to local media, including diasporic media. Focusing on a multicultural neighbourhood in north London, Georgiou explores the relation between how people encounter difference in the everyday and how they experience it in media. Her findings demonstrate the complexity – and almost paradoxical nature – of locals' relationship to where they live. The neighbourhood in question is somewhat typical of London, in that it is immensely diverse yet characterised by self-segregation, where ethnic communities (including white ethnicities) tend to stick to their own. Georgiou finds that media shapes people's understanding of Others in negative ways which then get localised, but this fear of the Other is then countered by ordinary, everyday encounters. In other words, ethnic segregation breeds insecurity and fear of Others, but this is somewhat mitigated by the inevitable 'crossing of paths' in real life. As Georgiou (ibid.: 273) states, 'the brief and uncommitted communication in the urban street is a moment where urban dwellers build their confidence in the continuity of their environment'. Locals, on the one hand, will talk about how certain communities self-segregate, but then will also talk warmly about the multicultural nature of the environment, which Georgiou describes as the 'dialectic of communicative conviviality'. Basically, 'convivial separation' (ibid.: 277) sums up the experience of living with difference in a multicultural city like London. As such, the mediation of multiculture clearly shapes people's experience of difference – but this is cut though by their real-life experiences in complex ways.

In terms of the effect of the negative representation of migrants, what I take from Georgiou is that media effects are never straightforward and are complicated by everyday experience, which if not causing publics to doubt media, certainly complicates the process of reception. It should be underlined that Georgiou is focusing on a very multicultural area of London. To add to this account, I draw from an important sociological study on the reception of then British Home Secretary Theresa May's notorious *Go Home* campaign (Jones et al., 2017) that explores how it was received differently in different places in the UK. This particular campaign created a sense of good (deserving) versus bad (opportunist) migrants, which increased fear and feelings of precariousness among racialised groups, as well as a strong polarisation of opinions within communities. What both these studies underline through close and sensitive qualitative analysis of communities in their everyday contexts is that the consumption of 'negative' representations of minorities is complex but no less powerful and divisive.

To conclude this section, I underline the point that we need to be careful about suggesting a causal relationship between media representation and public attitudes. Rather, media, including popular culture alongside press discourses, create a *hegemonic field of meaning* through which voter attitudes, social policy, immigration laws, foreign policy and everyday experience are formed. It is in these circumstances that the current crisis is experienced. However, one glaring omission in this chapter so far has been the impact of digital media on the mediation of migrancy. Social media in particular is an important context to explore since it blurs the lines between production and consumption: as users consume, they produce new content. (This is the topic of Chapter 10.) But in relation to the subject of migrancy I want to finish this chapter with a case study on the tragic death of Syrian refugee Aylan Kurdi to explore the impact of social media as well as to unpack further the debatability of racism in the current conjuncture.

BOX 7.1 Case Study

Aylan Kurdi

On 2 September 2015, photographer Nilüfer Demir took a picture of a dead three-year-old Syrian boy, Aylan Kurdi, washed up, face down on a beach near the Turkish city of Bodrum. His body was still intact and he was wearing the clothes he was travelling in. Within hours, the images were dramatically diffused through social media, followed by global mainstream press. The images produced a massive discursive response in the form of indignation and protest on social media – through the #CouldBeMyChild hashtag – at Western governments for the inhumane treatment of migrants. This ran counter to so much of the negative news coverage that the migrant crisis had generated. But does the dissemination of what Olesen (2018: 668) calls 'injustice photographs' represent the democratising powers of the internet?

Some critical media scholars argued that the coverage was disingenuous. Why the sudden focus on Kurdi when migrants had been drowning in the Mediterranean prior to 2015? Critical race scholar Nadine El-Enany (2016) argues that it was because of Kurdi's whiteness (in contrast to darker migrants, whose washed-up bodies did not solicit the same response or outpouring of compassion). Others argued that the coverage produced negative ideological effects. By the very nature of social media like Twitter, which limits discourse to 280 characters, Kurdi is dehistorcised; the #CouldBeMyChild hashtag omitted any recognition of the specificity of colonial histories and present Western excursions and interference abroad that force people to flee their homelands (El-Enany, 2016; Khiabany, 2016). For Chouliaraki and Stolic (2017) in their exploration of the nature of photos of refugees that circulate online, the spread of such images serves to wipe the hands of responsibility of the European; as the refugee is decontextualised from politics and history, refugees are effectively presented as a problem elsewhere, and certainly not the responsibility of the host nation.

A deeper argument that takes more seriously the apparatus of the internet comes from Gavan Titley (2019). For Titley, the debatability of racism that is the topic of his analysis is shaped also by what Andrew Chadwick calls 'hybrid media systems' that combine old and new. Titley draws from digital media and race scholar Sanjay Sharma to explore the varied ways in which racism and anti-racism are expressed, contested and become an object of fascination on social media, producing a digital mash-up (or indeed at times, a *pile-up*). Titley describes content such as the images of Kurdi as 'digital ephemera' that disappear as quickly as they spread, decontextualised and recontextualised, fused with material across new media and traditional media, accumulating new forms of commentary and interpretation along the way. It is this 'communicative context' that enables the debatability of racism.

With regard to the case of Alyan Kurdi, Titley's main interest is in a controversial cartoon titled 'Migrants' that was published in the French satirical comic *Charlie Hebdo* (that previously was the victim of a terrorist attack where staff were shot and killed by Islamic Fundamentalists during an editorial meeting). This cartoon was controversial for its 'joke' that if Kurdi had survived his journey across the Mediterranean he would have grown up to be a molester in Germany (referring to an incident in Cologne where women were allegedly sexually assaulted by gangs of immigrants). Using this example, Titley demonstrates how the Kurdi tragedy gets folded into a wider discourse about the threat of migrants. But rather than decried as racist, the cartoon generated as much defence as it

(Continued)

did criticism. The debate about whether the cartoon was racist – as it took place on- and offline – became about upholding liberal, secular, *European* values in the face of a multiculturalist, Islamist threat. Titley's point is that in order to understand the nature of this debate, we cannot divorce it from its communicative context. His argument is that it is the very architecture of the internet and the cascades of digital ephemera that it produces – via memes, trolling, clicktivism and other digital techniques – which in its very circulation generates masses of commentary and counter-commentary, that turns the flagrant racism of the cartoon into something open to debate.

What the case of Aylun Kurdi shows is that there is always the potential to produce alternative or counter-narratives that challenge negative framings of migrants. But the nature of new racism is such that these counter-narratives become subsumed into dominant discourses around migrancy. As Titley describes, the making of migrants and race, especially in the context of the new digital communication environment whose very political economy relies upon the churn of content, has turned the racist treatment of migrants into something to be debated, rather than something to eliminate.

7.4 Conclusion

The negative treatment of the migrant in media is clear. But in this chapter I wanted to complicate the picture without downplaying the racism itself that shapes media's portrayal of migrants, reducing them to highly reductive tropes. In that regard I framed my analysis in terms of 'crisis', which at once referred to the ongoing 'migrant crisis', as covered in news media, and a 'crisis in hegemony', which has led to significant ruptures in national politics across a number of different contexts, characterised by the rise of the populist-right.

Framing my approach in this way – indeed, according to the postcolonial cultural economy framework – entails a historical approach that situated the mediation of migrancy within broader histories of empire and nationalism. It also pays closer attention to media and the complex dynamics at play in the fields of production and consumption. The main aim was to demonstrate how dominant ideology takes control of these spheres but in complex ways that are always being contested and always producing contradiction. I also presented a case study on the media coverage of Aylan Kurdi to demonstrate the particular impact of digital media upon the mediation of migrancy. The overall theme has been to show that racism in media has become subject – or rather, content – to debate, enabled by the nature of the hybrid media systems that characterise contemporary communication. Despite the damning findings of media and policy research, and protestations from campaigners, activists and indeed audiences, migrant coverage seems immutable, and there remains a lack of an alternative language to speak about migrancy in news media in particular. The reason for this is the slippery nature of nationalism which is able to deflect accusations of racism. Put another way, it is precisely through how racism has become itself a media discourse to be debated, that allows the racist treatment of migrants to reproduce.

Migration is a fact of life and a permanent fixture in news and politics, and as such will offer media scholars a churn of new media texts to analyse and deconstruct. However, gaps in the fields remain. More work is needed that explores how media coverage of migrancy is consumed in the context of people's everyday *media lives*, including in mediated and unmediated contexts, in order to see how they really shape people's attitudes to migrants. This needs to entail a consideration of both news and entertainment media. Moreover, journalism studies needs to focus more on the operation of ideology in the newsroom, which takes both the agency of journalists and the political economy of the news industry equally seriously, grounded in an analysis of nationalism, empire and capitalism. Further research is needed also into the making of migrants in the context of social media (for those researchers who have the stomach for it), but that does not divorce such an analysis from the everyday.

7.5 Recommended and further reading

As covered, Gavan Titley's (2019) *Racism and Media* is one of those rare texts that crosses over both critical media studies and the sociology of race and racism, and adds serious value to each discipline. Titley's argument about how, in this time of 'postrace', racism has become something to be debated rather than immediately denounced explains so much that happens around race in contemporary media culture (as any single viewing of Piers Morgan discussing racism demonstrates). Preceding Titley was Charles Husband's (1975) influential text *White Media and Black Britain: A Critical Look at the Role of the Media in Race Relations Today*, which provides an early yet still valuable example of a content analysis approach to news media and immigration.

For an overview of immigration and news media in the British context, Smith and Deacon (2018) have produced a useful survey of the literature as well as the historical context, albeit mostly focused at the level of representation.

One area of research that is (a) under-recognised in media studies of migration, and (b) brings a much-needed focus on the everyday experience of migrant life and its mediation comes from researchers adopting ethnographic methods. One example referenced in the chapter is the work of Myria Georgiou, and in particular her book *Media and the City: Cosmopolitanism and Difference* (2013) (see also Miyase Christensen's (2012) article 'Online Mediations in Transnational Spaces: Cosmopolitan (Re) Formations of Belonging and Identity in the Turkish Diaspora'). A similar approach but more rooted in the field of urban studies comes from Les Back, a sociologist of race who is particularly attentive to popular culture. His article 'Moving Sounds, Controlled Borders: Asylum and the Politics of Culture' (2016) provides a unique empirical study of a grassroots community media initiative based around a music collaboration involving London-based Asian dance music DJs and Czech and Polish Roma musicians that led to the making of a CD called 'Asylum' (see also

Back's *Migrant City*, co-authored with Shamser Sinha (2018)). Employing a similar multi-media method, Lucila Vargas's (2009) book *Latina Teens, Migration, and Popular Culture* focuses on a group of transnational migrant teens and how they use media to make sense of their experiences and create attachment and belonging to both their old and new homes.

BOX 7.2 Key Theme

Ghosts, zombies and fear of the Other

Media studies of migrants generally focus on news media, but what can popular culture reveal about the dominant culture's feelings about – or indeed, *fears* of – migrants?

While nation states appear to care little about migrant lives, they cannot escape the ghosts of these migrants that come to haunt the national psyche. Drawing from Jacques Derrida's notion of the *spectre* of Marx, Avery Gordon (2008) develops the concept of 'hauntology' to explore how ghosts from the past – specifically victims from racial injustices – haunt the present. Such hauntings contribute to the postcolonial melancholia that Paul Gilroy conceptualises to describe the neurosis produced by Britain's unresolved relationship with its own empire and the atrocities upon others committed in its name. Film is one space where such apparitions appear. For instance, film scholar Glen Mimura (2009) demonstrates how the USA's internment of Japanese Americans during the Second World War, while resolved as far as the state is concerned, nonetheless produces spectres that haunt Asian American cinema in the work of filmmakers who were not even alive at the time.

Paul Gilroy (2012) himself uses the figure of the zombie to describe Britain's disturbed relationship with its own multiculture. As he states in his inimitable style:

> Those menacing, spectral figures of torrid, tropical modernity provide an appropriate avatar for vernacular culture here and now. Like Britain's stubbornly undead diversity, zombies are terrifying to the power and destabilising of the order that pronounced their death. Their resilient labour, superhuman physical strength and apparently limitless subaltern aggression bespeak the historically unprecedented perils and corrupting cultural contamination of unfree, creole formations. (2012: 384)

Certainly, in recent years we have seen a resurgence of zombies in popular culture, whether in film (*28 Days Later, Shaun of the Dead, World War Z*), television (*The Walking Dead, Z Nation*) and video games (*Last of US*, the *Resident Evil* franchise). What these films share in common are images of *swarms* of zombies overrunning, contaminating and cannibalising isolated communities of people. As the quote from Gilroy above suggests, zombies are relentless and not fully human – recognisable but irreconcilably different. Indeed, to what extent do the images of zombies that appear in popular culture speak to the fears of the nation? To be clear, I am not suggesting that these depictions of zombies are intended as anti-migrant allegories. However, as psychoanalytical approaches to

(Continued)

media demonstrate, fears and desire of the Other operate at the level of subconscious and manifest symbolically in media culture (Young, 1996a). My point is that forms of popular culture that do not directly represent migrants can nonetheless be particularly revealing about how the nation sees the Other.

Discussion

Think of some examples of how migrants appear in popular culture. How does it compare to their negativised treatment in the news?

Note

1   It is worth noting how different migrants have been stigmatised over time, starting with the Irish and Jews and then moving on to Commonwealth migrants (specifically from the Caribbean and South Asia), and then, more recently, Muslims and Eastern European migrants. It is important to note that the stigmatisation of these groups has entailed a form of negative racialisation.

8

Islamophobia and Media

What is Islamophobia? In what ways is it a distinct form of racism?
What roles do media play in perpetuating Islamophobia as racism?
How does Edward Said's concept of Orientalism help us understand con-
temporary representations of Islam in media?
How does Islamophobia involve an 'articulation' of race, religion and
gender?

8.1 Introduction

The term 'folk devil' has been used by sociologists to describe figures in society perceived as 'deviant' and a threat to the social order and collective values. Inevitably,
these folk devils are racialised. During the national crisis in 1970s Britain, as covered
in *Policing the Crisis* (Hall et al., 2013 [1978]), the young black man became a folk
devil, and that remains the case. But in recent times, *the Muslim* has emerged as a new
folk devil – perhaps the one most feared – who is seen as a threat to the West, both to
its culture and its physical security. This chapter explores the nature of contemporary
Islamophobia in society, and media's role in reinforcing – or challenging – essentialist
ideas about Muslims, whether at home or abroad.

Islamophobia refers to the fear of the faith of Islam, which is seen as a threat
to the West. As we shall explore, it also captures anti-Muslim discrimination. This
chapter considers how media perpetuate (and challenge) Islamophobia. As shall
become evident, there are strong parallels between the representations of Muslims
and migrants, which, in news media in particular, share many of the same negative framing techniques; indeed, the terms 'migrant' and 'Muslim' have become
conflated. But there is also something very particular about media's treatment of

Muslims, and specifically the nature of Islamophobia, compared to other racisms. In popular debate Islamophobes will deny being racist as they spout hateful pronouncements about Islam (and either directly, or by implication, Muslims themselves). But while there has been a tendency to sideline the issue of race in sociological studies of Muslim experience, there is an increasing understanding that Islamophobia entails a form of racialisation.

In this chapter I frame the discussion of media Islamophobia explicitly in terms of race. But I want also to underline the distinctiveness of Islamophobia in relation to other forms of racism. As we shall see, the making of Muslims as a 'race' involves a particular *articulation* of race with religion and, as I will demonstrate, gender as well. To reiterate, there is something very specific about the hostility towards Islam as religion that needs to be acknowledged. As such, this chapter asks how is race being made in media's representation of Muslims? Following the postcolonial cultural economy framework, answering this question demands a historical approach, and a consideration of the structural and the ideological, of production and consumption as well as representation.

In the first section of the chapter I unpack the nature of Islamophobia as a contemporary form of Orientalism, before examining the ways in which it can be considered a process of racialisation (without denying the particularity of the West's attitudes towards Muslims and Islam itself). I then focus on media more directly and look at the treatment of Muslims pre- and post-911 – including a discussion of the veil – as a way of exploring the gendered as well as racialised nature of Islamophobia and how it has changed through history. I then focus on how Muslims have attempted to contest and challenge Islamophobia in media, which shows how media's treatment of Muslims, while mostly reductive and essentialist, is always under contestation. I finish the chapter with a case study on supposedly sympathetic portrayals of Muslims that appear in popular culture – focusing on the work of Evelyn Alsultany in particular – which captures the slippery nature of contemporary Islamophobia and the ideological challenges it poses.

8.2 Orientalism, Islamophobia and racialisation

In order to understand the nature of contemporary Islamophobia that manifests in media we need to situate it within the context of Orientalism, following the work of Edward Said. As explained in Chapter 3, for Said, Orientalism is a body of knowledge that the West or 'Occident' has amassed about the 'Orient' that is represented as both Other and inferior. When Said refers to the 'Orient' he is mostly preoccupied with the Near East, and in *Covering Islam* (1981) (the third book of his so-called *Orientalism* trilogy) he focuses more directly, as the title suggests, on the West's depiction of and the subsequent claims it makes about Islam. In a nutshell, while the West sees itself as naturally superior, the Islamic world is nonetheless seen as a constant and ominous threat.

For Said, Orientalist discourse represents the Islamic world as absolutely, irreconcilably different from the West. It is constructed as oppressive (especially towards women), outmoded, anti-intellectualist, restrictive, extremist, backward and the cause of worldwide conflict. Even though all religions have their fanatical members, religious fundamentalism only seems to apply to Islam. As Said summarises, Muslims are painted as 'oil suppliers, as terrorists and, more recently, as bloodthirsty mobs' (Said, 1981: 6). Said's model of Orientalism, as covered in Chapter 3, has received criticism, for the selective nature of his arguments, the lack of interest in contradiction or contestatory narratives within the discipline of 'Orientialism', and for painting as monolithic an image of the Occident as Orientalists conceived the Orient. Nonetheless, while the original edition of *Covering Islam* was published at the turn of the 1980s, all of the stereotypes listed above remain troublingly familiar. For Sivamohan Valluvan (2017: 233), in a more recent piece on nationalism and the treatment of different migrants, the Muslim is still seen as 'a misogynist, indolent, communal, violent, fanatical, sectarian and, perhaps most invidiously, as protean and unpredictable'.

Contemporary representations of Islam, as shaped by Orientalist discourse, are framed within a narrative around the 'clash of civilisations'. According to this narrative, Islam and the West are two global orders that exist in a fundamental antagonism – the West has the power but Islam is a significant counter-force. What is unique about this relationship is that neither are contained by a particular nation; as such, it is not a territorial battle in a straightforward sense, but one based on ideas, values and beliefs. Moreover, it is the key antagonism that defines the current global conjuncture. But why is it the 'West' rather than 'Christianity' *versus Islam*? Once again, Edward Said provides the most perceptive explanation, that furthermore explains much about contemporary representations of Islam:

> At present 'Islam' and the 'West' have taken a powerful new urgency everywhere. And we must note immediately that it is always the West, and not Christianity, that seems pitted against Islam. Why? Because the assumption is that whereas 'the West' is greater than and has surpassed the stage of Christianity, it's principal religion, the world of Islam – it's varied societies, histories, and languages notwithstanding – is still mired in religion, primitivity, and backwardness. Therefore, the West is modern, greater than the sum of its parts, full of enriching contradictions and yet always 'Western' in it cultural identity; the world of Islam, on the other hand, is no more than 'Islam', reducible to a small number of unchanging characteristics despite the appearance of contradictions and experiences of variety that seem on the surface as plentiful as those of the West. (Said, 1981: 10)

Thus, using the 'West' in this dichotomy immediately alleviates it as modern and superior to Islam. But while Islam threatens the West's cultural identity, the clash of civilisation discourse is also shaped by the political-economic context, specifically, the loss of Western power in the Middle East and the subsequent loss of control over oil prices, which in turn challenges the economic might and consequent political authority of the US (Poole, 2002). In other words, the discourse around a clash of civilisations emerges from a combination of the perennial crisis in (Western) national identity and a geopolitical context where the military, political and economic authority of Western nations – primarily the US and the UK – is being challenged.

The threat of Islam – whether real or imagined – has led to an attempt to re-centre the West, within which Islamophobia is one response. Indeed, for sociologist Amir Saeed (2007), Islamophobia is the contemporary manifestation of Orientalism. Islamophobia is defined as hostility towards Islam and anti-Muslim prejudice in general (ibid.). However, there are some conceptual problems around Islamophobia, specifically that it paints Islam as a singular thing and refers only to the fear of Islam as a religion, rather than the fear of the people who follow it (Meer, 2013). As a consequence, Saeed (2007) highlights how some sociologists prefer 'anti-Muslim', as Islamophobic discrimination is less about Islam itself and more about the treatment of Muslim peoples. The danger of making this distinction, in my view, is that while anti-Muslim prejudice is frowned upon, Islamophobia – as a critique of Islam – is seen as somehow acceptable, or at least open to discussion. Either way, Islam and Muslims are seen as a threat to Western secular democracy, multiculturalism and integration (Meer et al., 2010; Saeed, 2007). The function of Islamophobia in this way is to keep the Muslims 'at a distance and impersonalised' (Poole, 2002: 45).

This leads on to the question of whether Islamophobia should be considered a form of racism. A common retort among Islamophobes is that they cannot be racist since *Islam is not a race*. In this regard, much like the debatability of racism (Titley, 2019), as covered in the previous chapter, 'Islam is not a race' acts as a discursive strategy that prevents the discussion about Islamophobic discourse being construed as racism, which would be seen as socially unacceptable (in polite conversation at least). But Western understandings of Islam are imbued with racialised ideas of the Other (Riley, 2009; Meer, 2013). There are ideas of race attached to being Muslim – based on perceived physical attributes and cultural difference. As an example, the way that Muslims are put under surveillance, denied citizenship rights and detained without trial entails a form of racial profiling, based on their appearance as much as their beliefs. In the period after 9/11 Sikh Americans who wore turbans/beards found themselves on the receiving end of excessive security measures at airports and racial violence on account of being mistaken for Muslims. In other words, a component of Islamophobia is an essentialised idea of racial difference. For Williamson and Khiabany (2010: 86), 'religion has come to stand in for race, complete with attributes that they are attached to this "singular" community'.

But that is not to say that Islamophobia is like any other racism. More precisely, Islamophobia should be understood as a distinct form of racism based on a particular articulation with religion (Modood, 1992; Meer and Nayak, 2013). For Saeed (2016: 31), 'the new floating signifier is not "colour" but religion and specifically Islam or Muslims', entailing assumptions about religion, class and nation in conjunction with race.

Saeed continues, 'it could be suggested that the issue of asylum seekers/refugees has been conflated with the issue of Islamic fundamentalist terrorism to create a new form of racism and thus, it may be argued, to create another dimension of exclusion' (ibid.). Therefore, much like the signifier 'race', 'Muslim' is contingent and gets articulated with race and other identities in very particular ways within a given moment. As Claire Alexander (2017: 15) states, 'Contemporary Islamophobia builds on, feeds off, transforms and adds to a store of racial, ethnic and religious stereotypes'.

In this regard Islamophobia is a historical phenomenon. A form of Islamophobia emerged in the very first encounters between Islam and Christianity in order to justify European colonial conquest and military expansion into the Middle East. Following the Enlightenment, Islam was constructed not in opposition to Christianity but as an antithesis to modern Europe's foundation in rationality and reason. Islamophobia in its contemporary form remains shaped by these legacies of colonialism and Enlightenment, but is activated in this context by postcolonial melancholia and the crisis of multiculturalism that followed 9/11, as covered in Chapter 4. For Holohan (2006), events such as 9/11 and the War on Iraq in particular have intensified the discourse of a fundamental clash between Islam and the West. Thus, foreign and domestic policy and mediated discourses around the crisis of multiculturalism combine and interact in order to produce the Islamophobia that defines the current conjuncture. To return to the question of Islamophobia's particular articulation of race and religion, as media studies scholar Elizabeth Poole (2002: 48), sums up:

> A dislike of Islam cannot be seen as the defining feature of hostility towards Muslims; it includes a complex mixture of xenophobia and racism. The supposed shift from skin colour to cultural practices as the 'ethnic signifier' has increased Muslims' visibility, given that being a Muslim often comprises an explicit projection of both.

To recap, Islam is constructed as a cultural and physical threat to the West. The relationship between Islam and the West is based on a long history but one that has been shaped by various crises at certain points in history. The antagonism between them, rather than real, has been constructed in particular ways, in particular times and particular places, for particular reasons – based on structural and ideological factors. So it's contingent rather than a taken-for-granted fact. Nonetheless there is a discursive continuity in the way Islam has been represented that goes back to early Christian encounters with Islam. But this discourse is not unchanging and reappears, as stated, in different forms at different times.

8.3 How media make Muslims

Having unpacked the character of anti-Muslim prejudice in the West, this section considers how Islamophobia is constituted in media. As stated in the introduction, media studies of the representation of Muslims produce similar findings as studies of migrants (a reflection of how 'Muslim' has become conflated with 'migrant'). Essentially, media marginalises Muslim voices and renders them invisible, but when they do appear they are negativised. Elizabeth Poole (2002), who has produced in-depth, longitudinal studies of Islamophobia and media, demonstrates how Muslims are seen as a threat to national security, a threat to mainstream values, inherently different and a disruptive presence in public life.

When we think of contemporary Islamophobia it is tempting to see its roots in the terrorist attack of '9/11', and as we shall see, 9/11 did indeed see a change in the way Muslims are covered in news media. However, it should be stressed that Islamophobia in its modern form goes back further than 9/11. While there was a moment when Islam had receded in the Western imaginary, this changed in the 1970s with the 1973 oil crisis, followed by the Iranian revolution in 1979 and the Iran hostage crisis (Said, 1981). These key (and mediated) moments in history both gave birth to modern Islamist movements and reanimated Western antagonisms towards Islam (Poole, 2002; Ahmed and Matthes, 2017). In the UK, debates around the integration of Muslims at home were set in motion by the Rushdie Affair of 1989, where a number of British Muslims protested against the publication of Salman Rushdie's novel *The Satanic Verses* for its perceived blasphemy. Rushdie received a *fatwa* from the then Ayatollah of Iran, whereby journalists began to connect British Muslims to global Islamist movements. This is where we begin to see the discourse around the *crisis in multiculturalism* emerge in politics and media. As Poole (2002: 51) puts it, 'For the UK, the Rushdie Affair was the catalyst for the struggles around identity that are currently being played out across Europe'.

However, 9/11 represented another key rupture. Following 9/11, there was a massive increase in news stories on Islam, which were predominantly negative, based on a 'clash of civilisations' rhetoric. More precisely, after 9/11 there is a greater association made between Muslims and terrorism; Muslims are no longer just a cultural threat, but also a threat to national security. In order to explore the shift in media discourse around Islam I want to focus on the issue of the veil, which in turn provides a deeper insight into how race is made in relation to media's treatment of Muslims.

8.3.1 Representing the veil

As Williamson and Khiabany (2010: 93) state, '[i]t has become impossible to talk about Islam without reference to women and impossible to talk of Muslim women without reference to the veil'. The 'veil' has become the symbol of Islamic difference. This conflation with the veil to Islam is interesting in itself, and a part of essentialising, Islamophobic discourse. There are a number of misconstructions around the veil: it is not unique to Islam and a form of it features in many other religions; rather than the product of religious doctrine, the veil is more closely linked to class, ranking and status; and rather than one veil there are many different types of veils/styles/fashions involving different levels of 'cover'. Nonetheless, the veil is seen as an 'all encompassing symbol of repression' associated solely with Islam (Macdonald, 2006: 8). As such, the veil – like all of Islam and Muslim experience – is dehistoricised and decontextualised within the clash of civilisation discourse (Ahmed and Matthes, 2017).

The role of the veil in the Western imaginary has its roots in colonialism, where it contained a sexual/erotic element, especially connected to the idea of *unveiling*. Feminist scholar Myra Macdonald (2006) states that the desire to unveil the Muslim woman was, on the surface, about making the Other conform to the colonial culture. But the politics of unveiling also constitutes a long colonial discourse of 'laying them bare' (ibid.: 9), with all the sexual connotations that such an expression holds. Orientalist discourse fetishises unveiling, as made evident in depictions of the harem, which was seen as barbaric and premodern in terms of the physical subordination of women, but also alluring, the source of sexual fantasy. Macdonald adds that depictions of the harem in art and photography that circulated in the West were actually overly exotic representations rather than grounded in reality (a form of 'imagined geography' as Said would put it). Nonetheless, this depiction takes hold and the fantasy around the unveiling of the Arab woman becomes a recurrent theme in modern Western popular culture, from cartoons like Disney's *Aladdin*, to *Carry On…* films, to adverts selling package holidays to the Near East.

Following 9/11, the allure of the veil begins to dissipate. In the UK, then Labour Home Secretary Jack Straw drew controversy when he stated that Muslim women should remove their veils for the sake of community relations. This received much attention in the news media, who largely supported his claims, not least for the way it fitted into dominant frames regarding Islam and the West, with the former seen as backward, uncivilised, decisive and incompatible with Western values of democracy and freedom (Khiabany and Williamson, 2008). But following Straw's comments, the figure of the veiled Muslim woman features increasingly in news media in particular. There are several dominant discourses that shape news coverage of the veil. First is that the veil symbolises the gender oppression that is supposedly inherent to Islam, and is particularly prominent in the newspaper columns of white liberal feminists such as Julie Birchall and Suzanne Moore (Rashid, 2016). Second is a discourse around the veil as symbolic of the Muslims' refusal to adapt to 'our way of life', that British multiculturalism is too tolerant, and that Britain is suffering from the tyranny of a 'culture' imposed by a minority (Khiabany and Williamson, 2008; Meer et al., 2010). A third discourse is one that disturbingly conflates the veil with migrants and, in turn, terrorism (Kapur, 2002; Cloud, 2004; Khiabany and Williamson, 2008). The veiled Muslim woman is not merely oppressed, but a terrorist threat.[1] This has had dangerous implications in terms of both domestic and foreign policy. For sociologist Naaz Rashid (2016), such a discourse serves to legitimate counter-terror programmes and the domestic surveillance of Muslim populations in particular, which has led to the detention and mistreatment of many innocent Muslims. For Rashid, such rhetoric around female empowerment is disingenuous or, indeed, ideological, as it constitutes a wider discourse on the civilising mission of anti-terrorist policy, based on the assumption that Muslims are at best passive, and at worse voluntarily housing terrorists.

While there is absolutely a paternalistic/misogynistic element to media discourses around the veil and unveiling, the debate around veiling is also racialised. Khiabany and Williamson (2008) are more forceful in arguing that the discourse around the veil is less about the specific topic of female oppression and more about racism. As they say,

> while many feminist commentators have emphasised the important gender issues related to representations of the veil, we will suggest that, even as the veil retains gendered dimensions, it functions in this new climate to erase previous depictions of Muslim women as victims and to produce a new veiled image of 'fundamentalism' that contributes to the demonisation of Muslims as a whole. (2008: 71)

In other words, while Western critiques of the veil were once about the liberation of women, it is now used as a device to Other and denigrate the broader Muslim population. In this way, the discussion about the veil and unveiling is in fact a way of managing citizenship – who belongs and who does not. Media depictions of Muslim women – whether in the news or popular culture – reveal very little about the actual experience of Muslim women (and do not do justice to the complexity of debates around the veil within Muslim communities (Rashid, 2016)). Perversely, media representation of the veil renders Muslim women hypervisible yet silences them in the process. But ultimately, discourse around the veil means that the Muslim community is once again essentialised (and racialised). This is how race is made in the representation of Islam – through a particular articulation of gender and religion.

8.3.2 Complications in production and consumption

So far, the focus has been on how Muslims continue to be represented according to Orientalist discourse, but also how such discourse is racialising. But how does Islamophobia actually manifest in media and what are the effects? Or put another way, how is it *constituted in* media production and consumption? In a rare foray into the question of media production, Edward Said (1981: 43) describes media as 'cultural apparatus' that has determined very selectively what Westerners should and should not know about Islam and the Muslim world. Echoing the arguments of the Schiller-McChesney school of political economy (see Chapter 3), for Said this occurs through the strong alignment between media and the (US) political and military establishment and the role of so-called 'experts' on the Middle East, who appear neutral but have strong ideological affinities. In this way, Said paints media as a tool of the state, which in turn is in the hands of Western Imperialists, which explains the reductive treatment of Islam. But is it as straightforward as that? Is it simply the case that media spews a neocolonial ideology which spreads into society unobstructed? How does a closer focus on production and consumption complicate the picture?

Taking media production initially, there remain very few concerted studies of how media representations of Muslims are physically made. The studies that do tackle this issue parallel the research covered in the previous chapter on migrants, focusing on two issues in particular: the role of primary definers and the lack of diversity in (news) media. To recap, primary definers are the experts, commentators and officials who become the main source of new stories. In the context of news coverage around Islam, such primary definers – who are effectively spokespeople for the dominant culture – essentially get to define Islam and Muslims. Politicians, for instance, gain privileged access to the media and are allowed to talk freely about Muslims (Rashid, 2016). Poole (2002) finds that when Islam in the news is covered, it is usually left to a non-Muslim (for the sake of 'objectivity') to present Islam to the public. In this way, Islam is constructed within an 'ethnocentric ideological (secular) framework' (ibid.: 99). However, emphasising complexity, Meer et al. (2010: 218) find that 'there is a proliferation in the inclusion of Muslim voices in Britain', going so far as to describe it as a 'progressive development where it opens up the public sphere to the expression of a variety of Muslim "differences"'. Nonetheless, while Poole (2002: 99) acknowledges that Muslim groups are managing to make some gains with regard to access within media, they 'lose control of the meaning' at the point of production where primary definers are effectively allowed to reproduce dominant ideological frames.

The Islamophobia that circulates across news media in particular can also be explained in terms of the industry's institutional whiteness, though once again, the picture is slightly more complicated than we may assume. In one of the few studies of news production and the representation of Muslims, journalism studies researcher Peter Cole (2006) finds that editors of regional newspapers with high racial/ethnic populations acknowledge there is a lack of diversity in the newsroom and that this is problematic. But there is a feeling as well among editors and journalists that professional ethics are enough to prevent explicitly Islamophobic coverage. Nonetheless, as Poole (2002) finds, the negative coverage of Islam is produced through news norms and uncritical, conservative modes of thought rather than the individual Islamophobic views of non-Muslim journalists. For instance, editors, while looking for newsworthy stories, are steered into producing sensationalist content that reproduces Orientalist tropes (Saha, 2012). In the UK, the Press Complaints Commission (PCC) (now replaced by the Independent Press Standards Organisation) has guidelines for the reporting of 'race' in its code of practice in order to prevent unfair discrimination and prejudice against racial and ethnic minorities (Saeed, 2016), but complaints about race and religion in particular are very rarely upheld (Petey, 2006; Saeed, 2016).

What effect do Islamophobic discourses in media have on audiences? As I have made clear throughout this book, the effect of media upon audiences is very difficult, if not impossible, to measure. Nonetheless studies of audiences produce very interesting insights into how knowledge about Islam and Muslims is received. Mirroring findings from research on the consumption of media representations of migrants, there is some evidence from studies based on survey methods to suggest that personal interaction with Muslims can negate negative media discourses among non-Muslims (Abdalla and Rane, 2007; Ahmed and Matthes, 2017). However, Elizabeth Poole (2002, 2011) has produced a more nuanced account in her own study of the reception of news stories on Muslims. Poole adopts a critical cultural approach based on Stuart Hall's encoding/decoding model that places less emphasis on how media effects audiences, and instead focuses on how media texts produce particular preferred meanings and how individuals bring their own interpretative frameworks to these texts, which shape whether they accept these preferred meanings or not. In this research, Poole conducts focus groups with three groups: (1) Muslims, (2) non-Muslims who have contact with Muslims, and (3) non-Muslims who do not have any contact with Muslims, asking each group to reflect upon and discuss particular new stories that feature Muslims. Unsurprisingly, Muslims adopt oppositional positions towards messages that negativise Islam, while non-Muslims who have no contact with Muslims are more likely to accept the preferred meanings of the dominant culture.

But the most interesting finding is that non-Muslims who have contact with Muslims are nonetheless more likely to accept preferred (Islamophobic) meanings. Non-Muslims who live in multicultural areas are sensitive to issues of discrimination, equality and fairness when it comes to race, but remain ignorant about religious issues and are likely to adopt dominant ideas about Islam as an oppressive and restrictive religion. For Poole (2002: 53), media produces 'cultures of ignorance' where even liberal-minded non-Muslims who have Muslim friends consume preferred readings from media texts about Muslims out of a fear of talking about religion. As such, Poole finds that contact alone is not sufficient to negate negative assumptions. In a nutshell: 'the media appear to act as an important resource for public knowledge of Islam but limit the way in which Muslims are known' (ibid.).

8.4 Contesting Islamophobia

The purpose of the previous section was to stress the complexity – particularly in relation to production and consumption – that underpins how media make race with regard to Islam and Muslims. As Poole (2002) states, it is not the case that media presents one stereotype of Muslims; rather, it takes the diversity of British Muslim experience and reduces them to a few (Orientalist) tropes. In stressing complexity – particularly at the level of production and consumption – rather than weakening our critique, it actually deepens our understanding of Islamophobia, underlining how it is a very particular type of racism shaped by the political-economic and socio-cultural conditions of a given moment. In this section I want to focus on the attempts of Muslims to contest the reduction and racialisation of Muslim culture in media. The danger of research into Islamophobia and media is that it paints Muslims as powerless victims without agency. But there are numerous studies that have demonstrated the active ways in which Muslims are challenging racist discourse around Islam, while articulating alternative ways of being – although these interventions can often struggle against the sheer size and influence of the dominant culture.

While Islamophobia in media has led to Muslims turning away from mainstream news in favour of alternative news sources from a Muslim perspective (Ahmed, 2006; Saeed, 2016), we see also more active forms of contestation, in terms of campaigns run by Muslims that attempt to challenge Islamophobia in media (Alsultany, 2012; Echchaibi, 2013). One recent example in the UK is the 'Riz Test', based upon the principles of the feminist 'Bechdel Test', which exposes the disturbingly reductive ways in which Muslims are portrayed in popular culture in particular.[2] Media researcher Tanja Dreher (2010) coined the notion of 'community media interventions' to describe activities that attempt to challenge mainstream racist discourse, such as The Arab Council of Australia's 'Rating the Media' project, where users draw attention to media misrepresentation/misinformation. Yet while emphasising the value of these efforts of activists, Dreher questions the extent to which these interventions actually result in being heard. While they are multiple, very few interventions have impact, hindered by perceptions of the interest of audiences and what media producers think audiences want. As she states, community media interventions remind us that 'speaking up does not guarantee being heard, but rather depends on being granted an audience' (Dreher, 2010: 99). For this reason, Dreher argues that we need a politics of listening; to quieten the inner (white) voice. This is where media power is located – who is heard rather than who gets to speak.

A more informal practice of contestation comes in the form of online communities. Such networks act as communities of resistance and empowerment for Muslims. This is what Amir Saeed (2016) finds in his analysis of *#MuslimApologies* on Twitter, where young Muslims used humour to challenge the idea that Muslims need to apologise for terrorism and fundamentalist ideas. Using a subcultural frame, social media researcher Dhiraj Murthy (2010) provides a critical account of the Taqwacore scene – a community of Muslim punk bands and fans, which amazingly started as a fictional comic book story (written by a white man) but inspired young Muslims to form real-life bands. Murthy observes how this scene spread primarily through the internet, bringing together Muslim punks from across the globe, and in doing so has created counter-narratives of Muslimness and what it means to be Muslim, including challenging and subverting Orientalist tropes. However, in making this argument

Murthy is careful not to overly extol the democratising potential of the internet; as he states, '[t]he Internet is hardly a space devoid of power relations' (Murthy, 2010: 185). Murthy argues that dominant ideology still shapes the internet and that online diasporic groups in particular are more often complicit in 'continuing, rather than disrupting, offline hegemonies' (ibid.: 186), especially gender hierarchies.[3] Murthy is trying to maintain a critical perspective – understanding the potential of the scenes, not least in terms of challenging Islamophobia in the case of Taqwacore, but how safe spaces online can also end up as 'cocoons' (ibid.: 191). For Murthy, gendered and racial hierarchies persist online as much as offline.

One of the indirect ways in which media provides resources for Muslims to contest and resist dominant hegemonies is through the making and consumption of popular culture. While the representation of Muslims is generally reduced to a handful of reductive tropes, especially in the news, Muslims are creating their own spaces, whether in the mainstream or 'underground', which are presenting alternative narratives around what it means to be Muslim – whether in television (Saha, 2013; Conway, 2014), film (Macdonald, 2011; Illott, 2013) or music (Alim, 2006; McMurray, 2008; Miah and Kalra, 2008). But the emotional and affective properties of popular culture itself can become a resource for Muslims, as explored by popular music scholar Nabeel Zuberi (2017) in his essay 'Listening while Muslim'. Zuberi, a British Pakistani living in Auckland, draws attention to the rich history of Muslims in popular music who articulate Muslim experience in radical and novel ways. But what Zuberi's essay shows is how music by non-Muslims (who do not address issues of being Muslim) can still be meaningful for Muslims, that is, Muslim identity. It is the sound itself that produces emotions and affects that can speak and gel with Muslim experiences in their full diversity. As he states, 'Music listening offers spaces to explore the limits of identities and the possibilities of alternative ways of being' (Zuberi, 2017: 34). So music acts not only as a form of resistance but also as a resource that helps Muslim listeners to challenge and deal with Islamophobia and negotiate the anxieties that arise as a Muslim living in the West and beyond. As he watched from New Zealand as the War on Iraq unfolded, Zuberi made a playlist that featured an eclectic list of (mostly non-Muslim) acts, including Public Enemy, The Buzzcocks, Heaven 17, Ennio Morricone and The Pogues. Speaking of the playlist, he says:

> These music enabled me to process geopolitics intimately from a distance. Most of the tunes did not refer to this political context, but their titles and lyrical fragments resonated with the moment of impending doom and military disaster. The sounds gained more meanings as well as eliciting familiar pleasures. These are the coping mechanisms of the voracious music consumer drawing on DJ culture to respond to post-9/11 discombobulation. (ibid.: 40)

The power of Zuberi's account is in demonstrating the affective power of culture, especially evident in music, which goes beyond questions of signification and representation. But affect can be instrumentalised by the dominant culture too. To unpack the ideological function of affect with regard to Islamophobia I want to end with a case study on the work of media scholar Evelyn Alustany and the study of supposedly sympathetic representations of Muslims in US popular culture.

BOX 8.1 Case Study

Simplified complex portrayals of Muslims

BBC drama *Bodyguard* (2018) has been the corporation's most successful and popular drama series in the multichannel era. It begins with a police officer foiling a terrorist attack by two Muslim would-be suicide bombers (including a veiled woman called Nadia Ali). But while the issue of terrorism remains the focus of the series, the plot line goes beyond the usual 'clash of civilisations' narrative and is instead a story about corruption within the British political establishment.

In some ways this typifies the way Muslims have been portrayed in television drama, which, while using the issue of Muslim terrorism/fundamentalism as a plot device, almost goes out of its way to avoid reproducing negativised tropes around Muslims. This was a pattern that American media scholar Evelyn Alsultany (2012) found after 9/11: that while the news appeared to be fulfilling the Islamophobic agenda of the Bush Administration, US network television drama was in fact full of sympathetic portraits of Arabs and Muslims. She has found that 9/11 in fact did not mark a turn from 'negative' to sympathetic representations, but rather a shift from the novelty of having a few sympathetic representations of Arab and Muslim identities to one where it becomes a standardised trope. As she states, 'After 9/11 these strategies, especially that of including a "good" Arab American to counteract the "bad" or terrorist Arab, came to define the new standard when representing Arabs' (Alsultany, 2012: 11). As such, Alsultany's aim has been to explore what these sympathetic representations are contributing amid the more dominant meanings circulating about Arabs and Muslims and the threat of Islam post-9/11.

Adopting a critical cultural studies approach, Alsultany's argument is not about celebrating positive representations over negative ones, but rather seeing what seemingly 'positive' representations are doing. Her argument is that in postrace discourse the American Other is portrayed sympathetically in order to project the US as an enlightened and inclusive society, even though the state practises racialist policies against Muslims. It achieves this by producing 'simplified complex representations' (ibid.: 21) of Muslims, that is, representations which appear complex and nuanced but are actually simplistic and still utilise familiar tropes. The key element of her argument is that simplified complex representations work by producing an 'excess of affect' (ibid.: 16), referring to the strong feelings of sympathy that are evoked when we watch stories of oppressed Muslim women, or a particular characterisation of Muslim men. Alsultany finds that these storylines, which present multiple perspectives and more sympathetic accounts of Muslims, nonetheless portray a narrative that depicts the racial profiling of Arab and Muslim identities as an unfortunate, but necessary consequence of the *War on Terror*. But they also imply that as soon this moment passes, multiculturalism and racial equality will prevail in the US again; after all, complex simplified representations of Muslims and Arabs suggest that we're making multicultural progress (because these characters had

(Continued)

not previously been created to deserve our feeling). As such, these affective responses serve an ideological function as they make the audience feel good about what they're watching, which in turn allows the justification of racist policies enacted upon Muslim populations at home and abroad.

To return to *Bodyguard*, the complexification of Nadia Ali's character occurs through the exposing of the police, military, security agents and government officials as themselves a threat to national security. But ultimately, none of these details detracts from the fact that Nadia is ultimately a Muslim suicide bomber who seeks to murder innocent Brits.

8.5 Conclusion

Studying how Muslims appear in media demonstrates the distinctive nature of Islamophobia that entails a particular articulation of race, religion and gender in the making of race. But while the Islamophobic portrayal of Muslims appears stark, I wanted to stress complexity and contestation. How media makes Muslims (and race in the process) is shaped by multiple factors, as Elizabeth Poole (2002: 54) sums up in the following quote:

> Explanations for the absence of diversity in media images of Islam are apparent in theories on the interplay of politics and society, on the historical conflictual relationship between Islam and the West, on current political processes including globalisation and fragmentation, on the politics of differentiation and ethnicity, with religion adding an extra dimension to hostility, and on institutional news practices operating within a market framework.

In this quote Poole encapsulates the postcolonial cultural economy approach – and the need to unpack the different historical, material and ideological layers through which race-making practices in media take place. As a consequence, the emphasis is on complexity, but that does not mean that we should understate the power of racism/Islamophobia. As Poole states, it is not the simple case that media presents one Islam as a threat to the nation; rather, media takes the diversity of British Muslim experience and reduces it to a few tropes that lead to a fairly homogeneous representation of British Muslims.

In terms of future work, ongoing geopolitical tensions regarding the West and the Middle East will provide researchers with plenty more new cases by which to explore the representational frameworks employed to depict Muslims and Islam. But following the critical cultural approach to media and race, the question for researchers should not be whether the knowledge produced by media about Muslims is correct, but what is this knowledge and what impact does it have? In addition to textual analyses of media texts that such a line of enquiry entails, more research is needed in production studies of the making of Muslims in media, as well as audience studies, especially those grounded in ethnographies of everyday media practices (including online and offline), in order to explore what knowledges are informing and are being made in the production and consumption of media texts – including both news *and* popular culture (the latter of which is neglected in media studies of Islamophobia). Moreover, more work is needed on the different forms of contestation by Muslims that are happening online and in popular culture in particular. We have entered an interesting moment in the cultural industries, with issues of diversity high on the policy agenda. This is providing some unique opportunities for Muslims and other racial/ethnic minorities, which is the theme of the next two chapters.

8.6 Recommended and further reading

Elizabeth Poole's (2002) *Reporting Islam: Media Representations and British Muslims* is slightly dated now in terms of its examples but the findings still resonate strongly with contemporary media depictions of Muslims and Islam. Moreover, it provides an outstanding illustration of a critical cultural approach to texts and audiences; the audience research element is particularly nuanced and a good template for media scholars wanting to do this kind of research. For an overview of news coverage of Muslims from a variety of perspectives covering a range of topics, see the edited collection by Elizabeth Poole and John Richardson (2006) *Muslims and the News Media* (although, except for a chapter by Peter Cole, the study of production contexts remains a gap). This provides a good survey of the dynamics of Islamophobia media culture.

The edited collection *After Charlie Hebdo* (Titley et al., 2017), uses the 2015 Paris attacks to think through contemporary Islamophobia in the context of 'postrace' society. In doing so it explores issues from the relationship between liberal tenants of freedom of speech to the activisation of anti-Muslim prejudice across traditional and social media. *After Charlie Hebdo* exemplifies the historical or conjunctural approach to race and media that this book is calling for.

While the examples referenced thus far focus more on news media, there have been some interesting studies on Islamophobia in popular culture. Bethany Klein's (2011) 'Entertaining Ideas: Social Issues in Entertainment Television' is not about Islamophobia *per se*, but provides an interesting insight into a Channel 4 drama on terrorism and British terrorism legislation based on an interview with the writer/director (see also Saha, 2012). Kristian Petersen is a scholar of Islamic Studies with a keen interest in popular culture (see Petersen, 2017). His (2019) essay on the Oscar-winning actor Mahershala Ali is particularly interesting for its focus on black American Muslim identity and, in turn, anti-black racism in certain Muslim communities based on a study of how Ali's Oscar win was received and made sense of in Pakistan.

BOX 8.2 Key Issue

Antisemitism in media

Relations between Jews and Muslims are generally perceived as antagonistic. But while both groups are placed in opposition, they actually share the same fundamental trait as *racialised religious subjects* (Murji and Solomos, 2005; Meer, 2013; Renton and Gidley, 2017). Antisemitism, like Islamophobia, involves racialisation, where Jewish people are spuriously associated with a set of physical characteristics as well as behaviours/cultural practices. However, Jews are no longer seen as the same threat as they once were. For anthropologist Matti Bunzi (2007), antisemitism was invented in the late nineteenth century to protect the ethnic purity of the nation state, but as the nation state became less significant, Jews became less of a threat. That is absolutely not to suggest that antisemitism has disappeared, as Jews still experience racist attacks and hate crimes. But in terms of British media, Jews are not vilified in the same way as other minorities, and when Jewishness is represented, it is in terms of particular mores and sensibilities (for example, 'Jewish humour') rather than in terms of ethnic absolutism. In fact, a very specific antisemitic trope is the belief that Jewish people 'run' and profit from the media, rather than being marginalised by it (see Carr, 2001).

While antisemitism had slipped off the British news agenda, it became a major issue again in the late-2010s as the Labour Party, under its new socialist leader Jeremy Corbyn, was accused of being institutionally antisemitic. While I do not wish to wade into this debate here, it should at least be acknowledged that while antisemitism is usually linked to the far right, there exists a very particular Leftist form of antisemitism, associated with conspiracy theories about Jewish economic and political power, but that also stems out of criticism of Israel, which is articulated as anti-Zionism but too easily becomes conflated with Judaism as a whole.

What is interesting about the criticisms of the Labour Party over its antisemitism is that it came from members of the political and media establishment who historically have not been particularly invested in issues facing British Jews. (The same right-wing press who vilified Corbyn for his antisemitism had in fact used antisemitic tropes in its coverage of the previous Labour leader Ed Miliband; see Gaber, 2014.) It also came from newspaper editors and columnists who believe that members of the Labour Party, specifically the *multiculturalists* within its ranks, are too accommodating of Islam and Muslims. This needs further analysis than I can afford here, but the point is that antisemitism in this particular moment is linked to Islamophobia. For Nasar Meer (2013), Jews have generally been racialised negatively, but at times certain sections of Jews have been racialised *positively*, sometimes in relation to the negativisation of other Jews, for instance, longer established Western Jews in London in contrast to Jews coming in from Eastern Europe. In the media coverage of the Labour Party accusations, Jews have been racialised positively in relation to Muslims. But this is not to make a point that Jewish people are afforded more privileges than Muslims. Rather, the argument here is that racism is slippery and that the process of racialisation is always relational. Right now, the mainstream media and politicians are quick to denounce attacks on Jews, but we should be alert to the racial debris of antisemitism that still mars contemporary media culture.

(Continued)

Discussion

What does it mean to be racialised *positively*?

Notes

1   This trope in fact dates back to the French colonial image of the veiled Muslim woman as a dangerous element in the Algerian resistance to French rule, hiding weapons under her burqa, as famously described by Franz Fanon (see Khiabany and Williamson, 2008).

2   To pass the test a Muslim character needs to fulfil one of the following criteria: (1) Talking about being the victim of or the perpetrator of terrorism? (2) Presented as irrationally angry? (3) Presented as superstitious, culturally backwards or anti-modern? (4) Presented as a threat to a Western way of life? (5) If the character is male, is he presented as misogynistic? Or if female, is she presented as oppressed by her male counterparts? Needless to say, very few representations of Muslim fail.

3   While Murthy does not address this issue, there is the issue of the surveillance of Muslims online by security services, including creating databases on potential threats (Fekete, 2006), an issue that I will address in more detail in Chapter 10.

9

The Production and Circulation of Blackness in Media

Why do representations of black people appear to remain so consistent over time?

What is the value (and limitations) of 'stereotype' in understanding the making of blackness?

In what ways is the commodification of blackness ambivalent?

How is blackness made in the 'postrace' era?

9.1 Introduction

This chapter focuses on media's making of blackness, mainly in the context of popular culture. This involves an account of stereotyping and the ongoing demonisation/exoticisation of black culture. But it is also about how black cultural producers have widened the regime of representation. The focus on blackness is not to diminish the significance of Asianness or Latinx or indigenous culture in popular culture. Indeed, I write this regretfully, well aware that these cultures receive far less attention in discussions of race and media culture. But there is something very particular about how black people are denigrated in real life but are seemingly celebrated in popular culture. Black expressive culture generates masses of media content (and profit), particularly in film, television and music industries. (One of the most curious facts about global popular music is how its very basis is in the musical forms created by an enslaved and oppressed population of black people; see Hesmondhalgh and Saha, 2013: 184.) Indeed, studying how blackness is produced and circulates in media provides an exemplary case of the contradictions of how media make race. It is an exploration of how historical representations of blackness reproduce in media, with what on the surface looks like little variation. But adopting the postcolonial cultural economy framework, I place a strong emphasis on complexity, contradiction and contestation.

Before I begin, I want to stress two caveats regarding the discussion of how media make blackness. First, we need to move beyond a discussion of whether a representation of blackness is correct or not. While it is relatively straightforward to call out a stereotypical representation of black people, attempting the inverse and identifying authentic black experience is a much bigger challenge. Instead, our focus here is on what representations of blackness *are doing*. Second, the commodification of black culture does not have to just mean the production of bland, co-opted and weak approximations of black/minority life and culture (Hesmondhalgh and Saha, 2013). Indeed, black cultural producers themselves *self-commodify* and in a way that can open up representational practices and broaden the regime of representation.

This chapter starts with a discussion of 'blackness' itself, and how blackness is made in media. In the section that follows it considers the making of blackness specifically in relation to racial neoliberalism, where contradictions become more apparent. In the third section, I explore how normative constructions of blackness are contested in terms of production and consumption. Once again, my primary interest is in the British context, although it is impossible not to consider global forms of blackness.

9.2 The making of blackness

What do I mean by 'blackness'? To start answering the question we need to unpack the meaning of 'black'. In the UK, following mass immigration after the Second World War from Commonwealth countries (or indeed, the former colonies), the term 'black', rather than referring to people of African descent, was instead used to describe all racial and ethnic minorities, and, like the term 'coloured', was racist in character. In the 1970s the term 'Black' (now with a capital 'B') was co-opted by minoritised groups (including Asians as well as Afro-Caribbeans) and became the banner under which they would mobilise in the face of the severe racial provocation and discrimination that they were experiencing in society at the time (Gilroy, 1987; Brah, 1996). In other words, 'Black' became a political category designed to forge solidarity across different racial and ethnic communities. But as Stuart Hall identifies, while 'Black' was crucial to the anti-racist movements of the time, it was soon rejected by Asians and non-Afro-Caribbean Others, who found the term did not describe their particular experience. In more contemporary times we observe a plethora of racial and ethnic identifications adopted by racialised groups, such as 'Asian' or 'Muslim', or even 'brown', especially after 9/11, with 'black' now generally associated with those of (selected) African descent (Alexander, 2002: 554).

What black actually means is highly contested and takes *essentialist* and *anti-essentialist* forms. The essentialist version claims that being black contains intrinsic qualities/characteristics that are biologically determined. This particular idea of black is what undergirds racist logics, but also appears in the politics of black nationalism, as Gilroy (1993) demonstrates. The anti-essentialist version of black, on the other hand, rejects the spuriousness of biological, exceptionalist ideas of race. Instead, 'black', like 'race', is a floating signifier, is historically contingent (as the above delineation of 'black' in the British context demonstrates), and changes meaning over time and space. Black identity and experience is hybrid, fluid and plural (Hall, 1997d). Black people do not share DNA but rather the history of slavery/colonialism which is what produces commonality and community. The impact of intersectional theorists in particular has been in exposing how forces of homophobia/transphobia/sexism/classism/disablism collide with racism leading to different types of oppressions for different black people – again denying the idea that there is one singular black experience. Thus, to refer to 'black*ness*' is to underscore how the category 'black' is mutable and multiple, and is constantly being made and remade, from the top-down and the bottom-up, in different arenas and fields, including media. As Herman Gray (2005: 19) puts it, 'blackness' indicates 'the shifting cultural fields and social relations and the material circumstances in which black people operate. [It refers to] the discursive work – cultural practices, social meanings, and cultural identifications – that black people use to negotiate and construct meaningful lives'. This is the definition of 'black' that I work with.

As stated, the focus of the chapter is on how media make blackness, and what these representations *are doing*. Having established the meaning of blackness, I now want to consider what shapes it, namely, racial ideology and racial neoliberalism (as a political-material force).

9.2.1 The construction of blackness 1: Ideology

In order to understand how dominant ideology shapes blackness, we need to return to the concept of the stereotype. Stereotypes as a concept need to be handled carefully; following postcolonial theorist Homi Bhabha, stereotypes are *not* mere distortions of reality (as this would suggest there is something objective behind them), but rather, they are simplified representations. Stuart Hall (1997c: 257) calls stereotyping a form of 'amplified typification', that is, the process of reducing people to a number of essential qualities and traits, which are in turn exaggerated and simplified, and in turn again, fixed. Stereotypes are implicated in power and the reproduction of power and are often directed towards the subordinated. As a form of power/knowledge, they produce the idea of the norm (and who fits it) and the Other (those who do not). The power of dominant ideology is to convert stereotypes into truths. Even when we recognise that they are clear exaggerations, the power of stereotypes is that we come to believe they have a hint of truth within them.

Stereotypes of blackness work according to a binary form of representation, framed within sharp, oppositional extremes. As Hall (1997c: 254) starkly demonstrates, while white people are defined in terms of their intellectuality, black people are seen as more emotional and in touch with feelings – feeding into the 'emotion/intellect, nature/culture binary oppositions of racial stereotyping'. Moreover, the black subject comes to embody both sides of the binary. For instance, according to Kara Keeling (2007: 81), the construction of black women is such that 'in the black woman, femininity appears as either excessive or deficient'. Hall (1997c) uses the concept of naturalisation to explain how black people are reduced to nature; that any identifiable biological or cultural traits are a fundamental part of their nature and make up. It is implied that this is fixed, an essential quality of blackness that cannot change.

As stated, the construction of blackness is historically contingent and shaped by key historical moments, including (1) the fifteenth century, which marked the initial contact between European traders and West African nations, and also marked the start of the slave trade, (2) the moment of the European colonisation of Africa and the period of High Imperialism, and (3) the post-Second World War migrations from former colonies. The role of racial ideology through each of these historical moments was to construct the black subject as Other in order to create and maintain racial hierarchies while the world was going through massive upheaval. Hall (1997c) identifies three narratives around blackness that have persisted through history. Black people are either (1) explicitly degraded (seen as lazy, criminal, deviant, feckless), (2) sentimentalised (referring to tropes of the *noble savage*, Uncle Tom, the 'Mammy' figure, or (3) 'happy natives', particularly in the form of black entertainers. While the last two narratives might appear 'positive', they are nonetheless simplified and reinforce racial hierarchies. Each of these tropes have their roots in colonialism/slavery and still persist in modern-day representations of black people.

Most troubling of all is how black people themselves can sometimes reproduce hegemonic ideas of blackness. Fulfilling white fantasies of blackness sometimes comes as a conscious choice, in order to attain some level of social/cultural – and economic – recognition. But this also happens at the level of the subconscious, the tragedy of which Frantz Fanon so powerfully captures in *Black Skins White Masks* (1986 [1967]). Adopting a similar psychosocial register to Fanon's, Stuart Hall (1997c) attempts to makes sense of the hyper-masculinity and chauvinism of rap music. For Hall, black men adopt the stereotype of overly-sexual in response to their infantilisation by white society. He describes how this is rooted in slavery where black men were deprived of certain supposedly male attributes – familial responsibility, ownership of property – which acted as a form of symbolic castration. In response the black male asserted himself in the only way he was allowed – through 'caricature-in-reverse' (1997c: 263), that is, hypermasculinity and super-sexuality (see also hooks, 2004). The point for Hall is that this 'logic' works on two levels – a conscious and overt level, and a subconscious and hidden level; white people fear (the stereotype of) black people on a conscious level but envy them on a subconscious level. On the inverse, Hall argues that when black men act 'macho', they consciously challenge the stereotype of black men as childlike, but at the subconscious level they reinforce the white fantasy of the over-sexed, over-endowed black male. Thus, black people are trapped within the binary structure of the stereotype.

Racial ideology also produces normative versions of blackness that ignore other black identities and experiences. It excludes sexual and gendered Others in particular (Martin, 2015). Drawing upon Maria Lugones' notion of 'the modern/colonial gender system', Anima Adjepong (2019) explores how legacies of empire impose a gender binary and instigate *heteropatriarchy*, that is, the combination of male-dominated society with heterosexual coupling, as the norm. This serves to silence black queer women in particular who are not valued in this system. Similarly, Kara Keeling (2007) explores the encounter between heteropatriarchy and representations of black 'masculine' queer women in particular. The figure of the 'black butch-femme', as Keeling puts it, is potentially radical in how it destabilises raced, gendered and sexualised norms. As an example, Keeling considers the deliberately 'masculine' appearance of women in the Black Panther Party (BPP), which sought to challenge the representation of black women as passive or secondary in the black nationalist movement. But looking across popular culture, Keeling finds that when the black butch-femme appears, they are often subsumed into a heterosexual context – where their same-sex desires are erased, reifying blackness as masculinity in particular. This sheds a particular light on Beyoncé's 'appropriation' of the figure of the BPP woman during her famous half-time performance at the 2016 Super Bowl, which represented them in a more sexualised manner. Once again, the black subject is split into binary oppositions.

9.2.2 The construction of blackness 2: Capitalism

Racial ideology by itself is not enough to explain the reproduction of historical tropes of Otherness/blackness. As stressed throughout this book, race-making practices are shaped by the political economy of media. For instance, in her account of blackness as brand on US network television, media scholar Jennifer Fuller (2010) explains how both the marginalisation/stereotyping of blackness occurs according to market logics. Firstly, network channels are reliant on advertising and therefore need to maximise audiences, and as a consequence consider it too risky to produce programming solely for black audiences which represent a relatively small and poorer portion of the market, resulting in fewer black people on television. Secondly, if the producers of a black-cast show want it to be green-lit, it has to demonstrate crossover appeal, the result being a representation of black people that is easy to digest by the 'mainstream' white audience. While of course ideologies of race are at play in these processes, it is the political economy of media – specifically, a commercialised system based on advertising – that leads to their reproduction.

Herman Gray makes the strongest case for why we need to take the commercial context of the making blackness seriously: as he states, cultural practices 'must be theorised from inside the commodity form and inside market relations … it is within the realm of commercial culture and representation that we are constantly being constituted and positioned, as well as reconstituting ourselves collectively and individually' (Gray, 2004: 7). These are the terms in which I express how media *make* race and studying the production process behind representations of blackness is a key component of this project. In this quote, Gray is alluding to the process of commodification which is a determining force upon the making of blackness. For instance, for bell hooks (1992), the fetishisation and sexualisation of black women occur precisely though the commodification of difference. Consuming racialised sex in commodity form is a (safe) way for white people to transgress through the encounter with black sexuality as it does not disrupt racial hierarchies. It is through the commodification of gendered blackness that white privilege is reinforced.

But as I stressed in Chapter 4, commodification needs to be understood as a fundamentally ambivalent process, which has enabling and constraining tendencies. Racial identities are made through their commodification; as Gray makes clear in the aforementioned quote, the making of blackness is as much about self-commodification as it is about the dominant culture's commodification of blackness (Saha, 2018). Indeed, media industries provide opportunities for structural poor black people to accrue capital from the performance of their own racial identities, as we shall see shortly (Quinn, 2013a). The point, though, is that commodification of blackness can both reify and destabilise normative forms of blackness. It is these dynamics that I want to unravel further in the rest of the chapter when I look more closely at how media make blackness.

However, before I do so, following the postcolonial cultural economy, we need to situate our analysis within the given historical context, namely racial neoliberalism. As explored in Chapter 4, according to neoliberalism, the market is the best way to allocate public resources, founded on the idea of the subject as a rational, efficient, consumer. In this regard human freedom is increasingly defined in terms of consumer sovereignty. Following neoliberal ideology, individualisation has replaced community, consumer freedom has replaced social justice. In terms of media within the racial neoliberal conjuncture, the politics of representation is now defined in the name of *diversity*, and has been marked by a shift in the regime of representation. This has a had a profound effect on the production and circulation of blackness and is the theme of the following section.

9.3 The making of blackness in the context of racial neoliberalism

As stated, there has been a shift in the way blackness has been represented in media. In the context of the UK, early portrayals of black men were as the criminal Other and as a social problem (Gilroy, 1987; Malik, 2002; Malik and Nwonka, 2017). Black women and queer folk were invisible. This changed somewhat in the 1980s via the Black Film Workshop movement (Ross, 1995) where black people started getting access to the means of cultural production, spawning the *new ethnicities* moment (see Chapter 2) that was a counter-hegemonic response to racial stereotyping and the reductive ways in which black people were being treated in media. Multicultural policy across the arts also enabled British-born black cultural producers to articulate new Black British identities. *UK Blak* – the title of an album by soul singer Caron Wheeler (1990) – captured the new cultural mood (see also Jazzy B and Soul II Soul, Neneh Cherry, Maxi Priest, and Monie Love), and moreover showed black British popular culture had commercial value. The new black arts was anti-essentialist and syncretic – including collaborations between Black Britons and British Asians (Back, 1995) – and a break from black defined by racism alone (Gilroy, 1991). Having said that, it should be stressed that the representation of blackness at the time was still defined by narrowcasting/ghettoisation, and a limited range of representations of black experience, with black cultural producers labouring under the weight of the burden of representation (Mercer, 1994; Ross, 1995).

From the late 1990s onwards we see the demise of multicultural policy and a shift to an emphasis on 'diversity', that was less about catering for specific racial and ethnic groups and instead about bringing those groups into mainstream programming (Malik, 2013a). The extent to which this has been a progressive shift has been contested by race and media scholars (Nwonka, 2015; Malik and Nwonka, 2017; Saha, 2018) and has instead been read as a particular characteristic of racial neoliberalism. The rejection of multicultural in favour of diversity has impacted how media make blackness in two ways.

First, blackness is *over-determined*. As covered in the previous chapter, Gavan Titley (2019) argues that race has become media content in itself (see also Hasinoff, 2008). The commodification of blackness goes back to the birth of popular culture, but under racial neoliberalism media formats themselves have become racialised according to conceptions of black, which is particularly evident in music in the case of rap (Fitts, 2008). In the UK we see this in the emergence of the new 'urban' genre that moves across music, film and television. This is the interest of Sarita Malik and Clive Nwonka (Malik and Nwonka, 2017; Nwonka and Malik, 2018), whose approach incidentally, exemplifies the critical cultural approach to media.

Malik and Nwonka provide a detailed historical analysis of the ascendency of 'urban' film and television in the UK. They set this against the rise in urban subculture more generally, including the 'popularising of black cultural products', whether UK Garage and Grime music or the commercialisation of urban clothing. Initially, *urban* connoted edginess but was not particularly dangerous; while clearly racialised, the label *urban* effectively removed 'black' and with it any reference to race/racism. In addition, the authors find that while the emergence of *urban* was organic, it also served the social inclusion agendas of politicians, specifically the *New Labour* government with its commitment to both social justice *and* market imperatives, exemplifying its 'Third Way' policy and by extension the neoliberal version of diversity (Nwonka, 2015). As Malik and Nwonka (2017: 427) state, '"urban" initially acted as a commercial pseudonym that by the early 2000s was offering the illusion of inclusivity through the "positive" mainstreaming of black youth subculture'. This also aligned with global forms of blackness – particularly out of the US – and the historical association of black with all that is edgy and cool (Fuller, 2010).

But, returning to the UK, there was a shift where *urban* was re-racialised as something dangerous. Malik and Nwonka (2017) observe how a spate of social disorder in inner-city areas, including rioting, knife and gun crime and 'black on black' violence, and the inevitable sensationalist news headlines that followed (based around racialised discourse of the gang problem), created national anxieties again around young black men. The urban crime narrative that came to prominence in the news led to a new subgenre in film and television: the (black) urban crime drama that 'reproduces dominant discourses of black criminality' (ibid.: 430). Examples included *Bullet Boy* (2004), *Life and Lyrics* (2006), *Kidulthood* (2005), *Rollin' with the Nines* (2008), *Adulthood* (2008), *1 Day* (2009), and *Shank* (2010), which all explored facets of black urban life and criminality. The authors recognise that these films potentially offer a counter-hegemonic narrative around gun grime, connecting gang violence to wider socio-economic issues. But when decontextualised, they reinforce media discourses around black criminality as an '"underclass" deliberately pursuing a subculture of criminality' (ibid.: 431). Thus, this new negativised – yet intensely profitable – inflection of *urban* reinforces notions of a black 'underclass', 'laying their own lives to waste, a decontextualised interpretation that consequently strengthened hegemonic narratives of black criminality' (ibid.: 429).

In some ways there is nothing new about how a particular exoticised, masculinist version of blackness has become the hegemonic representation of blackness. But Malik and Nwonka's argument is that this has been enabled by the new 'diversity' paradigm in the creative industries (and here they bring in a political economy analysis). The UK Film Council has come under a lot of pressure for the lack of diversity in the productions it has funded and, as such, it has placed a strong emphasis on financing more black-made films; as one industry figure said about the funding of *Bullet Boy* there was an urgent need to '*just get something black made*' (Nwonka and Malik, 2018: 11, my emphasis). But in order to fulfil an industry tick-box, films need to demonstrate that they are both commercial and *diverse*. As such, films that feature representations of race that play on dominant themes of blackness (that have demonstrated commercial value) get privileged over films that depict racial experience in more ambiguous or challenging ways. Thus, within the diversity paradigm, the crime drama effectively becomes the dominant filmic/televisual context within which black people appear, shaped by racial ideology and economic imperative.

The second way that the current diversity paradigm under racial neoliberalism has shaped blackness lies in how it gets subsumed into an ideology of what cultural studies scholar Jo Littler (2017: 153) calls 'postracial neoliberal meritocracy'. The idea of postracial neoliberal meritocracy is founded on two ideas, both neoliberal in character: (1) the notion that we live in a meritocracy where everyone can equally succeed, and (2) postracialism as the idea that racial inequality is a thing of the past. Meritocracy in general is such a powerful ideology that it can even be internalised by racialised groups. For instance, black British actor John Boyega drew criticism for suggesting that minority actors should stop 'complaining' about racism in creative and cultural industries as it is 'not going to benefit us' (Waring, 2016). He went on to say, 'Be the change you want to be. Be the change. And continue and focus' (ibid.). While Boyega subsequently apologised for appearing to downplay the experience of racism, the discourse underlying his comments exemplifies the discourse around postracial meritocracy. As Gray (2013a: 772) puts it, post-racialism is 'a constituent element of a contemporary regime of race, racial difference has solidified into postra-cial discourses of multiculturalism, diversity, and colour blindness'. Consequently, according to postracial neoliberal meritocracy, minorities no longer should receive support from the state, otherwise this would give them an unfair advantage (which in turn would be *racist*).

A discourse of postracial neoliberal meritocracy is particularly evident in reality television, which 'neutralises racial difference, in order to put all contestants on a level playing field, and simulate a world where meritocracy rules; common humanity and sameness are emphasised over difference' (Malik, 2014: 34). This can be productive, but as Malik continues, the fact is that neo-imperialism/neoliberalism has damaged cosmopolitanism; in the context of public service media, the turn to creative diverse policy has depoliticised representations of black folk (Malik, 2013b: 515). We get a hypervisiblity of blackness in media but learn very little about black experience, let alone race (and racism).

Media scholar Kristen Warner's (2015a, 2015b) work on the trend of colour-blind casting in the US critiques the perceived progressiveness of such practices, and in doing so highlights the ideological workings of postracial neoliberal meritoc-racy. In one example, Warner (2015b) critically examines Shonda Rhimes – one of the most powerful showrunners in American television, and one of the very few black women. Rhimes goes out of her way to create diverse casts without defining her characters by their race. As such, her shows are rarely about racial issues, or rather, they take a back seat to supposedly more 'universal' issues. Rhimes basically employs *blindcasting*: casting diverse characters for un-racially defined characters. Her shows are praised for their diversity. But not only do they very rarely explore the specific diversity of characters, they also present a postracial world where 'all the sins of the past are absolved in the heroic efforts of a few dissidents during the Civil Rights era' (ibid.: 638).

For Warner, blindcasting inadvertently produces stereotypes through a lack of specificity, alienating 'characters of colour from the material realities of racism' (ibid.: 642), and she provides a close critical analysis of her texts to prove this point. But Warner is also interested in how Rhimes talks about her career – a careful negotiation of acknowledging her experience of being a black woman, and the challenges that this brings, but also not wanting to define herself by her racial identity by stressing her work ethic (and talent). For Warner, Rhimes effectively racially neutralises herself (ibid.: 635):

> the way she self-presents as a colourless female writer is a discursive strategy deployed to divest race from its cultural contexts for herself and her cast. That is to say, in the same manner that Rhimes disavows any racially specific politics, her cast of characters practices a similar strategy that results in difference that is only skin-deep. (ibid.: 636)

In this way, Rhimes – through her own narration of her career and the shows she makes – fulfils neoliberal postracial meritocracy, where race (and by extension, racism) is subsumed, or to put it more provocatively, *white-washed* (ibid.: 633). For Herman Gray (2013a) the turn to blindcasting has perversely led to a decline in black-scripted television. Such a practice hollows out 'race' from references to social inequality and social injustice and replaces it with an idea of difference as market niche, brand identity and in turn the accumulation of private property and wealth. Hence, race becomes a lifestyle marker. Under racial neoliberalism this form of difference poses no threat to the nation or the market. This is in sharp contrast to earlier depictions of blackness that were seen precisely as a social threat.

This section has shown how blackness is made in the context of racial neoliberalism. It has led to 'new racial regimes' (Gray, 2013a: 772) where racialised, 'abject and marginal' groups have gone from invisibility and exclusion, to exaggeration, to proliferation/hypervisibility. The fact that blackness is either over-determined or subsumed into a race-less version of diversity appears a contradiction, but they are opposing sides of the same 'diversity' coin. Within racial neoliberalism blackness is everywhere and nowhere in media.

9.4 Contesting normative constructions of blackness

The preceding account would suggest that under the conditions of racial neoliberalism the making of blackness will always be a reductive process. But needless to say, this is not the whole picture, not least for the fundamental reason that it ignores the agency/activity of producers and audiences.

With regard to the latter, in his study of the international syndication of African American television, Tim Havens (2013) demonstrates the at times radically divergent ways in which international audiences consume American blackness. (Havens' argument is that media executives' perception of audience tastes and practices towards black-cast shows then becomes the 'lore' that shapes the production of blackness at home.) Havens highlights how audiences from Scandinavia to South African (a) consume these depictions of blackness readily and eagerly, and (b) in both radical and conservative ways. His approach, which tracks the social life of 'black television', demonstrates the complexity of the production and circulation of blackness. Despite the executive's, or indeed the academic's, attempts to present totalising accounts of what versions of blackness *work* in media (I include myself in this), the human beings involved, whether producers, intermediaries and audiences, are unpredictable. Or to put it more precisely, following Herman Gray, black expressive culture is structured by different macro and micro elements, including the political economy of media and other cultural institutions, social conditions, broader political struggles and cultural discourses, not least 'disputes among blacks about difference, class, community, mass collective action, authenticity, and, of course, representation' (Gray, 2005: 18). Once again, the stress is on complexity for the simple reason that the social worlds within which blackness circulates are complex in themselves.

If we return to the question of media specifically, hegemonic representations of blackness are *always* under contestation. This is particularly the case where bottom-up forms of convivial culture and multicultural drift are allowed to emerge organically, particularly in public service media which has a remit to cater for the diverse populations of the nation. For Sarita Malik (2013b: 515), drawing from Gilroy, convivial culture becomes a potential 'manoeuvre for managing the potential challenges of living with multiculture (and the interactions it offers)'. In a rare foray into daytime television, Paul Gilroy himself comments upon lifestyle programmes such as DIY shows, that obligingly feature racial and ethnic minorities as the lead subjects (in order to fulfil diversity policy) that nonetheless reduce 'the exaggerated dimensions of racial difference to a liberating ordinaryness. From this angle, "race" becomes nothing special, a virtual reality given meaning only by the fact racism endures' (Gilroy, 2004: 131). Thus, even though I maintain that diversity discourse is a product of racial neoliberalism, it nonetheless produces ambivalent effects, including depictions of multiculture that demonstrate the 'ability to live with alterity without becoming anxious, fearful or violent' (ibid.: xi).

Hegemonic representations of blackness are also actively contested by black cultural producers. As I have covered elsewhere (Saha, 2018), while commercial settings provide some opportunities for black cultural producers as media companies look to give their products a sense of 'quality' or 'edginess' or 'coolness' (Banet-Weiser, 2007; Fuller, 2010; Quinn, 2013b), spaces that are (relatively) autonomous of corporate production have been particularly enabling for black cultural producers. The *new ethnicities* moment was driven by black symbol creators working independently on the edges of media and art worlds. In more contemporary times Aymar Jean Christian

(2018) – the only academic I am aware of who has their own television network – demonstrates how web television in particular is opening up regimes of representation, especially for intersectional black identities. While they are constrained by algorithmic governance (see Chapter 10), they still have the potential to break through and reach wider audiences, enabled by black queer networks (offline as well as online) in particular. Similarly, Francesca Sobande (2017) shows how black beauty vlogs on YouTube produce forms of solidarity between black women who turn to the online platform as mainstream media content alienates them. As she states, 'young Black women in Britain, as media spectators, often feel strengthened rather than manipulated by Black women's vlogs. This is in contrast to the downright sense of alienation, misrecognition and neglect they often experience when watching mainstream television' (Sobande, 2017: 663). How digital media make race is the topic of the following chapter.

Following Sobande's work in particular, and retuning to the subject of audiences, an analysis of consumption reveals something different about how representations of blackness work; even what we might interpret as a particularly regressive depiction of blackness can achieve something positive in a different context. As covered in Chapter 2, audience studies scholars provide a more nuanced appreciation of the pleasures and meanings that different groups and people get from these representations. What I want to reiterate now is how media is the very material which individuals – particularly racialised groups – use to reconstitute themselves and maybe even transgress the cultural/social locations that constantly attempt to contain and police them (Gray, 2004: 5). And to stress once again, a single text does not produce one ideological effect; instead, a media text is complicit in a number of different (political) discourses. How we consume them (and the extent to which we take on preferred meanings of the dominant culture) depends on where we are positioned within a particular discourse.

As has become a recurrent theme, the study of the making of blackness in relation to race, culture and media is deepened by a focus on everyday media practices. Popular music scholar Caspar Melville's (2019) take on London's rich black music culture has a strong emphasis on conviviality and how these scenes challenged racial divisions of the city – in terms of both production and consumption (in fact, Melville blurs the role of producer and consumer in the context of the nightclub or warehouse party). As he puts it, London's black music scene 'explored new ways in which culture could be inhabited collectively. In ways both deliberate and contingent, these musical scenes involved collaboration between young people from different sides of what the great American sociologist W. E. B. Du Bois (1903) identified as "the color line", and hosted lived multiculture on the dancefloor' (Melville, 2019: 1). Melville focuses on how London's black music scene was and continues to be shaped by postcolonial migration, and the ethnic reconfiguration of society as it becomes post-industrial. Moreover, strongly influenced by the *new ethnicities* tradition, Melville identifies new articulations of British blackness that came out of these scenes but demonstrates how these were always syncretic in character based on collaboration between London's diverse communities. So blackness was foregrounded but very much based on community, commonality and solidarity; anyone could join these scenes, you just needed to be open. The dance floor of black music spaces produces alternative visions of how we can better live together. As Melville stresses, this was an ambivalent process, 'where gains were often temporary, but it was also one within which new forms of interculture emerged that transformed the city' (ibid.: 2). As he continues:

> I offer evidence that while black Atlantic musical culture may have receded as the central force in articulating a black subjectivity in the late twentieth century, in the spaces of the warehouse party, the rave and the jungle club, even when produced using digital technology, this music and its cultures served as a vital resource to build and sustain multicultural forms of sociality and, to use Gilroy's own term, politically significant multicultural 'conviviality'. (ibid.: 9)

Melville provides another example of how convivial culture can emerge organically within media worlds. But what I take more broadly from Melville's social and cultural history of black British music is how any account of race, media and culture cannot ignore the urban as the place where culture emerges.

BOX 9.1 Case Study

Making the black athlete and national identity

This chapter has predominantly tackled the making of blackness in the context of popular culture and capitalism. The preceding discussion on multiculture and conviviality, however, alludes to how media constructions of blackness contribute to our understanding of national identity. One field of research that is useful here is sport studies and its regular engagement with the question of media. Sport is a relatively neglected area of study in recent critical scholarship, dismissed as nothing more as leisure and therefore of trivial interest. But for cultural studies scholar Ben Carrington (2010: 3), sport is deeply implicated in the 'making and re-making of race beyond its own boundaries'. The feats of black athletes have challenged racist ideas of the natural biological superiority of the white male. But this has meant that racism has had to shift and slip in order to keep racial hierarchies in place in the face of black sporting achievements. One way is through the commodification of blackness, which has constrained and reified black bodies, casting upon them superhuman powers (Gilroy, 2000), or reinforced racial ideas around savagery and animalistic qualities (Carrington, 2010). But black athletes also get instrumentalised in a way that reflects a nation's multicultural progress – especially the nation's celebration of its black representatives in international competition. This appears to be a progressive shift but it is something critical sports studies scholars of race are deeply ambivalent about.

Daniel Burdsey (2016) provides a particularly nuanced analysis of the reception of British Somalian Muslim long-distance runner Mohamed 'Mo' Farah. Following his successes at the London 2012 Olympic Games, Farah was hailed in the media as symbolic

(Continued)

of Britain as a healthy and successful multicultural nation as he provided yet another iconic image of Black British athletes draped in the Union Flag. Burdsey acknowledges that such images contribute to the feeling of a more confident black British identity, as a consequence of multicultural drift. However, he nonetheless wants to show how the representation of Mo Farah 'reflected exclusionary, and at times contradictory, attitudes around Britishness, Islam, migration, multiculture and citizenship' (Burdsey, 2016: 14).

Burdsey finds that Farah's black Muslim identity – and his relatively cosmopolitan, transnational background and supposedly 'moderate' religious values – have produced ambivalence in his coverage in the British press. Farah is painted as a migrant success story, but in a manner that reinforces the good migrant/Muslim versus bad migrant/Muslim dichotomy. Moreover, his success is represented in a way that is less about overcoming racial/religious barriers and more about the 'success' of British liberal values. Farah was painted as a good *black-Muslim-migrant* in order to make him tolerable, which entailed Farah to an extent playing down his Muslim black identity (as Fortier (2008) argues, Black British athletes in underlining their sense of belonging to Britain often find that they have to deny their blackness in the process). And as Burdsey argues, in the process he is used to reinforce the dominant culture's hegemonic values of Britishness (and its intrinsic whiteness) rather than truly celebrate British multiculturalism and the achievement of its black and brown citizens. Burdsey (2016: 20) is basically thinking through the 'extrapolation of Farah's personal triumph to signify a narrative of national "multicultural" accomplishment' that hides the racial marginalisation and subjugation that characterises black experience. Rather than a symbol of multicultural success, the representation of Farah reinscribes hegemonic core values around nation. In other words, his success (and his blackness and Muslimness) is instrumentalised or exploited for the sake of espousing British values rather than truly recognising black and Muslim experience.

9.5 Conclusion

The aim of this chapter has been to explore how media make blackness, where hegemonic representations of race take hold (and reproduce through history although they also take new forms) but are always being contested. Within the current conjuncture, black people are no longer invisible but hyper-visible, as audiences demand more diverse characters. But to what extent does this fulfil the logic of neoliberal postracial meritocracy? Conversely, in what ways has the regime of representation around blackness broadened, a consequence of multicultural drift, but also the very purposeful interventions of black cultural producers and their collaborators, that reject and subvert, as Molina-Guzmán (2013: 220) puts it, the 'adherence to whiteness as the normative aesthetic for ethnic and racial minority bodies'. To what extent do these articulations of difference deny a form of identity politics that governs who belongs to the group and who does not, and instead produces forms of community, commonality and solidarity? This brings us to the question of audience, and how they themselves make sense of and contest the meanings of blackness that circulate across offline and online media.

This chapter has exposed patterns, changes and continuities in how media make blackness, but with an emphasis on complexity and contestedness. Future studies on this topic, especially those concerned with representation and discourses around blackness, need to similarly make a point of searching for contradiction. This is not for the sake of intellectual contrarianism. Instead, a focus on contradictory cases can be the most illuminating about the current conjuncture. Indeed, studies of texts in particular need to avoid slipping into simplistic normative terms of whether a particular representation of black people is correct or not, and instead think through what such representations are doing in the given moment. Once again, this entails a historical approach, as underlined by the postcolonial cultural economy. In addition, there are still huge gaps to fill in terms of research into production and audiences. The new digital forms of production/consumption provide a particularly rich area in which to investigate race-making practices, as the next chapter demonstrates.

9.6 Recommended and further reading

In terms of current conjuncture, Kristen Warner's (2015) *The Cultural Politics of Color-blind TV Casting* provides an excellent critique of the supposedly progressive act of blindcasting. Jo Littler's (2017) *Against Meritocracy* (especially Chapter 5) also provides a valuable account of postrace media culture, in relation to the concept of meritocracy, where race has become something that is both commodified (in the name of diversity) and denied. Read together, these two books explain so much of what we are seeing in terms of blackness, especially on streaming services like Netflix and Amazon Prime.

Elsewhere there has been some outstanding work on the politics of representations of blackness that is bringing a much-needed emphasis on the *contextual* as much as the *textual*. Clive Nwonka has produced a sustained body of work that explores the dynamics of both representation and production in black British film and cinema that combines film studies, cultural studies and critical policy research. Also focusing on production and more engaged with the intersections of race and sexuality is Alfred Martin Jr's (2021) *The Generic Closet: Black Gayness and the Black-Cast Sitcom*, and Aymar Jean Christian's (2018) *Open TV: Innovation beyond Hollywood and the Rise of Web Television*. In terms of audiences Darnell Hunt's (1997) *Screening the Los Angeles 'Riots': Race, Seeing, and Resistance* remains an important contribution to audience studies, and one of the few focused on blackness. The opening chapter also provides an excellent critical overview of cultural studies and the subject of race. In more recent times, Francesca Sobande's (2020) *The Digital Lives of Black Women in Britain* is an important work on Black British women's media practices in the digital context.

BOX 9.2 Key Theme

Black Studies and media

One field of increasing influence that I have not mentioned in this chapter but is very relevant for the study of blackness in media is what is broadly referred to as 'Black Studies'. Black Studies emerged out of African American studies, and in turn Africana Studies, and is predominantly interested in the experience of black people in the United States. While it is an interdisciplinary field, Black Studies has at its core the question of culture, and as a consequence media features frequently in its analysis, where the images and sounds of blackness become the material in which to examine black life, black culture, and black politics more generally.

Situated squarely in the humanities, Black Studies provides a new angle in which to tackle the topic of race, culture and media. Firstly, it emphasises aesthetics and performance over representation. (For a particularly interesting example of this approach see Dhanveer Brar's (2015) close textual reading of James Brown and the aesthetic strategy of rupture.) As such, it helps counter the tendency in media studies of race to frame its analysis in reductive terms of media bias, stereotype or misrepresentation, and instead produces an account of the making of blackness more in keeping with Stuart Hall's new ethnicities formulation, which understands blackness as a contested field of representation (see Brar and Sharma, 2019). Secondly, it is more explicitly linked to the decolonial project, the decentering of whiteness and, as a consequence, the foregrounding of black feminism and queerness in particular (Spillers, 1987; Keeling, 2007). In doing so it innovates new modes of theorisation and writing as part of the project of deconstructing white hegemonic knowledge production – as an example see Kwodo Eshun's (2018) sonic fiction or Fred Moten's (2014) experimentations with theory and poetry.

For some critical race scholars, Black Studies' highly abstract theorisation, its lack of interest in (or indeed outright rejection of) the empirical, and its predominant interest in modernist forms of black culture (that is seen as exemplifying black radical aesthetics) will limit its appeal. But as stated, Black Studies' emphasis on aesthetics, which is crucially always situated within a historical analysis, offers an alternative path out of the dead-end that follows a sole focus on the representational politics of race.

Discussion

What might a focus on black aesthetics and performance capture that the concept of 'representation' does not?

10

Digital Race/Racism

In what ways is the internet an inherently white space?
Does the internet reflect racism offline, or does it produce new types of racism online?
How can digital technologies be racially biased?
In what ways can new digital platforms be an enabling space for racialised groups?

10.1 Introduction

It almost feels too obvious to say that the production and consumption of culture – and by extension, race – increasingly takes a digital form. While the death of traditional media – whether watching linear television, going to the cinema, or buying books or records – has been greatly exaggerated, the production/consumption of new or digital media is increasing rapidly, along with internet usage more generally. By digital media I am referring to streaming services, digital news media, video games, and social media in particular, accessed through a range of online technologies, such as personal computers, smart televisions, tablets, games consoles and smartphones.

This chapter asks, how do digital media make race? Put another way, how do digital technologies impact upon race-making practices? The tendency is to think of technology as neutral, immune to cultural biases, developing independently, propelled purely by scientific advancements. According to this perspective, the online world merely replicates the dynamics of race/racism in the offline world. As this chapter will demonstrate, such a view is not just naïve but also deeply problematic. The explosion of 'Web 2.0' – the latest iteration of the internet, which has online participatory culture at its core, leading to the huge popularity of social networking sites – is having a profound effect on social interactions, dynamically transforming the nature of online 'racial inclusions and exclusions' in particular (Sharma, 2013: 47). That is, new media technologies are shaping the making of race online in very particular ways. Following sociologist Ruha Benjamin (2019), the internet is a 'Black box' that takes the dynamics of race from the 'real' world as its input, but produces different types of racialising outputs. I should add that I make this argument while careful not to slip into a form of technological determinism that problematically assumes that technology holds all explanatory power, let alone can be separated from wider political economic/socio-cultural processes and developments. Instead, my core argument is that within the current conjuncture, the making of race online provides a further example of the logics of racial neoliberalism.

This chapter, then, is not about ascertaining the extent to which race/racism as embodied/expressed in the digital realm reflects the real world. Rather, as set out Chapter 2, it understands that racial identities are made online; the digital provides further material from which we constitute our racial identities. The same goes for racism itself, where, as suggested, the internet produces particular racialising dynamics. Drawing from the burgeoning field of race digital studies, in this chapter I provide a critical account of how race is made online, framed by a critical cultural analysis focused on media. It is split into two main parts. The first focuses on how racism manifests online, in terms of racist commentary on social media, racist visual representations (as embodied in video games, for instance), and in terms of the architecture of the internet itself, including supposedly scientific tools such as algorithms and the use of big data. In the second half of the chapter I focus on how racialised groups flourish online, including the creation of 'counter publics' and alternative communities more generally (particularly migrant/diasporic groups), and the production of media content on new digital platforms that allow racialised groups to produce alternative narratives to those found in 'mainstream' media. Adopting the postcolonial cultural economy approach, the chapter situates the various case studies within their historical context, namely racial neoliberalism, with an emphasis on the ambivalence of digital race-making practices in contemporary times. There is something very new, but also very old, about how these processes occur and how they are shaped by racial ideology and capitalism.

10.2 Racism online

As covered in Chapter 2, the birth of the internet contained within it utopian aspirations. This had positive implications for racial minorities, where the anonymity of the web, and the ability to create brand new identities, was going to supposedly create a genuinely postracial space (Nakamura, 2013 [2002]; Daniels, 2013;

Sharma, 2013). When the internet was more text-based, the ability to escape racialisation certainly felt attainable (although as Nakamura (2013 [2002]) shows, race still persisted in this version of the web), but this has become less the case as the web has become much more visual. Since then, the idea of the internet as post-racial has been roundly dismissed as a pernicious myth, by academics, researchers and users alike. While racialised groups turn to digital spaces to get away from the discrimination, marginalisation and exclusion they encounter in mainstream media, once online they find that they cannot entirely escape racial imagery and discourse (see Sobande et al., 2019). The internet has certainly not delivered the utopian, postracial world that was initially promised.

As this chapter will demonstrate, digital environments are anything but race-neutral. As Sanjay Sharma (2013: 46–47) states: 'The internet has always been a racially demarcated space … a manifold set of sociotechnical practices, generative of digital privileges and racial ordering'. Indeed, the main aim of this section is to demonstrate how the internet reproduces racial hierarchies, albeit in a novel way. This perhaps is no surprise considering the institutional whiteness of Silicon Valley (Daniels, 2013; McIlwain, 2019). Black people in particular have been historically marginalised within and excluded by the tech industry, and this is mirrored in the very infrastructure of computing itself, where whiteness is the norm and blackness is 'the social problem' that necessitates computational solutions in order to be fixed (Benjamin, 2019; McIlwain, 2019). Indeed, many critical race scholars of technology have drawn attention to the internet as an intrinsically white space. This was particularly evident in the early days of personal computing, featuring DOS commands like 'Master Disk' and 'Slave Disk', the ubiquitous white hand as cursor, and the original emoji set in Unicode 7.0 that featured no black/indigenous emojis and stereotyped the ethnic/racial groups that did feature (Nakamura, 2013 [2002]; Daniels, 2013; Matamoros-Fernández, 2017). As digital race scholar Jessie Daniels (2013) argues, whiteness is the internet's default setting. This becomes the frame through which I now analyse the different variations of racism that manifests on online media.

10.2.1 The representation of race online

For Lisa Nakamura and Peter Chow-White (2012), we have seen the proliferation rather than the erasure of race on the internet, as made evident in the volume of visual representations of race that circulate on digital platforms. Much like representations of race offline, for Nakamura (2008), the politics of representation online is shaped by colonialism. Daniels (2013) uses Stuart Hall's notion of 'spectacle of the Other' to explore how race becomes an object of the white gaze online. This is particularly evident in video games where race becomes exotic spectacle (Nakamura and Chow-White, 2012). For instance, in first-person shooter video games, foreign (brown) Others are the designated enemy and their deaths are normalised (Leonard,

2004), in action-adventure games like *Grand Theft Auto*, domestic racialised and ethnic minorities are stereotyped and vilified (Chan, 2005), while in video sports games blackness is reduced to images of 'hyperphysicality, hypermasculinity, and hyper-sexuality' (Gray, 2012: 262).

But if this suggests that the spectacle of the Other online basically replicates what happens in traditional media, there is something very specific about race in video games; it is not just about how users consume stereotypical images of racialised Others when they play video games, but 'how they *perform* them' (Nakamura and Chow-White, 2012: 8, my emphasis). Cultural studies scholar David J. Leonard (2004: 1) provocatively describes sport video games that feature highly racialised charac-terisations as amounting to a 'high-tech form of blackface', for the way that they allow white creators and players to become black. He also echoes bell hooks (1992) in her famous 'Eating the Other' essay, when he describes how 'these games elicit pleasure, playing on white fantasies as they simultaneously affirm white privilege through virtual play' (ibid.). Thus, video sports games give the white subject a sense of transgression through the relatively safe consumption of the Other. Moreover, the engagement with the Other in this way, as hooks (1992: 22) puts it, 'reinscribes the status quo', as it is fundamentally about control. As Leonard (2004: 03) adds, 'As blacks supposedly control sports in the real world, video games allow white players to not only become the other, but to discipline and punish'.

10.2.2 Racism online

The example of gaming also opens up the discussion of how racist language festers online. Online gaming in particular is characterised by users expressing explicit rac-ism, sexism and homophobia in their interactions with those who are identified as Other. As digital race scholar Kishonna Gray (2012) finds the use of such language has become so normalised that it provokes little reaction from the black gamers who accept it as a feature of gaming culture. Such is the whiteness of the gaming scene (even though a significant portion of gamers do not fulfil the white, male stereotype (Shaw, 2012)) that racialised and gendered Others are demarcated as *deviant* (Gray, 2012) or *space-invaders* (Leurs, 2012). Moreover, online gaming exposes a double power dynamic where white users can take advantage of the anonymity of the inter-net to make racist pronouncements without impunity, while minoritised Others do not themselves have the privilege to mask their identities as their racial/gendered/sexual identities invariably come to be revealed (see Gray (2012) for a close analysis of how this happens).

While I have used the specific example of online gaming, the same dynamics of racism relate to the nature of digital commentary on the internet more broadly, whether comments/tweets made on social media (Cisneros and Nakayama, 2015; Matamoros-Fernández, 2017; Murthy and Sharma, 2019) or comments posted on online newspaper articles (Hughey and Daniels, 2013; Gardiner, 2018; Titley, 2019). The general finding is that there is a proliferation of racist sentiment online, again taking place as it does in a context where people can remain anonymous and post messages with relatively little editorial intervention.

The last point regarding the (ineffective) policing of racial harassment online is a common feature in research on racism online. Social media platforms certainly appear reluctant to act upon racial harassment, illustrated by vague policies, arbitrary enforcement of rules and somewhat glib pronouncements on freedom of speech (Matamoros-Fernández, 2017; Titley, 2019). For Ruha Benjamin (2019: 23), 'Twitter's relatively hands-off approach when it comes to the often violent and hate-filled content of White supremacists actually benefits the company's bottom line'. This raises issues about the very economics of the internet. Social media relies upon a sustained tempo of online commentary (Titley, 2019) that, as shall be explored, becomes content to be monetised, leading to what feels like a deluge of 'racist digitalia' (Gilroy, 2012: 381). In other words, it is not the case that racism is an unfortunate feature of online discourse on social media, rather, digital platforms provide affordances that facilitate a particular type of online racism to flourish. For Murthy and Sharma (2019: 195), racism 'pervades social relations – both off- and online – and has been deeply embedded in the formation of Western modernity and technological innovation'. Put another way, the internet has racialising dynamics built into it. Benjamin (2019: 5–6) coined the concept of 'New Jim Code' (a reference to Jim Crow and the formal and informal structures that excluded, isolated and denigrated black people in America in the pre-civil rights era) to describe 'the employment of new technologies that reflect and reproduce existing inequities but that are promoted and perceived as more objective or progressive than the discriminatory systems of a previous era'. Benjamin's point here is that the supposed neutrality of the net hides its racialist tendencies.

Before I explore this in more detail, the operation of web 2.0, through which so much of our media is now consumed, needs to be set against the context of racial neoliberalism, which has shaped its development. While the internet's original formation was very much rooted in Libertarian ideology, and the fundamental belief in personal freedom in terms of free market principles (Matamoros-Fernández, 2017: 934), in the shift towards neoliberalism we have seen the increasing commercialisation of the internet where platforms are led by economic interests. (Tech companies are now among the biggest and the most valuable in the world.) Value in web 2.0 is generated by identity construction so it can create more focused, targeted user-generated content, based upon the neoliberal language of efficiency (Leurs, 2014; Benjamin, 2019). While white, Western males remain the key target consumers, as we shall see, ethnicity and race become markers in which to sell – or more likely, withhold – certain products and services. For digital race scholar and activist Safiya Noble (2013: 8), 'Much of the Internet's use, for commercialism, academic, and military purposes, reinforces entrenched ideologies of individualism and a definition of the self through consumption'. It is in this way that web 2.0 fulfils the logic of racial neoliberalism, based around a discourse of 'diversity', where racial and ethnic identities effectively become commodified, reduced to market niches or branded lifestyles. To unpack this further, I am going to demonstrate how generic online processes, namely, big data, user tracking/surveillance and algorithms, fulfil the logics of racial neoliberalism.

10.2.3 Web 2.0's racialising dynamics

Web 2.0 has generated huge amounts of data – or indeed, *big data* – where all our online likes, clickthroughs, links and preferences are saved and sold in order to pro-duce targeted content and advertising. For internet researchers, big data represents a treasure trove of material by which to generate elaborate network maps and visualisa-tions that explore the nature of social processes online. But a dangerously neglected feature of big data is how it itself reproduces power inequalities and 'inherently dis-criminates against already marginalised subjects' (Leurs and Shepherd, 2017: 211). Big data is not neutral. As stated, big data allows governments and companies to seg-ment populations/audiences, which is then used to include/exclude them from cer-tain products/services. Moreover, the way in which such data are used to essentially automate who gets access and who does not (again, in the name of efficiency) has seen it applied to the management of national borders. Governments increasingly use automated social sorting in order to control the flow of people, or more precisely keep out unwanted others. This includes biometric techniques used to monitor asy-lum seekers/migrants at borders and the monitoring of social media for the purpose of policing (Leurs and Smets, 2018). As digital researchers Koen Leurs and Tamara Shepherd (2017: 214) show:

> For those privileged subjects carrying desirable passports, e-borders and iris scans sustain liquid flow across borders and planetary nomadic mobility as an effortless normality. By contrast, undesired subjects have to provide fingerprints – a genre of biometric data with a long history of criminal connotations – to be cross-referenced among a host of other identifiers in data-based risk calculations.

In this way Leurs and Shepherd describe border control technologies as 'residual colonialism' (ibid.: 215).

Muslim populations in particular come under surveillance in the name of security. For Fekete (2006), European governments, briefed by EU heads of state, senior police, civil servants and security services, see foreigners from the 'Islamic World' as a threat to the security of the nation, and as such have facilitated the surveillance of Mus-lims online. This includes creating databases on potential threats – including groups and individuals – based on computer scanning (see also Gürses et al., 2016). The point is that the surveillance of Muslims goes beyond collecting data on individu-als with actual connections to terrorism, but to include Muslims who have no such connections. As Benjamin (2019) shows, the same processes have been applied to black and Latinx communities in the US, who by virtue of having particular racially/ ethnically coded names and living in particular zip codes have been algorithmically placed in databases for gang members (including children). For Benjamin (2019), the surveillance of black people in particular is historical; new media technologies have not created something new but facilitated something that has always been a fact of black experience. Hence, anti-black racism is the very infrastructure as well as the output of new media technologies (see also McIlwain, 2019).

The same surveillance strategies are used for commercial purposes. As already mentioned, marketers build group profiles to ascertain which population segments are preferred for certain companies and their products, and which ones are less desirable (Nakamura and Chow-White, 2012: 12). But as Ruha Benjamin (2019: 34) puts it, 'there is a slippery slope between effective marketing and efficient racism'. For instance, drawing from their direct experience working in compliance, Leurs and Shepherd (2017) describe how minorities with clean credit cards were denied mobile phone contracts because of racist stereotyping; as a supervisor explained, 'those Somalis, they never pay' (ibid.: 213). To reiterate, the data systems which are used by banks, companies and state institutions, which are designed to process huge amounts of personal data in order to make quick decisions or make predictions, work on algorithms that rather than being neutral and objective contain cultural biases, not least for the reason that 'people are still making the decisions at every step of the process' (ibid.: 214).

This brings us onto the issue of algorithms, while rooting the discussion again more squarely in the question of media. Algorithms, whether helping us select televisions shows or recommending products, may appear as if they are serving us convenience, to help us navigate the huge amounts of products in the digital market space. But, once again, research shows that rather than being neutral, algorithms have cultural biases around race, gender and class built into them via the cultural biases of the (mostly white men) who created them (who use white, hetereosexual identity as the norm). As race and digital media scholars Photini Vrikki and Sarita Malik (2019: 275) state: 'Where people, with their own prejudices, racisms and biases, may previously have served as gatekeepers to the CCIs [cultural and creative industries], now algorithms have replaced them in the digital space, with no guarantee that systems of representation or inequalities are addressed'. Datasets contain within them racial biases that algorithms reproduce rather than fix. In this way, technology amplifies racism under the guise of objectivity and neutrality. Returning to marketisation and the issue of 'efficiency', Benjamin (2019: 18) shows how, through tailored marketing, Netflix entices black viewers to certain movies by using posters that foreground black supporting cast members, making movies appear more diverse than they really are. What is particularly disturbing about this process is, as Benjamin notes, Netflix does not actually ask users to provide information on their racial/ethnic identities.

Rather, racial profiles are constructed based on our viewing data and how we respond to certain programmes. This follows niche marketing logic that uses race and other identifiers to differentiate people and place them into markets to be targeted with specific content. Technology facilitates this kind of audience segmentation but in the process turns to racial stereotyping and exoticisation in order to entice those audiences. As Benjamin states, niche marketing 'has a serious downside when tailoring morphs into targeting and stereotypical containment' (ibid.: 21).

The main purpose of this section has been to underline how technology, rather than being neutral, objective or scientific, contains and reproduces racialising dynamics. Following Benjamin (2019: 40), racism is the input that goes into the making of technology – 'part of the social context of design processes' – that leads to novel forms of racism as its output. In addition, I demonstrate how racism in the context of web 2.0 is shaped by racial neoliberalism, which allows explicit racism to manifest in the form of digital commentary, the churn of which provides social media with content to be monetised, as racial identities are transformed into niche marketing categories in order to sell/withhold products, services and even citizenship rights. But as Noble (2013) argues, it is not simply to say that technologies produce racist ideologies in a straightforward way, or that they are inherently racist. Instead, they reflect and reinstate racial ideologies of the societies within such technologies are formed.

10.3 How racialised groups flourish online

While this paints a somewhat bleak picture of the internet, Safyia Noble (2013) does point out that when users engage with such technologies they exist in a dynamic relation where they create content together. And for Noble, this at times can go against the grain of the dominant ideology. Noble, in effect, describes a dialectical tension in the making of race and gender online; digital technologies reproduce social relations but also create new ones based on our engagements with them. In what follows we look at how the internet and new digital platforms can be an enabling space for racialised groups.

10.3.1 Digital anti-racism

As much as the internet has seen a festering of racist discourse, digital technologies have allowed minorities to expose racism, for instance, using smartphones to capture bigots on public transport or incidents of police brutality that are then shared instantaneously online. (As I write this, #GeorgeFloyd – the latest African American man to be murdered by the police – is trending on Twitter, including disturbing video and images of him being choked to death by a police officer.) Moreover, diasporic groups use 'digitised tactics' (Kumar, 2018: 3) to raise awareness of political struggles across the globe.

The dominant culture is being held accountable perhaps more than at any point in history, and this has been enabled by the dialogic nature of digital communication.

The concept of alternative public spheres is one way in which digital race theorists have attempted to make sense of the political mobilisations of anti-racists that occur online (Leurs et al., 2012; Carney, 2016; Vrikki and Malik, 2019). Sarah J. Jackson and Brooke Foucault Welles (2015), for instance, coined the term 'networked counter publics' to describe the online spaces where marginalised communities come together, deliberate and form community bonds, and in doing so challenge dominant knowledge. Based on analyses of the hijacking of the New York Police Department's PR campaign #myNYPD (Jackson and Welles, 2015), and also the creation of the #Ferguson hashtag instigated by a young black woman following the fatal shooting of teenager Michael Brown (Jackson and Foucault Welles, 2016), they describe how these particular networked counter publics emerged, producing community though different rhetorical devices, such as humour and rage. Their key argument, however, is how these counter publics not only challenged but helped shape mainstream media narratives, giving coverage to stories that would have ordinarily gone undetected. Their case studies show how the architecture of Twitter in particular allows counter publics to mount fairly impactful interventions within mainstream discourse. As they say,

> It is clear from our findings that Twitter functions as a useful tool for counter publics to share in-group knowledge and experience about police brutality and that through the strategic use of Twitter these counter publics have the power to motivate the mainstream public sphere to take note and respond. (ibid.: 948)

But while the notion of counter publics and alternative public spheres has clear resonance when thinking through the digital practices of anti-racist activists, as Gavan Titley (2019) argues, the contestation for racism might be better understood as a permanent fixture of online discourse. In a study of racist commentary and counter-commentary on YouTube, Murthy and Sharma (2019: 204) describe non-hostile and hostile commentary as 'entangled' – that is, part of the same. They argue that 'Race-talk on YouTube, and on the Internet more broadly, needs to be situated in terms of the complex relationship between online media, techno-sociality and the motility of racism' (ibid.: 205). In effect, Murthy and Sharma, like Titley, imply that racism and counter-racism is the condition of everyday online social life, or moreover, it is built into the very architecture and economy of web 2.0.

10.3.2 Digital diasporas

While the internet enables anti-racist mobilisations and interventions, digital media enables racialised Others in their everyday lives. I am especially referring here to the way that migrants and diasporic groups create communities through digital media – the focus of digital migration studies in particular (Leurs and Smets, 2018).

Digital migration scholars demonstrate the way that new technologies help migrants create a connection between home and each other – whether personal communication (social media, email) or media (diasporic news media, digital television) (Hedge, 2016; Leurs and Smets, 2018). They also address the different contexts in which such technologies are employed, from the fraught, such as negotiating borders and structural issues involving SIM cards and remittances, to the relatively banal, such as the use of online discussion boards that help members of a diaspora meet and share ideas/opinions/experiences (Leurs et al., 2012). Digital migration researcher Radha Hedge (2016) uses the concept of 'digital diasporas' to cover migrant media practices from the use of technologies to stay in contact with home, including the consumption of media from the homeland, to the way it is used for activism and political mobilisations. In doing so, Hedge makes two important arguments. Firstly, the use of digital media is always located in the social; as she says, 'electronic space of media and the space of sociality are already deeply interconnected' (ibid.: xxx). In other words, digital practices are embedded in the everyday. Secondly, Hedge highlights how the making of culture is always ongoing in the local context, which in turn shapes global culture flows. In this way digital technologies facilitate diasporic cultural production. Digital diasporas do not just involve transporting sounds, images and words from the homeland to the country of arrival. Rather, they highlight a more dynamic relation, where diasporic digital cultural production is 'connected to and at the centre of a transnational circuit of aesthetic exchange and commodity flows' (ibid.: 92). Hedge shows us how digital technology is itself a form of material culture that migrants use to constitute themselves and their identity and culture. Moreover, it is an ambivalent relationship – technology not only connects but can also produce exclusions (not least in terms of the 'digital divide'– see Box 10.2 for a critical account of this concept).

On this last point, Koen Leurs and Kevin Smets (2018: 8) warn digital migration researchers to be careful of slipping into both 'techno orientalism' that fetishises the migrant's use of new technologies (for instance, the ubiquitous image of a refugee at a border trying to get mobile reception), and technological determinism that centres digital media as starting points for research into migrant experience that can overvalorise the use of those media in the process. As Hedge (2016) reminds us, digital diasporas often emerge out of the traumatising experience of dislocation and expulsion that characterise forced migrations in particular. Sometimes the supposedly empowered use of new media technology is deeply ambivalent; Hedge (ibid.), for instance, uses an example of South Asian workers in the United Arab Emirates who send selfies of themselves in front of impressive buildings back home, designed to mask the dire working conditions in which they find themselves. Indeed, in real life there can be fear over the use of technology, related to the issues of surveillance mentioned in the previous section. But the online practices of migrants can themselves be the subject of racist discourse, for instance the fear that social media radicalises migrant populations or facilitate bubbles and self-segregation, therefore exasperating multicultural relations (Leurs, 2014).

A lacuna for some of this research on migration and diaspora is the topic of race. While digital migration scholars address war, conflict, persecution and climate disaster that lead to forced migration, the historical role of racism that structures the access to and experience of digital technology in particular could be made more explicit in this research. Another issue which is absent that I want to tackle now is how members of a diaspora use digital communities to construct their sense of racial and ethnic identities. For instance, Sobande et al. (2019: 4) use the notion of 'online embodiment' to describe how individuals rearticulate their identities online, particularly though photos, videos and avatars. Similarly, Jessie Daniels (2013: 699) refers to how 'people use the Internet to both form and reaffirm individual racial identity and seek out communities based on race and racial understandings of the world'. Such practices are sometimes read as a form of cultural resistance. Two studies mentioned in previous chapters that have particular resonance here include Dhiraj Murthy (2010) on the online Taqwacore scene, which creates a space for Muslim punks to articulate their identities beyond the gaze of both mainstream Western public culture and dominant Muslim communities, and Francesca Sobande (2017) on the consumption of YouTube vlogs by black women as a rejection of mainstream television (that disavows black women). In another study of black British women's online practices, Sobande et al. (2019) explore their relationship to black American content that dominates the internet, finding a form of *glocalisation* that helps these women connect to social justice issues like Black Lives Matter. They describe how black British women create their own content and engage with the content of other black women cultural producers internationally, providing 'linkages between the thoughts, lived experiences and cultural memories of Black African-Caribbean women in Britain and elsewhere' (ibid.: 10). In this way, the authors read this activity as 'potentially resistant media practices [including] the rejection of British mainstream media, as well as their active, and possibly financial, support of online alternatives' (ibid.: 7). But if notions of cultural resistance may sometimes be over-determined, it is worth reminding ourselves that such spaces can reproduce other types of social hierarchy (Murthy, 2010). Leurs et al. (2012) find that the use of online message boards can be a fraught experience for young Muslims who occasionally find online interactions alienating, especially when encountering particular types of religious doctrine, as emerged in their interviews with young Dutch Moroccan women about their experience and use of such forums.

10.3.3 The new digital 'creatives of colour'

In the aforementioned study, Leurs et al. (2012: 166) see these discussion boards as a form of alternative media where Moroccan-Dutch youth are able to 'discuss and reframe dominant images circulating in news media'. This returns us to the question of 'media' in terms of the production of symbolic content. While the lines of production and consumption have been blurred in the digital world, the studies I have drawn upon have nonetheless focused mostly on online practices of consumption. In this section I want to focus more on production of new media by racialised groups – or 'creatives of colour' – which in turn sheds new light on the inner workings of the postcolonial cultural economy.

By new media content I am referring to podcasts (Florini, 2015; Vrikki and Malik, 2019), web series (Christian, 2011; Day and Christian, 2017), blogs (Brock et al., 2010) and YouTube videos (James, 2015; Hedge, 2016; Sobande, 2017). Using the frame of subaltern counterpublics, Vrikki and Malik (2019) provide a neat overview of the value of this new media, in terms of giving voice to the marginalised, providing them with the autonomy to tell their stories, and in doing so, allowing them to expose inequalities that exist in society. Research on this topic has focused on the cultural politics of the new self-produced media in three ways. Firstly, is how such media create alternative spaces for racialised groups beyond mainstream media. Digital race scholar Andre Brock (2012) draws parallels between the Black women weblogs of his study and black women beauty salons, where conversations are kept within a space beyond the ears of the people outside. Sobande (2017) similarly finds that YouTube videos made by black women give access to the 'backstage' of those black women's lives. Even though the women in the study who consume these 'vlogs' understand that they are staged (and commercialised), they describe how they nonetheless feel authentic and real (see also Hedge (2016) on South Asian women food blogs). Secondly, the self-produced media of racialised groups online frequently draws attention to social justice issues. In their study of black and Asian podcasters in Britain, Vrikki and Malik (2019: 280–281) describe how such podcasts have strong interactions with activism, describing 'a symbiotic relationship between the current wave of black and Asian youth-led podcasts and forms of anti-racist resistance in the UK'. In this way, this *new* new media proliferates anti-racist discourse. Thirdly, the media referenced allow intersectional voices to flourish in particular (Vrikki and Malik, 2019). The work of Aymar Jean Christian, media scholar and founder of Open TV, an online platform for intersectional television, provides a highly original empirical insight into how queer/black filmmakers use online streaming platforms to tell their stories. Christian et al. (2020) innovate the term 'platforming intersectionality' to describe how such platforms allow identities that were previously invisible to emerge. Web series work with very different logics and speak directly to audiences without the need to appease advertisers, conform to formats or even chase ratings. This allows them to produce more socially conscious programming as well as to give voice to formally disavowed voices (Day and Christian, 2017).

What I find valuable in the research referenced is how the authors are all careful not to make utopian pronouncements about the digital. For instance, Christian et al. (2020) make the crucial point that the success of intersectional television depends upon offline queer communities and not just online ones. Moreover, each of the studies referenced in some way demonstrates how these new media are not necessarily anti-corporate/commercial, and in doing so they provide a nuanced account of the relationship between these digital spaces and capitalism. Indeed, the new generation of minority digital production often struggle to make money unless they deal with corporate media. As Vrikki and Malik (2019: 284) state in relation to their empirical study of black and Asian podcasters, 'Even if this counterpublic makes possible alternative forms of self-representation, this does not equate to a state of equality'. They find that while podcasters are happy to operate on the margins in terms of having the freedom to create communities beyond the white gaze, this in effect limits their ability to 'crossover'. As a consequence, many podcasters look for sponsorship deals or join podcasting networks that are run by the same white gatekeepers as are found in traditional media. In this way they fall foul of the same inequalities that blight mainstream creative and cultural industries.

Essentially, we need to avoid a romanticised narrative around these alternative media that over-determines their autonomy or resistance. Indeed, what the postcolonial cultural economy approach highlights are the interactions between racial ideology *and* capitalism which shape race-making practices online. As Hedge (2016: 85) shows, the production of culture online appears organic and grassroots, and to an extent it is, but it is also 'embedded within the market logics of a digital economy and a culture of individuation'. Referring to her study of South Asian women migrants who write food blogs, sharing recipes with members of the diaspora, but also connecting (or hoping to connect) with the wider community of food bloggers, immediately implicates these women within 'an entrepreneurial frame of communicative capitalism where every recipe and post is likely to be counted or rated for its popularity and circulatory muscle' (ibid.: 84). So despite the community's best interests, 'it is coaxed into formation and regulated by algorithms, aggregators, and technical manipulations' (ibid.: 84). As Sobande et al. (2019) acknowledge, online embodiment can be empowering for the racialised Other, but it involves producing social media content for free, from which huge media companies profit. Moreover, as a further fulfilment of racial neoliberal ideology, individuals create their racial/gender/sexual identities in a way that connects to marketing/branding strategies. As Sobande et al. (2019: 10) state, 'digital environments can simultaneously aid and limit potentially oppositional media practices; stressing the restricted nature of online experiences that may be regarded as liberating'. Returning to the question of anti-racism online, Noble (2013: 12) makes a particularly salient point about how (racialised) identity operates 'in a dialectical tension between the struggle for social justice organised around collective identities and histories, and the commercialisation and ownership of such identities to sell products, services, and ideologies for profit'. This is the nature of race-making in the context of racial neoliberalism. Digital environments *do* offer new potential routes and opportunities for creatives of colour. But much like 'traditional' media, the outcomes are always ambivalent.

BOX 10.1 Case Study

Black Twitter: A way of making race that contributes to its undoing…

The emphasis that I have placed on ambivalence throughout this book is not to simply say that anything goes with regard to race, culture and media. Rather, the purpose is to turn our attention from the question of whether 'race' is being represented correctly to what is an articulation of race doing in a particular moment. This is illustrated by the phenomenon of *Black Twitter*. Black Twitter stems from the curious fact that black people in America are a disproportionately large presence on Twitter (see Brock, 2012). Black Twitter is an online community where black users tweet to each other about news and popular culture using a very particular black American vernacular (although this has become more international in recent times). Involving inventive memes and hashtags, Black Twitter is both critical, tragic, radical and hilarious. Very often these hashtags become dominant trending topics on Twitter. Unsurprisingly, many digital researchers refer to Black Twitter as an exemplary counter public (Graham and Smith, 2016; Hill, 2018; Kuo, 2018).

It is tempting to approach the topic of Black Twitter in terms of the extent to which it represents the authentic expression of black people, or more simply, in terms of the question: what makes Black Twitter *black*, but again, this in some ways is the wrong question. Instead, a more generative question is to ask what is Black Twitter *doing*? For Andre Brock (2012: 531), Black Twitter's online articulations of Black discursive culture illustrate both how culture shapes online social interactions and how Twitter's interface and discursive conventions 'helped to frame external perceptions of Black Twitter as a social public'. He makes this argument through a study of the hashtag. Firstly, he finds that it is an expression of signifyin', often based around explicitly Black American references that in turn invites participation from closely affiliated and linked members of the same community (which help hashtags spread, or indeed trend quickly). Secondly, hashtags additionally allow the mainstream to 'peer in' and see black discourse unfold (without much care from Black Twitter itself, the users of which are not performing for the mainstream gaze). Thirdly, in the context of Black Twitter, hashtags are racialised – or indeed become signifyin' hashtags – which effectively 'set the parameters of the discourse to follow' (ibid.: 538). What unfolds is a form of antiphony – or call and response – a particular characteristic of Black Atlantic cultural traditions (see Gilroy, 1993). In this way Black Twitter, shaped by history and enacted through the architecture of Twitter, is defiantly *anti-postrace*.

Sanjay Sharma (2013: 54), based on his study of racial hashtags – or what he calls 'Blacktags' – conceptualises the term 'digital-race assemblage' as an alternative way to approaching – or rather, evading – the question of whether Black Twitter is the authentic expression of black people or not. As he argues, 'Understanding race as an "assemblage" acknowledges the oppressive force of racial categorisation and the violence of racism, yet seeks to activate the potential of race to become otherwise' (ibid.: 54). Therefore, the cultural politics of Black Twitter is not about the politics of representation but instead focuses on how race is being made through technology, and how web 2.0 (its related devices, its interfaces, its discursive conventions) enables us to articulate our racial/gendered/sexual identities in potentially disruptive ways. When it spills into the offline social world, these racialised articulations can lead to new forms of becoming. So when thinking through the cultural significance

(Continued)

of Black Twitter, Sharma argues that it is not because of the 'idiosyncratic set of eth-
noracial dispositions' supposedly associated with black people in the US (as this
would veer dangerously close to essentialism), but rather it is down to the 'array of
qualities and connections *vis-à-vis* the technocultural assemblages of Twitter' (ibid.: 61).
To put it more simply, what makes Blacktags 'black' or whether they are 'radical' is not
really the point. Instead, it's about what makes them go viral, or what makes them 'contagious digital objects' (ibid.: 62), or once again, *what they are doing*. In turn, this leads
us to think through how Blacktags are made and enabled technologically. For Sharma,
Blacktags, rather than fully liberatory, 'interrupt the whiteness of the Twitter network'
(ibid.: 63), which invariably spills into reality. Therefore, drawing from Brock and Sharma,
studying the practices of a particular group of black people online on Twitter provides an
illustration of how digital media make race. More significantly, in my view, their analyses
show us how race-making practices online can contribute to the very undoing of race.

10.4 Conclusion

The purpose of this chapter has been to show the particular nature of race-making
practices online. It is tempting to assume that the making of race online replicates
what happens offline, if only for the reason that you cannot divorce what happens in
the digital world from the 'real' – the digital practices of racialised groups in particular are always embedded in the social world, especially in their urban contexts (see
Georgiou, 2013; Leurs, 2014; James, 2015). However, there's something very distinct
about what digital technologies – and the internet specifically – do to race. Drawing
from Ruha Benjamin's (2019) work, racism and race-thinking from the 'real' world is
the input, which the internet turns into distinct outputs. To illustrate this argument,
this chapter included a discussion of the structure of the internet (including the
political economy of social media), digital diasporic communities and the new media
being produced by racialised Others on the digital platforms of web 2.0. The underlying argument of the chapter is that web 2.0, through which so much of our digital
production/consumption now takes place, is shaped by racial neoliberalism, which
in turn shapes race-making practices. But racial neoliberalism takes a particular form
online. To begin with, rather than postrace, social media encourages the expression
of clearly defined, racial/ethnic identities as they are easier to put into niches that
can be monetised in the form of targeted advertising. Moreover, online media rely
upon the constant churn of content, which explains huge tech companies' lacklustre
policing of online racism, since the commentary and counter-commentary generated provides likes and tweets that again can be monetised.

As digital technologies evolve, this will give researchers a wealth of new case studies to explore. But it is crucial in my view that future research into digital race/racism
always situates its analysis within the context of racial neoliberalism in order to better understand racialising dynamics as they unfold online. There is a tendency in my
view to overstate or over-valorise the online practices of racial and ethnic minorities,

especially in a context where social justice discourse on social media feeds tech companies rather than challenges them. Obviously, the picture is much more complicated than that, in which case the ambivalence of such practices needs more unpacking – against the backdrop of racial neoliberalism. The value of the postcolonial cultural economy approach in this regard is how it takes seriously the dynamics of production, distribution and consumption together as well as questions of ideology and the political-economic, placing particular phenomenon in their historical context.

10.5 Recommended and further reading

One of the key figures in digital race studies is Lisa Nakamura, including her books *Digitizing Race: Visual Cultures of the Internet* (2008) and *Cybertypes: Race, Ethnicity, and Identity on the Internet* (2013 [2002]). Nakamura's work will be of particular interest to those interested in the visual making of race online.

There has been a spike in books published in recent years that have examined the racialised architecture of web 2.0. Many of these were referenced in this chapter and are worthy of deeper engagement, specifically, *Algorithms of Oppression: How Search Engines Reinforce Racism* by Safiya Noble (2018), *Race after Technology* by Ruha Benjamin (2019) and *Black Software: The Internet & Racial Justice, from the AfroNet to Black Lives Matter* by Charlton McIlwain (2019). McIlwain's book in particular gives a fascinating, in-depth history of the black presence in the development of online technology since the computer revolution of the 1960s.

One topic I did not address in this chapter was far-right activism. Sociologist Les Back (2002) was the first to coin the concept of 'cyber-racism' in his study of white nationalism online. Jessie Daniels' book (2009) *Cyber Racism: White Supremacy Online and the New Attack on Civil Rights* is another study of online manifestations of white supremacy, based on a study of teenager interactions with 'cloaked' far-right websites, in terms of the question of media literacy (finding that youth switch between cloaked sites and legitimate sites while not always recognising the difference).

Throughout this chapter I have referred to 'offline' and 'online', 'real' and 'virtual' worlds through gritted teeth, as the distinction is much more blurry than that. The various works of Koen Leurs and his colleagues referenced in the chapter do an important job of situating online practices in everyday life. Providing a particularly interesting case study in this regard is sociologist/cultural studies researcher Malcolm James (2015) and his ethnography of young people in an east London youth club who produce a controversial grime video which is then posted online and circulated within the community with potentially dangerous ramifications for the producers. This example demonstrates how real life and online worlds spill into each other and provides yet another important example of how race-making practices – in terms of production as well as consumption – need to be situated within their urban contexts.

BOX 10.2   Key Issue

Digital divide?

It might surprise some readers that I have not framed this chapter's discussion of online racial inequalities in terms of the well-known concept of 'digital divide'. Why not do so?

In 2011 Nigerian-American author Teju Cole tweeted a response to the trending hashtag #firstworldproblems. Compiled together his message was as follows:

> I don't like this expression 'First World problems.' It is false and it is condescending. Yes, Nigerians struggle with floods or infant mortality. But these same Nigerians also deal with mundane and seemingly luxurious hassles. Connectivity issues on your BlackBerry, cost of car repair, how to sync your iPad, what brand of noodles to buy: Third World problems. All the silly stuff of life doesn't disappear just because you're black and live in a poorer country. People in the richer nations need a more robust sense of the lives being lived in the darker nations. Here's a First World problem: the inability to see that others are as fully complex and as keen on technology and pleasure as you are. (Quoted in Madrigal, 2011)

Cole's series of tweets raise interesting questions about the 'digital divide'. Digital divide refers to inequalities in access to digital technologies, between global north/south and white/black (intersected by class, gender and age in particular). Such inequalities exist in terms of access to technology and digital literacy and, fundamentally, who has access to information and who does not. As suggested, the 'digital divide' has particular ramifications for racialised groups (Leurs, 2012; Daniels, 2013).

While the notion of 'digital divide' on the surface seems grounded in social justice, it has its limitations. To begin with, it is far too simplistic. For instance, black youth use mobile technologies more than their white counterparts but may experience lack of access in the digital spheres of education and economics (Nakamura and Chow-White, 2012). More problematically, digital divide literature relies on fairly essentialist views of the global south, as Cole's tweets allude to, as well as racialised groups (Daniels, 2013). For Brock et al. (2010), digital divide is often discussed in terms of digital illiteracy, which in turn has a civilising tone; the *civilised* have a natural affinity with technology, whereas the *uncivilised* (racialised) masses do not have the same sophistication or intelligence.

Digital divide rhetoric in the context of social research also produces problems in that it makes race/ethnicity a causal variable in research into inequalities in digital access, which ignores critical context. Jessie Daniels (2013) critically examines a common discourse that Asian Americans are more wired while other minorities are less so, arguing that it problematically 'conceptualises race as a causal variable in Internet studies in ways that replay the spectacle of the Other while reaffirming whiteness as normative' (ibid.: 70). In other words, such conceptualisations merely reinforce the idea of the internet as normatively *white*, which white people can navigate unfettered.

Fundamentally, the notion of 'digital divide' assumes that digital technology is unambiguously good (Nakamura and Chow-White, 2012). As this chapter demonstrates, having access to online technologies can be dangerous for certain groups, limiting their access to services and goods, or putting them under surveillance in the name of

(Continued)

security. Either way 'digital divide' should be treated as a discourse that we approach critically, rather than the normative terms in which we explore racial inequalities in the digital realm.

Discussion

Considering the limitations of the concept of 'digital divide' as discussed, how should we measure digital inequalities with regard to race? What dimensions/manifestations of inequality should be considered?

11
Conclusion

In the case studies that made up Part III we explored the different dimensions that shape how media makes race in each of these contexts. This was enabled by what I define as the postcolonial cultural economy approach to race, culture and media. To conclude this book, I want to briefly recap what I mean by postcolonial cultural economy, which describes both the object of analysis and a theoretical framework. I then revisit one of the key ideas of the book: the shift from an analysis of *how media represent race* to *how media make race*. The purpose is to reiterate the value of such a reframing, specifically in terms of what it means for race, media and social justice.

11.1 Recap: Postcolonial cultural economy

Postcolonial cultural economy is a theoretical framework, but more broadly can be used to explain the media context through which race – specifically, meanings of race – are made. As I outlined in Part II of the book, there are a number of structural forces that come together to shape this terrain.

The first are legacies of empire, the root of which, in the context of the West, is where the modern idea of race first emerges. This explains the consistency in the ways that racialised Others are represented in media throughout history – constrained within a binary system that was first set in place during colonialism – although we need to recognise that new forms and meanings around race emerge at different moments in time (and as such we also need to be careful about proclaiming that contemporary representations of race spring directly out of the colonial moment).

The second structural force I explored was capitalism, and specifically racial capitalism. This understands that the development of capitalism – where colonialism played a central rather than incidental role – relied upon both the economic exploitation and the racial subjugation (including both disavowal and cultural stigmatisation) of the Other. The material and cultural domination of racialised groups continues into the current conjuncture, but this time with neoliberalism the main form of governance. Racial neoliberalism in this sense emphasises individualisation, entrepreneurship and private property (which are the terms in which 'diversity' is valorised), as well as the idea that society is now postrace, leading to the denial of racism as a structural inequality.

The third force is nationalism. This is shaped by the history of empire, but also globalisation and counter-currents of cosmopolitanism/multiculturalism. In the context of global capitalism, borders are porous when it comes to commodities, information and finance, but hardened when it comes to the flow of people, specifically those from the *darker nations*. The right-wing nationalists who have come into ascendency in the Anglophone nations are caught in-between a desire for unfettered capitalism (including the exploitation of cheap labour home and abroad) and a desire to protect the (racial) purity of the nation. Despite national efforts to curb entry, globalisation has made populations more diverse, and governments have had to implement various types of multicultural policies – including in the media sphere – in order to manage the increasing heterogeneity of the nation, but in a way that keeps the dominant culture in place.

The fourth structuring force I defined are media themselves. Most Western nations have a mixed media system consisting of commercial media and public service media (PSM). In the shift towards neoliberal policies, these media systems – including PSM – have become more marketisted and commercially-driven. This affects race-making practices, for instance in the shift from multicultural policy to *cultural/creative diversity* policy, which in turn is shaped by the interplay between legacies of empire, capitalism and nationalism/multiculturalism. But the reason that I treat media as an independent force is because of the distinctiveness of cultural production that contains its own logics (in contrast to other forms of industrial production, which broadly speaking share the same form), based upon the particular nature of the cultural commodity and its unique use value: originality and novelty. Thus, media production is characterised by a tension between, on the one hand, standardisation and homogenisation (as this keeps costs down) and, on the other hand, innovation/experimentation (in order to create original symbolic content). This shapes the making of race in very particular ways.

A fifth structuring force that was not included in Part II but was explored in Chapter 10 was technology, specifically digital technology. This includes the internet, through which so much of our media consumption takes place. As was demonstrated, this is a determining force upon race-making practices, specifically in the way that the very architecture of web 2.0 contains racialising dynamics. New digital technologies effectively take (racial) input from the material world and create new (racialised) outputs which in turn feed back into the material world.

Each of these structuring forces *determines* (in terms of setting limits/exerting pressures upon) race-making practices in media. But in each of the chapters I stressed ambivalence, whether it is the inherent instability of colonial discourse, the inevitable 'emergent tendencies' of race within capitalism, the possibilities of conviviality in the context of nationalism, or the structural need for difference intrinsic to media. Moreover, these forces always have a potential opposing force – people themselves. The media practices of individuals and communities may involve active resistance, contestation or rejection, or consuming and using media texts in ways that are radically different from the producer's original intentions. While the structuring forces outlined may ensure consistency in the ideological make-up of media content (although we should also recognise the potential for contradiction), the meanings transcoded in a single text multiply and proliferate the moment that text enters the social world. One particular meaning may remain dominant but we should not discount the 'ability for oppressed peoples to exercise agency in producing cultural forms that provide pleasure, entertainment, and fecund meanings that may not be apparent to the outside observer' (Hesmondhalgh and Saha, 2013: 190). As such, throughout this book I wanted to underline the relative stability of racial ideology which ensures that the broad meaning of race stays consistent throughout history, but to stress also the complexity of media culture in doing so. For some, this runs the risk of blunting the critique of media, but doing justice to this complexity will in fact sharpen our arguments.

While the above outlines postcolonial cultural economy as the space where race-making practices take place, it also describes a broad framework. This is a multidimensional approach that has three facets. First, it takes equally seriously structure and agency. In this book I have emphasised the influence of structural forces without slipping into structural determinism. Instead, the postcolonial cultural economy approach pays attention to the agency of cultural producers and audiences/communities, hence the emphasis on contestation.

Second, is the equal emphasis on production, texts and consumption. Studies of race and media focus mostly on the text and the question of representation, but this can only tell part of the story of how media make race. The postcolonial cultural economy approach advocates a contextual approach to the textual. Since the process of communication in media is primarily symbolic, unpacking and analysing these symbols in the form of media texts will naturally remain a key concern. But it is a mistake to assume that the production of meaning is a straightforward reflection of its producer. In fact, studying production contexts illuminates how exactly racial ideologies reproduce within media (and how they can be challenged) – knowledge that is beyond the scope of studies of representational politics. Moreover, media texts, as stated, can be read in multiple ways by different audiences. Sometimes texts that represent race in the most crude or reductive ways can provide pleasure and in fact be a source of rich meaning and empowerment for those very groups being represented.

Third, the postcolonial cultural economy approach is historical. At times I have referred to this as a conjunctural approach, which is associated with a particular Marxist method. Essentially, this aspect of the postcolonial cultural economy necessitates that studies of race-making practices are placed within their historical context, that is, the specific conditions of a particular historical moment within a given social formation. Racism, rather than being intrinsic to capitalism, as is sometimes mistakenly assumed, is contingent on wider historical forces – indeed, the forces I outline above. At various historical moments these forces will come together in particular ways, overlapping or contradicting each other, with some growing more powerful or influential over others. As such, a historical approach to race and media in this current moment needs to situate its analysis within the context of racial neoliberalism, the ideology of postrace and the ascendency of 'diversity' discourse. I would add that this approach not only illuminates the nature of racism in a given moment, but can also be equally revealing about media and its role in society in a general sense.

11.2 Revisiting: Media make race

One of the key arguments of this book is that any analysis of race, media and culture needs to shift from the question around how media represent race to *how media make race*. This is an explicit nod towards the constructivist idea of race that a critical cultural approach brings to bear upon the analysis of race and media. But it more directly comes out of a critique of the way that representation tends to be conceptualised in both race and media studies and activism. This returns to the point made in Chapter 1 regarding race, media and social justice.

When Stuart Hall originally started articulating the 'politics of representation' he did so in terms of this constructivist idea of race. In his 'New Ethnicities' essay, Hall (1988: 28) argues that a new generation of black and Asian cultural producers and artists had forced a (welcome) shift towards a new mode of representation where it is no longer about correcting negative representations of a particular racialised group, but is instead articulating *new* ethnic and racial identities that transcend cultural essentialisms and ethnic absolutisms. This argument is captured in a key passage from that essay that is worth quoting in full:

> Once you enter the politics of the end of the essential black subject you are plunged headlong into the maelstrom of a continuously contingent, unguaranteed, political argument and debate: a critical politics, a politics of criticism. You can no longer conduct black politics through the strategy of a simple set of reversals, putting in the place of the bad old essential white subject, the new essentially good black subject. Now, that formulation may seem to threaten the collapse of an entire political world. Alternatively, it may be greeted with extraordinary relief at the passing away of what at one time seemed to be a necessary fiction. … This does not make it any easier to conceive of how a politics can be constructed which works with and through difference, which is able to build those forms of solidarity and identification which make common struggle and resistance possible but without suppressing the real

heterogeneity of interests and identities, and which can effectively draw the political boundary lines without which political contestation is impossible, without fixing those boundaries for eternity. It entails the movement in black politics, from what Gramsci called the 'war of manoeuvre' to the 'war of position' – the struggle around positionalities. But the difficulty of conceptualizing such a politics (and the temptation to slip into a sort of endlessly sliding discursive liberal-pluralism) does not absolve us of the task of developing such a politics. (ibid.)

I finish this book with this quote to make the point that Hall might have been a little premature in assuming that a shift had already occurred. Instead, as Herman Gray (2013a) points out, we find an ongoing tendency to conceptualise representation in terms of a lack – whether in relation to visibility or the supposed accuracy of a portrayal. This is particularly evident in social media and other online forums where big film studios, television networks or publishing houses are called out for either the lack of diversity in their latest production or the stereotypical manner in which particular groups are being represented. But with regard to diversity, while it would be nice to see more black and Asian talent being recognised at the BAFTAs, if this is the extent of work around the politics of recognition, then this feels like a failure. With regard to critiques of representation of racial minorities, the application of normative terms like negative/positive, stereotypical/authentic, biased/truthful fails to capture the complexity of representational politics, as Hall highlights above, and the way in which the production of racial meaning is produced and circulates in society.

While the concept of representation by itself is not problematic, the way it is operationalised in discourse around race, media and social justice *is*. As Gavan Titley (2019) astutely highlights, in postrace times, where racism is no longer a social fact but something to be debated, the politics of representation, by which I mean the discourse typically found on social media based around ongoing critique and counter-critique over whether, say a particular television show, 'is racist' or not, has itself become media content that is then monetised by major tech companies. Put another way, the way in which the politics of representation is conducted online, in particular, has itself become commodified. This, I am saddened to say, is being fed by people with genuine concerns over the injustices that media depictions of race bring.

It is for this reason that we need to re-orientate our critical work around a notion of *how media make race*. Such a re-framing immediately draws attention to how race is not only a social construct, but how the construction of race is a process that is always ongoing. It also draws attention to the production *and* consumption of media, and how race is made in these social worlds, beyond the confines of the text. Moreover, an additional value of the frame *how media make race* is that it is explicitly anti-essentialist. In this book I have urged caution over the use of the term stereotype, and have deliberately avoided the question of cultural appropriation that is often the catalyst for racism as reduced to debate. The reason being is that both notions, if handled improperly, assume that behind every media representation is an authentic, fully realised (essential) racial subject. Cultural appropriation, in particular, assumes that racial identities or culture exist in an authentic pure state before it is cynically exploited by the dominant culture. It also contains within it assumptions about culture as property, something that certain groups have owner-ship over, who have the right to restrict its use to other groups. While we should be absolutely alert to and critical of the ways that the dominant culture in the context of corporate media mine the margins in order to extract surplus value, the discourse of cultural appropriation does not do justice to the way that culture actually works (which is why I frame this particular phenomenon in terms of commodification that better captures the complexity of this exploitative process). Instead of getting caught up in debates over cultural appropriation on social media (which becomes the free content that tech companies lap up), we should instead be asking, how is race being made in this particular instance? How exactly is race being exploited and what new meanings about race are being created?

The potential danger with this approach is that it reduces politics to the level of critique, and nothing more. On the one hand, as the final half of the Hall quote above suggests, the stress on contingency that the idea of *media make race* brings potentially slips into an 'endlessly sliding discursive liberal-pluralism' that basically says race can mean anything and everything depending on context. But on the other hand, if we adopt too strong a normative position on race, we end up reifying the very categories that we are trying to destabilise. But as Hall suggests at the end of the quote, just because the development of a coherent cultural politics of race is difficult does not mean we should not at least try. One route out of this conundrum that was suggested earlier is that we focus on strategies that *make race in a way that contributes to the very undoing of race*. This in some ways fulfils the requirements of the decolonial project as the task is not about finding a way to represent race 'correctly' or 'better' (a move that I have tried to problematise in every way) or calling for the removal of race totally from media narratives in order to halt racial discourse, but exposing (in order to start the process of dismantling) the structures of knowledge that produce the very idea of race. The emphasis on contingency that a critical cultural approach brings highlights how there is no right way to make race (as it all depends on context), but how there are a wide variety of aesthetic strategies that can contribute to its undoing.

A politics based around how media make race also draws attention to the need to fix inequalities in production and consumption. In recent years we have seen the ascendency of diversity discourse in creative and cultural industries, based on the recognition that racialised groups in particular are excluded from cultural produc-tion. The same applies to the field of consumption, where minoritised groups do not have the same access to media, or have to deal with media that does not value them as audiences, economically or culturally. While I have problematised the concept of 'diversity' in this book, the inequalities that I refer to take us beyond the question of aesthetic strategies and into the formulation of structural solutions, including at the level of political economy. This includes forms of regulation that afford minoritised groups greater access to the means of cultural production and ensure that they have creative autonomy to tell the stories they want to tell), and also financial and infra-structural support for cultural distribution which guarantees everyone has access to media/arts and no communities are left out.

To reiterate, there is no right way to represent race in media. But that does not mean there is no need for a politics of race-making. Media in the West are scarred by racism, and in turn, they contribute to the maintenance of racial hierarchies that not only reduce the life-chances of minorities but also prevent them from truly flourish-ing. As I have stressed in this book, however, how media reproduce racial ideologies is far from a straightforward process. Not only is it complex, but it is always under contestation from producers who are striving to transform the narratives of differ-ence, and audiences who, while presented with a limited palette, have the agency and creativity to transform media into material that can nourish and nurture and contribute to survival. A politics of race-making involves transforming media to make it a truly democratic sphere where everyone can participate. Media is not just about dissemination or distraction but difference itself. To paraphrase Stuart Hall, media is the theatre or forum where difference is both articulated and to be worked out. The challenge is to ensure that is open to all to participate in freely.

References

Abdalla, M. and Rane, H. 2007. *The impact of media representations on the understanding of Islam and attitudes toward Muslims in Queensland.* Griffith Islamic Research Unit, Griffith University for Multicultural Affairs, Queensland.

Adjepong, A. 2019. Voetsek! Get[ting] lost: African sportswomen in 'the sporting black diaspora'. *International Review for the Sociology of Sport.*

Ahmed, S. 2006. The media consumption of young British muslims. In E. Poole and J. E. Richardson, eds., *Muslims and the news media.* London: I.B. Tauris, pp. 167–175.

Ahmed, S. and Matthes, J. 2017. Media representation of Muslims and Islam from 2000 to 2015: A meta-analysis. *International Communication Gazette*, 79(3), pp. 219–244.

Alexander, C. 2002. Beyond black: Re-thinking the colour/culture divide. *Ethnic and Racial Studies*, 25(4), pp. 552–571.

Alexander, C. 2006. Introduction: Mapping the issues. *Ethnic and Racial Studies*, 29(3), pp. 397–410.

Alexander, C. 2017. Raceing Islamophobia. In F. Elahi and O. Khan, eds., *Islamophobia: Still a challenge for us all.* London: Runnymede, pp. 13–17.

Alexander, C. 2018. Breaking black: The death of ethnic and racial studies in Britain. *Ethnic and Racial Studies*, 41(6), pp. 1034–1054.

Alhassan, A. and Chakravartty, P. 2011. Postcolonial media policy under the long shadow of empire. In R. Mansell and M. Raboy, eds., *The handbook of global media and communication policy.* Oxford: Wiley-Blackwell, pp. 366–382.

Alim, H.S. 2006. Re-inventing Islam with unique modern tones: Muslim hip hop artists as verbal Mujahidin. *Souls*, 8(4), pp. 45–58.

Alsultany, E. 2012. *Arabs and Muslims in the media: Race and representation after 9/11.* New York and London: New York University Press.

Althusser, L. 2006 [1971]. Ideology and ideological state apparatuses (notes towards an investigation). In A. Sharma and A. Gupta, eds., *The anthropology of the state: A reader.* Oxford: Blackwell Publishing, pp. 86–111.

Amin, A. 2013. Full article: Land of strangers. *Identities: Global Studies in Culture and Power*, 20(1), pp. 1–8.

Anderson, B. 1983. *Imagined communities.* London: Verso.

Appadurai, A. 1990. Disjuncture and difference in the global cultural economy. *Theory, Culture & Society*, 7(2–3), pp. 295–310.

Augoustinos, M. and Every, D. 2007. The language of 'race' and prejudice: A discourse of denial, reason, and liberal-practical politics. *Journal of Language and Social Psychology*, 26(2), pp. 123–141.

Back, L. 1995. X amount of Sat Siri Akal! Apache Indian, reggae music and intermezzo culture. In *Negotiating identities: Essays on immigration and culture in present-day Europe.* Amsterdam: Rodopi, pp. 139–166.

Back, L. 1996. *New ethnicities and urban cultures: Racisms and multiculture in young lives.* Abingdon, UK: Routledge.

Back, L. 2002. Aryans reading Adorno: Cyber-culture and twenty-first-century racism. *Ethnic and Racial Studies*, 25(4), pp. 628–651.

Back, L. 2016. Moving sounds, controlled borders: Asylum and the politics of culture. *Young*, 24(3), pp. 185–203.

Back, L., Keith, M., Khan, A., Shukra, K. and Solomos, J. 2002. The return of assimilationism: Race, multiculturalism and New Labour. *Sociological Research Online*, 7(2), pp. 1–10.

Back, L. and Sinha, S. 2018. *Migrant city*. Abingdon, UK: Routledge.

Back, L. and Solomos, J. 2000. Introduction: Theories of race and racism. In J. Solomos and L. Back, eds., *Theories of race and racism: A reader*. Abingdon, UK, and New York: Routledge, pp. 1–32.

Bailey, O.G. and Harindranath, R. 2005. Racialised 'othering'. In Allan, S. (ed.) *Journalism: critical issues*. Maidenhead: Open University Press.

Bailey, O., Georgiou, M. and Harindranath, R. 2007. Introduction: Exploration of diaspora in the context of media culture. In O. Bailey, M. Georgiou and R. Harindranath, eds., *Transnational lives and the media: Re-imagining diasporas*. Basingstoke: Palgrave Macmillan.

Balaji, M. 2009. Why do good girls have to be bad? The cultural industry's production of the other and the complexities of agency. *Popular Communication*, 7(4), pp. 225–236.

Banet-Weiser, S. 2007. *Kids rule! Nickelodeon and consumer citizenship*. Durham, NC, and London: Duke University Press.

Banet-Weiser, S. and Mukherjee, R. 2012. Introduction: Commodity activism in neoliberal times. In R. Mukherjee and S. Banet-Weiser, eds., *Commodity activism: Cultural resistance in neoliberal times*. New York and London: New York University Press.

Banks, M. 2017. *What is Creative Justice?* CAMEo Research Institute for Cultural and Media Economies, University of Leicester.

Banks, M., Ebrey, J. and Toynbee, J. 2014. *Working lives in black British jazz* [Online]. Manchester: Centre for Research on Socio-Cultural Change. Available from: www.chrishodgkins.co.uk/wp-content/uploads/2015/01/Working-Lives-in-Black-British-Jazz.pdf [accessed 19 April 2017].

Beck, U. 2006. *Cosmopolitan vision*. Cambridge: Polity Press.

Benjamin, R. 2019. *Race after Technology*. Cambridge: Polity Press.

Bennett, S., Ter Wal, J., Lipiński, A., Fabiszak, M. and Krzyżanowski, M. 2013. The representation of third-country nationals in European news discourse: Journalistic perceptions and practices. *Journalism Practice*, 7(3), pp. 248–265.

Bhabha, H.K. 1990. *Nation and narration*. London: Routledge.

Bhabha, H.K. 1994. *The location of culture*. London: Routledge.

Bhambra, G.K. 2007. *Rethinking modernity: Postcolonialism and the sociological imagination* [Online]. Basingstoke: Palgrave Macmillan. Available from: www.britsoc.co.uk/NR/rdonlyres/18372B92-4E78-49E6-84A4-7C0D098841F3/0/PAM2008Winner.pdf [accessed 20 July 2015].

Bhambra, G.K. 2011. Cosmopolitanism and Postcolonial Critique. In M. Rovisco and M. Nowicka, eds., *The Ashgate Research Companion to Cosmopolitanism*. London: Routledge, pp. 313–328.

Bhambra, G.K., Nisancioglu, K. and Gebrial, D. 2018. Introduction: Decolonising the university. In G.K. Bhambra, K. Nisancioglu and D. Gebrial, eds., *Decolonising the university*. London: Pluto Press.

Bhattacharyya, G. 2018. *Rethinking racial capitalism: Questions of reproduction and survival*. London: Rowman & Littlefield International.

Billig, M. 1995. *Banal nationalism*. London: Sage.

Bobo, L. 1988. The Colour Purple: Black women as cultural readers. In D.J. Pribam, ed., *Female spectators: Looking at films and television*. London: Verso.

Born, G. 2005. Digitising democracy. *Political Quarterly*, 76(1), pp. 102–123.

Born, G. 2013. Mediating the public sphere: Digitization, pluralism and communicative democracy. In C. Emden and D. Midgley, eds., *Beyond Habermas: Democracy, knowledge, and the public sphere*. Oxford: Berghahn Books, pp. 119–146.

Born, G. and Hesmondhalgh, D. 2000. Introduction: On difference, representation, and appropriation in music. In G. Born and D. Hesmondhalgh, eds., *Western music and its others: Difference, representation, and appropriation in music*. Berkeley, CA: University of California Press, pp. 1–58.

Brah, A. 1996. *Cartographies of diaspora: Contesting identities*. London: Routledge.

Bramwell, R. 2015. *UK Hip-Hop, Grime and the city: The aesthetics and ethics of London's rap scenes*. London: Routledge.

Brar, D.S. 2015. 'James Brown', 'Jamesbrown', James Brown: Black (music) from the getup. *Popular Music*, 34(3), pp. 471–484.

Brar, D.S. and Sharma, A. 2019. What is this 'Black' in Black Studies?: The transition from Black British Cultural Studies to Black Critical Thought in U.K. arts and higher education. *New Formations*, 99.

Brock, A. 2012. From the blackhand side: Twitter as a cultural conversation. *Journal of Broadcasting & Electronic Media*, 56(4), pp. 529–549.

Brock, A., Kvasny, L. and Hales, K. 2010. Cultural appropriations of technical capital: Black women, weblogs, and the digital divide. *Information, Communication & Society*, 13(7), pp. 1040–1059.

Bunzi, M. 2007. *Anti-Semitism and Islamophobia: Hatreds old and new in Europe*. Chicago, IL: Prickly Paradigm Press.

Burdsey, D. 2016. One guy named Mo: Race, nation and the London 2012 Olympic Games. *Sociology of Sport Journal*, 33(1), pp. 14–25.

Burtenshaw, R. 2012. Raceocracy: An interview with Barnor Hesse – Part 1. *Irish Left Review*. [Online]. Available from: www.irishleftreview.org/2012/10/24/raceocracy/ [accessed 25 March 2019].

Cabanes, J.V.A. 2014. Multicultural mediations, developing world realities: Indians, Koreans and Manila's entertainment media. *Media, Culture & Society*, 36(5), pp. 628–643.

Carney, N. 2016. All lives matter, but so does race: Black Lives Matter and the evolving role of social media. *Humanity & Society*, 40(2), pp. 180–199.

Carr, S.A. 2001. *Hollywood and anti-Semitism: A cultural history up to World War II*. Cambridge: Cambridge University Press.

Carrington, B. 2010. *Race, sport and politics: The sporting black diaspora*. Los Angeles, CA: Sage.

Centre for Contemporary Cultural Studies, ed. 1982. *Empire strikes back: Race and racism in 70s Britain*. London: Centre for Contemporary Cultural Studies and Hutchinson.

Cere, R. 2011. Postcolonial and media studies: A cognitive map. In R. Cere and R. Brunt, eds., *Postcolonial media culture in Britain*. Basingstoke: Palgrave Macmillan, pp. 1–13.

Chakravartty, P. 2006. *Media policy and globalization*. Edinburgh: Edinburgh University Press.

Chakravartty, P., Kuo, R., Grubbs, V. and McIlwain, C. 2018. #CommunicationSoWhite. *Journal of Communication*, 68(2), pp. 254–266.

Chakravartty, P. and Roy, S. 2013. Media pluralism redux: Towards new frameworks of comparative media studies 'beyond the West'. *Political Communication*, 30(3), pp. 349–370.

Chakravartty, P. and Silva, D.F. da 2012. Accumulation, dispossession, and debt: The racial logic of global capitalism – an introduction. *American Quarterly*, 64(3), pp. 361–385.

Chan, D. 2005. Playing with race: The ethics of racialized representations in E-Games. *International Review of Information Ethics*, 4, pp. 24–30.

Chouliaraki, L. and Stolic, T. 2017. Rethinking media responsibility in the refugee 'crisis': A visual typology of European news. *Media, Culture & Society*, 39(8), pp. 1162–1177.

Christensen, M. 2012. Online mediations in transnational spaces: Cosmopolitan (re) formations of belonging and identity in the Turkish diaspora. *Ethnic and Racial Studies*, 35(5), pp. 888–905.

Christensen, M. and Jansson, A. 2015. *Cosmopolitanism and the media: Cartographies of change*. London: Palgrave Macmillan.

Christian, A.J. 2011. Fandom as Industrial Response: Producing Identity in an Independent Web Series. In R.A Reid and S. Gatson, eds., Race and Ethnicity in Fandom [Special issue]. *Transformative Works and Cultures*, 8. https://doi.org/10.3983/twc.2011.0250.

Christian, A.J. 2018. *Open TV: Innovation beyond Hollywood and the rise of web television*. New York: New York University Press.

Christian, A.J., Day, F., Díaz, M. and Peterson-Salahuddin, C. 2020. Platforming intersectionality: Networked solidarity and the limits of platform power. *Social Media and Society*, pp. 1–12.

Cisneros, J.D. and Nakayama, T.K. 2015. New media, old racisms: Twitter, Miss America, and cultural logics of race. *Journal of International and Intercultural Communication*, 8(2), pp. 108–127.

Cloud, D.L. 2004. 'To veil the threat of terror': Afghan women and the <clash of civilizations> in the imagery of the US war on terrorism. *Quarterly Journal of Speech*, 90(3), pp. 285–306.

Cohen, P. 1999. Through a glass darkly: Intellectuals on race. In P. Cohen, ed., *New ethnicities, old racisms?* London: Zed Books.

Cohen, S. 2002. *Folk devils and moral panics: The creation of the mods and rockers.* London: Psychology Press.

Cole, P. 2006. Mixed communities: Mixed newsrooms. In E. Poole and J. E. Richardson, eds., *Muslims and the news media.* London: I.B. Tauris, pp. 63–73.

Comaroff, J.L. and Comaroff, J. 2009. *Ethnicity, Inc.* Chicago, IL, and London: University of Chicago Press.

Conway, K. 2014. Little mosque, small screen: Multicultural broadcasting policy and muslims on television. *Television & New Media*, 15(7), pp. 648–663.

Crang, P., Dwyer, C. and Jackson, P. 2003. Transnationalism and the spaces of commodity culture. *Progress in Human Geography*, 27(4), pp. 438–456.

Daniels, J. 2009. *Cyber racism: White supremacy online and the new attack on civil rights.* Plymouth, MA: Rowman & Littlefield.

Daniels, J. 2013. Race and racism in Internet studies: A review and critique. *New Media & Society*, 15(5), pp. 695–719.

Day, F. and Christian, A.J. 2017. Locating black queer TV: Fans, producers, and networked publics on YouTube. *Transformative Works and Cultures*, 24.

De Beukelaer, C. and Spence, K.-M. 2018. *Global cultural economy.* London: Routledge.

Deuze, M. 2006. Ethnic media, community media and participatory culture. *Journalism*, 7(3), pp. 262–280.

Dirlik, A. 1994. The postcolonial aura: Third World criticism in the age of global capitalism. *Critical Inquiry*, 20(2), pp. 328–356.

Downing, J.D.H. and Husband, C. 2005. *Representing race: Racisms, ethnicity and the media.* London: Sage.

Dreher, T. 2010. Speaking up or being heard? Community media interventions and the politics of listening. *Media, Culture & Society*, 32(1), pp. 85–103.

Dudrah, R. 2006. *Bollywood: Sociology goes to the movies.* London: Sage.

Dwyer, C. and Crang, P. 2002. Fashioning ethnicities: The commercial spaces of multiculture. *Ethnicities*, 2(3), pp. 410–430.

Echchaibi, N. 2013. Muslimah Media Watch: Media activism and Muslim choreographies of social change. *Journalism*, 14(7), pp. 852–867.

El-Enany, N. 2016. Aylan Kurdi: The human refugee. *Law and Critique*, 27(1), pp. 13–15.

Erel, U., Murji, K. and Nahaboo, Z. 2016. Understanding the contemporary race–migration nexus. *Ethnic and Racial Studies*, 39(8), pp. 1339–1360.

Eshun, K. 2018. *More brilliant than the sun: Adventures in sonic fiction.* London: Verso.

Fanon, F. 1986 [1967]. *Black skin, white masks.* London: Pluto Press.

Fanon, F. 2001 [1965]. *The wretched of the earth.* London: Penguin Books.

Fekete, L. 2006. Racial profiling and the war on terror. In E. Poole and J. E. Richardson, eds., *Muslims and the news media.* London: I.B. Tauris, pp. 35–44.

Fish, S. 1997. Boutique multiculturalism, or why liberals are incapable of thinking about hate speech. *Critical Inquiry*, 23(2), pp. 378–395.

Fitts, M. 2008. 'Drop it like it's hot': Culture industry laborers and their perspectives on Rap music video production. *Meridians: Feminism, Race, Transnationalism*, 8(1), pp. 211–235.

Florini, S. 2014. Tweets, tweeps, and signifyin' communication and cultural performance on 'Black Twitter'. *Television & New Media*, 15(3), pp. 223–237.

Florini, S. 2015. The podcast 'Chitlin' Circuit': Black podcasters, alternative media, and audio enclaves. *Journal of Radio & Audio Media*, 22(2), pp. 209–219.

Fortier, A.-M. 2006. Pride politics and multiculturalist citizenship. *Ethnic and Racial Studies*, 28(3).

Fox, J.E., Moroşanu, L. and Szilassy, E. 2012. The racialization of the new European migration to the UK. *Sociology*, 46(4), pp. 680–695.

Fraser, N. 2008. Social justice in the age of identity politics. In G. Henderson and M. Waterstone, eds., *Geographic thought: A praxis perspective*. Abingdon, UK: Routledge, pp. 72–91.

Freedman, D. 2014. *The contradictions of media power*. London: Bloomsbury.

Fuller, J. 2010. Branding blackness on US cable television. *Media, Culture & Society*, 32(2), pp. 285–305.

Gaber, I. 2014. The 'othering'of 'Red Ed', or how the *Daily Mail* 'framed' the British Labour leader. *The Political Quarterly*, 85(4), pp. 471–479.

Gandy, O.H. 1998. *Communication and race: A structural perspective*. London: Arnold.

Gardiner, B. 2018. 'It's a terrible way to go to work': What 70 million readers' comments on the *Guardian* revealed about hostility to women and minorities online. *Feminist Media Studies*, 18(4), pp. 592–608.

Garnham, N. 1990. *Capitalism and communication: Global culture and the economics of information*. London: Sage.

Garnham, N. 2000. *Emancipation, the media, and modernity: Arguments about the media and social theory*. Oxford and New York: Oxford University Press.

Gemi, E., Ulasiuk, I. and Triandafyllidou, A. 2013. Migrants and media newsmaking practices. *Journalism Practice*, 7(3), pp. 266–281.

Georgiou, M. 2005. Diasporic media across Europe: Multicultural societies and the universalism–particularism continuum. *Journal of Ethnic and Migration Studies*, 31(3), pp. 481–498.

Georgiou, M. 2007. Transnational crossroads for media and diaspora: Three Challenges for research. In O. Bailey, M. Georgiou and R. Harindranath, eds., *Transnational lives and the media: Re-imagining diasporas*. Basingstoke: Palgrave Macmillan.

Georgiou, M. 2013. *Media and the city: Cosmopolitanism and difference*. Cambridge: Polity Press.

Georgiou, M. 2016. Conviviality is not enough: a communication perspective to the city of difference. *Communication, Culture & Critique*, 10(2), pp. 261–279.

Gilbert, J. 2019. This conjuncture: For Stuart Hall. *New Formations*, 96(96–97), pp. 5–37.

Gillespie, M. 1995. *Television, ethnicity and cultural change*. London: Routledge.

Gilroy, P. 1987. *There ain't no black in the Union Jack*. London: Hutchinson.

Gilroy, P. 1991. Sounds authentic: Black music, ethnicity, and the challenge of a 'changing' same. *Black Music Research Journal*, 11(2), pp. 111–136.

Gilroy, P. 1993. *The Black Atlantic: Modernity and double consciousness*. London: Verso.

Gilroy, P. 2000. *Between camps: Race, identity and nationalism at the end of the colour line*. London: Allen Lane.

Gilroy, P. 2004. *After empire: Melancholia or convivial culture?* Abingdon, UK: Routledge.

Gilroy, P. 2010. *Darker than blue: On the moral economies of black Atlantic culture*. Cambridge, MA: Harvard University Press.

Gilroy, P. 2012. 'My Britain is fuck all': Zombie multiculturalism and the race politics of citizenship. *Identities*, 19(4), pp. 380–397.

Gilroy, P. 2013a. '…We got to get over before we go under…': Fragments for a history of black vernacular neoliberalism. *New Formations*, 80(1), pp. 23–38.

Gilroy, P. 2013b. 1981 and 2011: From social democratic to neoliberal rioting. *South Atlantic Quarterly*, 112(3), pp. 550–558.

Goldberg, D.T. 2009a. *The threat of race: Reflections on racial neoliberalism*. Malden, MA, and Oxford: Wiley-Blackwell.

Goldberg, D.T. 2009b. Racial comparisons, relational racisms: Some thoughts on method. *Ethnic and Racial Studies*, 32(7), pp.1271–1282.

Gordon, A. 2008. *Ghostly matters: Haunting and the sociological imagination*. Minneapolis, MN: University of Minnesota Press.

Graham, R. and Smith, S. 2016. The content of our# characters: Black Twitter as counterpublic. *Sociology of Race and Ethnicity*, 2(4), pp. 433–449.

Gray, H. 1993. Review: Black and white and in color: *Enlightened racism: The Cosby Show, audiences, and the myth of the American Dream* by Sut Jhally and Justin Lewis. *American Quarterly*, 45(3), pp. 467–472.

Gray, H. 1994. Response to Justin Lewis and Sut Jhally. *American Quarterly*, 46(1), pp. 118–121.

Gray, H. 2004. *Watching race: Television and the struggle for Blackness*. Minneapolis, MN: University of Minnesota Press.

Gray, H. 2005. *Cultural moves: African Americans and the politics of representation*. Berkeley, CA: University of California Press.

Gray, H. 2013a. Subject (ed) to recognition. *American Quarterly*, 65(4), pp. 771–798.

Gray, H. 2013b. Race, media, and the cultivation of concern. *Communication and Critical/Cultural Studies*, 10(2–3), pp. 253–258.

Gray, H. 2016. Precarious diversity: Representation and demography. In M. Curtin and K. Sanson, eds., *Precarious creativity*. Oakland, CA: University of California Press, pp. 241–253.

Gray, K.L. 2012. Deviant bodies, stigmatized identities, and racist acts: Examining the experiences of African-American gamers in Xbox Live. *New Review of Hypermedia and Multimedia*, 18(4), pp. 261–276.

Gürses, S., Kundnani, A. and Van Hoboken, J. 2016. Crypto and empire: The contradictions of counter-surveillance advocacy. *Media, Culture & Society*, 38(4), pp. 576–590.

Hall, S. 1972. Encoding/decoding. *Culture, Media, Language: Working Papers in Cultural Studies*, 79, pp. 128–138.

Hall, S. 1980. Race, articulation and societies structured in dominance. In UNESCO, *Sociological theories: Race and colonialism*. Paris: UNESCO, pp. 305–345.

Hall, S. 1981. Notes on deconstructing 'the popular'. In R. Samuel, ed., *People's history and socialist theory (history workshop series)*. London: Routledge & Kegan Paul, pp. 227–239.

Hall, S. 1985. Signification, representation, ideology: Althusser and the post-structuralist debates. *Critical Studies in Media Communication*, 2(2), pp. 91–114.

Hall, S. 1988. New ethnicities. In K. Mercer, ed., *Black film: British cinema*. London: Institute of Contemporary Art, pp. 27–31.

Hall, S. 1992. The West and the rest: Discourse and power. In S. Hall and B. Gieben, eds., *Formations of modernity*. Cambridge, UK: Open University Press/Polity Press, pp. 275–332.

Hall, S. 1995. When was the 'the post-colonial'? Thinking at the limit. In I. Chambers and L. Curti, eds., *The post-colonial question: Common skies, divided horizons*. London: Routledge, pp. 242–260.

Hall, S. 1996. What is this 'black' in black popular culture? In K.-H. Chen and D. Morley, eds., *Stuart Hall: Critical dialogues in cultural studies*. London: Routledge, pp. 468–479.

Hall, S. 1997a. Introduction. In S. Hall, ed., *Representation: Cultural representations and signifying practices*. London: Sage, pp. 1–11.

Hall, S. 1997b. The work of representation. In S. Hall, ed., *Representation: Cultural representations and signifying practices*. London: Sage, pp. 13–74.

Hall, S. 1997c. The spectacle of the other. In S. Hall, ed., *Representation: Cultural representations and signifying practices*. London: Sage, pp. 223–290.

Hall, S. 1997d. Old and new identities, old and new ethnicities. In A.D. King, ed., *Culture, globalization, and the world-system: Contemporary conditions for the representation of identity*. Minneapolis, MN: University of Minnesota Press, pp. 41–68.

Hall, S. 2000. Conclusion: The multi-cultural question. In B. Hesse, ed., *Un/settled multiculturalisms: Diasporas, entanglements, 'transruptions'*. London and New York: Zed Books, pp. 209–241.

Hall, S. 2017a. *Familiar stranger: A life between two islands* (B. Schwarz, ed.). Durham, NC, and London: Duke University Press.

Hall, S. 2017b. *The fateful triangle: Race, ethnicity, nation* (K. Mercer, ed.). Cambridge, MA, and London: Harvard University Press.

Hall, S. 2016. *Cultural studies 1983: A theoretical history* (J. D. Slack & L. Grossberg, eds.). Durham, NC: Duke University Press.

Hall, S., Critcher, C., Jefferson, T., Clarke, J. and Roberts, B. 2013 [1978]. *Policing the crisis: Mugging, the state and law and order*. Basingstoke: Palgrave Macmillan.

Hall, S. and Massey, D. 2010. Interpreting the crisis. *Soundings*, 44, pp. 57–71.

Hardy, J. 2014. *Critical political economy of the media: An introduction*. London: Routledge.

Harindranath, R. 2005. Ethnicity and cultural difference: Some thematic and political issues on global audience research. *Particip@tions: Journal of Audience and Reception Studies*, 2(2); p. 2.

Harindranath, R. 2009. *Audience-citizens: The media, public knowledge, and interpretive practice*. London: Sage.

Hasinoff, A.A. 2008. Fashioning race for the free market on America's next top model. *Critical Studies in Media Communication*, 25(3), pp. 324–343.

Havens, T. 2013. *Black television travels: African American media around the globe*. New York: New York University Press.

Hedge, R. 2016. *Mediating migration*. Cambridge: Polity Press.

Hegde, R.S. and Shome, R. 2002. Postcolonial scholarship – productions and directions: An interview with Gayatri Chakravorty Spivak. *Communication Theory*, 12(3), pp. 271–286.

Herbert, E. (2018) Black British women filmmakers in the digital era: New production strategies and re-presentations of Black womanhood. *Open Cultural Studies*, 2(1), pp. 191–202.

Hesmondhalgh, D. 2018. *The cultural industries* (4th edn). London: Sage.

Hesmondhalgh, D. and Saha, A. 2013. Race, ethnicity, and cultural production. *Popular Communication*, 11(3), pp. 179–195.

Hesse, B. 2000. Introduction. In B. Hesse, ed., *Un/settled multiculturalisms: Diasporas, entanglements, 'transruptions'*. London and New York: Zed Books, pp. 1–30.

Hill, M.L. 2018. 'Thank you, Black Twitter': State violence, digital counterpublics, and pedagogies of resistance. *Urban Education*, 53(2), pp. 286–302.

Hoggart, R. 1957. *The uses of literacy*. London: Chatto and Windus.

Holohan, S. 2006. New Labour, multiculturalism and the media in Britain. In E. Poole and J.E. Richardson, eds., *Muslims and the news media*. London: I.B. Tauris, pp. 13–23.

hooks, bell 1992. *Black looks: Race and representation*. Boston, MA: South End Press.

hooks, bell 2004. *We real cool: Black men and masculinity*. London: Routledge.

Hughey, M.W. and Daniels, J. 2013. Racist comments at online news sites: A methodological dilemma for discourse analysis. *Media, Culture & Society*, 35(3), pp. 332–347.

Hultén, G. 2014. A vulnerable diversity: Perspectives on cultural diversity policies in Swedish public service media. In G. Titley, K. Horsti and G. Hultén, eds., *National conversations: Public service media and cultural diversity in Europe*. Bristol: Intellect Ltd, pp. 147–166.

Hunt, D.M. 1997. *Screening the Los Angeles 'riots': Race, seeing, and resistance*. Cambridge, UK, and New York: Cambridge University Press.

Huq, R. 1996. Asian Kool? Bhangra and beyond. In S. Sharma, J. Hutnyk and A. Sharma, eds., *Dis-orienting rhythms: The politics of the new Asian dance music*. London: Zed Books, pp. 61–80.

Huq, R. 2003. From the margins to mainstream? Representations of British Asian youth musical cultural expression from bhangra to Asian underground music. *Young*, 11(1), pp. 29–48.

Husband, C. 1975. *White media and black Britain: A critical look at the role of the media in race relations today*. London: Arrow.

Ilott, S. 2013. 'We are the martyrs, you're just squashed tomatoes!' Laughing through the fears in postcolonial British comedy: Chris Morris's *Four Lions* and Joe Cornish's *Attack the Block*. *Postcolonial Text*, 8(2), pp. 1–17.

Ilott, S. 2015. *New postcolonial British genres: Shifting the boundaries.* Basingstoke: Palgrave Macmillan.

Jackson, P. 2002. Commercial cultures: Transcending the cultural and the economic. *Progress in Human Geography*, 26(1), pp. 3–18.

Jackson, P., Thomas, N. and Dwyer, C. 2007. Consuming transnational fashion in London and Mumbai. *Geoforum*, 38(5), pp. 908–924.

Jackson, S.J. and Foucault Welles, B. 2015. Hijacking# myNYPD: Social media dissent and networked counterpublics. *Journal of Communication*, 65(6), pp. 932–952.

Jackson, S.J. and Foucault Welles, B. 2016. #Ferguson is everywhere: Initiators in emerging counterpublic networks. *Information, Communication & Society*, 19(3), pp. 397–418.

Jakubowicz, A. 2014. 'And that's goodnight from us': Challenges to public service media in a culturally diverse Europe – an antipodean perspective. In G. Titley, K. Horsti and G. Hultén, eds., *National conversations: Public service media and cultural diversity in Europe*. Bristol: Intellect Ltd, pp. 255–240.

James, M. 2015. Nihilism and urban multiculture in outer East London. *The Sociological Review*, 63(3), pp. 699–719.

Jhally, S. and Lewis, J. 1992. *Enlightened racism: The Cosby Show, audiences, and the myth of the American Dream.* Boulder, CO: Westview Press.

Jones, H., Saltus, R., Dhaliwal, S., Forkert, K., Davies, W., Gunaratnam, Y., Bhattacharyya, G. and Jackson, E. 2017. *Go home? The politics of immigration controversies.* Manchester: Manchester University Press.

Jong, J. de 1998. Cultural diversity and cultural policy in the Netherlands. *International Journal of Cultural Policy*, 4(2), pp. 357–387.

Kapoor, N. 2013. The advancement of racial neoliberalism in Britain. *Ethnic and Racial Studies*, 36(6), pp. 1028–1046.

Kapur, R. 2002. Un-veiling women's rights in the war on terrorism. *Duke Journal of Gender Law & Policy*, 9, p. 211.

Keeling, K. 2007. *The witch's flight: The cinematic, the black femme, and the image of common sense.* Durham, NC: Duke University Press.

Khiabany, G. 2016. Refugee crisis, imperialism and pitiless wars on the poor. *Media, Culture & Society*, 38(5), pp. 755–762.

Khiabany, G. and Williamson, M. 2008. Veiled bodies – naked racism: Culture, politics and race in *The Sun. Race & Class*, 50(2), pp. 69–88.

Kim, H. 2014. *Making diaspora in a global city: South Asian youth cultures in London.* London: Routledge.

King, J. 2014. Is Beyoncé a terrorist? Black feminist scholars debate bell hooks. *Colorlines.* [Online]. Available from: www.colorlines.com/articles/beyonce-terrorist-black-feminist-scholars-debate-bell-hooks [accessed 1 July 2020].

Klein, B. 2011. Entertaining ideas: Social issues in entertainment television. *Media, Culture & Society*, 33(6), pp. 905–921.

Kohnen, M. 2015. Cultural diversity as brand management in cable television. *Media Industries*, 2(2).

Kumar, P. 2018. Rerouting the narrative: Mapping the online identity politics of the Tamil and Palestinian diaspora. *Social Media+ Society*, 4(1), p. 2056305118764429.

Kuo, R. 2018. Racial justice activist hashtags: Counterpublics and discourse circulation. *New Media & Society*, 20(2), pp. 495–514.

Lentin, A. 2017. Decolonising epistemologies. *Alana lentin.net*. [Online]. Available from: www.alanalentin.net/2017/02/10/decolonising-epistemologies/ [accessed 25 January 2019].

Lentin, A. 2020. Coronavirus is the ultimate demonstration of the real-world impact of racism. *The Guardian*. [Online]. Available from: www.theguardian.com/commentisfree/2020/may/12/coronavirus-racism-bame-pandemic-race [accessed 20 May 2020].

Lentin, A. and Titley, G. 2011. *The crises of multiculturalism: Racism in a neoliberal age.* London: Zed Books.

Leonard, D. 2004. High tech blackface: Race, sports, video games and becoming the other. *Intelligent Agent*, 4(4.2).

Leong, N. 2012. Racial capitalism. *Harvard Law Review*, 126(8), pp. 2153–2225.

Leurdijk, A. 2006. In search of common ground: Strategies of multicultural television producers in Europe. *European Journal of Cultural Studies*, 9(1), pp. 25–46.

Leurs, K. 2012. *Digital passages: Moroccan-Dutch youths performing diaspora, gender and youth cultural identities across digital space*. Amsterdam: Amsterdam University Press.

Leurs, K. 2014. Digital throwntogetherness: Young Londoners negotiating urban politics of difference and encounter on Facebook. *Popular Communication*, 12(4), pp. 251–265.

Leurs, K., Midden, E. and Ponzanesi, S. 2012. Digital multiculturalism in the Netherlands: Religious, ethnic and gender positioning by Moroccan-Dutch youth. *Religion and Gender*, 2(1), pp. 150–175.

Leurs, K. and Shepherd, T. 2017. Datafication & discrimination. In M. T. Schäfer and K. van Es, eds., *The datafied society: Studying culture through data*. Amsterdam: Amsterdam University Press, pp. 211–234.

Leurs, K. and Smets, K. 2018. Five questions for digital migration studies: Learning from digital connectivity and forced migration in (to) Europe. *Social Media+ Society*, 4(1), p. 2056305118764425.

Lewis, J. and Jhally, S. 1994. The politics of cultural studies: Racism, hegemony, and resistance. *American Quarterly*, 46(1), pp. 114–117.

Littler, J. 2017. *Against meritocracy: Culture, power and myths of mobility*. London: Routledge.

Lopez, L.K. 2018. Asian American media studies. *Feminist Media Histories*, 4(2), pp. 20–24.

Macdonald, M. 2006. Muslim women and the veil: Problems of image and voice in media representations. *Feminist Media Studies*, 6(1), pp. 7–23.

Macdonald, M. 2011. British Muslims, memory and identity: Representations in British film and television documentary. *European Journal of Cultural Studies*, 14(4), pp. 411–427.

Madianou, M. and Miller, D. 2013. *Migration and new media: Transnational families and polymedia*. London: Routledge.

Madrigal, A.C. 2011. What's wrong with #FirstWorldProblems. *The Atlantic*. [Online]. Available from: www.theatlantic.com/technology/archive/2011/11/whats-wrong-with-firstworldproblems/248829/ [accessed 2 July 2020].

Malik, S. 2002. *Representing Black Britain: A history of Black and Asian images on British television*. London: Sage.

Malik, S. 2013a. 'Creative diversity': UK public service broadcasting after multiculturalism. *Popular Communication*, 11(3), pp. 227–241.

Malik, S. 2013b. The Indian family on UK reality television: Convivial culture in salient contexts. *Television & New Media*, 14(6), pp. 510–528.

Malik, S. 2014. Diversity, broadcasting and the politics of representation. In G. Titley, K. Horsti and G. Hultén, eds., *National conversations: Public service media and cultural diversity in Europe*. Bristol: Intellect Ltd, pp. 21–42.

Malik, S., Chapain, C. and Comunian, R. 2017. Rethinking cultural diversity in the UK film sector: Practices in community filmmaking. *Organization*, 24(3), pp. 308–329.

Malik, S. and Nwonka, C.J. 2017. Top boy: Cultural verisimilitude and the allure of black criminality for UK public service broadcasting drama. *Journal of British Cinema and Television*, 14(4), pp. 423–444.

Malone, A. 2010. Slaughter of the swans: As carcasses pile up and migrant camps are built on river banks, Peterborough residents are too frightened to visit the park. *The Daily Mail*. [Online]. Available at: https://www.dailymail.co.uk/news/article-1261044/Slaughter-swans-As-carcasses-pile-crude-camps-built-river-banks-residents-frightened-visit-park-Peterborough.html [accessed 27 May 2020].

Martin Jr, A.L. 2015. Scripting Black gayness television authorship in Black-cast sitcoms. *Television & New Media*, 16(7), pp. 648–663.

Martin Jr, A.L. 2021. *The generic closet: Black gayness and the Black-cast sitcom.* Bloomington, IN: Indiana University Press.

Matamoros-Fernández, A. 2017. Platformed racism: The mediation and circulation of an Australian race-based controversy on Twitter, Facebook and YouTube. *Information, Communication & Society*, 20(6), pp. 930–946.

Matthews, J. and Brown, A.R. 2012. Negatively shaping the asylum agenda? The representational strategy and impact of a tabloid news campaign. *Journalism*, 13(6), pp. 802–817.

Mayer, V. 2001. From segmented to fragmented: Latino media in San Antonio, Texas. *Journalism & Mass Communication Quarterly*, 78(2), pp. 291–306.

Mayer, V., Banks, M.J. and Caldwell, J.T. 2009. Production studies: Roots and routes. In V. Mayer, M. J. Banks and J. T. Caldwell, eds., *Production Studies: Cultural Studies of Media Industries.* New York: Routledge, pp. 1–12.

McClintock, A. 1995. *Imperial Leather: Race, gender, and sexuality in the colonial contest.* New York: Routledge.

McIlwain, C. 2019. *Black software: The internet & racial justice, from the AfroNet to Black Lives Matter.* Oxford: Oxford University Press.

McLaren, L., Boomgaarden, H. and Vliegenthart, R. 2018. News coverage and public concern about immigration in Britain. *International Journal of Public Opinion Research*, 30(2), pp. 173–193.

McMurray, A. 2008. Hotep and hip-hop: Can Black Muslim women be down with hip-hop? *Meridians*, 8(1), pp. 74–92.

Meer, N. 2013. Racialization and religion: Race, culture and difference in the study of antisemitism and Islamophobia. *Ethnic and Racial Studies*, 36(3), pp. 385–398.

Meer, N., Dwyer, C. and Modood, T. 2010. Beyond 'angry Muslims'? Reporting Muslim voices in the British press. *Journal of Media and Religion*, 9(4), pp. 216–231.

Meer, N. and Nayak, A. 2013. Race ends where? Race, racism and contemporary sociology. *Sociology*, 15 November, p. 0038038513501943.

Melamed, J. 2015. Racial capitalism. *Critical Ethnic Studies*, 1(1), pp. 76–85.

Melville, C. 2019. *It's a London thing: How Rare Groove, Acid House and Jungle remapped the city.* Manchester: Manchester University Press.

Mercer, K. 1994. *Welcome to the jungle: New positions in Black cultural studies.* New York: Routledge.

Miah, S. and Kalra, V.S. 2008. Muslim hip-hop: Politicisation of kool Islam. *South Asian Cultural Studies Journal*, 2(1), pp. 12–25.

Mimura, G.M. 2009. *Ghostlife of third cinema: Asian American film and video.* Minneapolis, MN, and London: University of Minnesota Press.

Mitra, R. and Gajjala, R. 2008. Queer blogging in Indian digital diasporas: A dialogic encounter. *Journal of Communication Inquiry*, 32(4), pp. 400–423.

Modood, T. 1992. *Not easy being British: Colour, culture and citizenship.* London: Runnymede Trust and Trentham Books.

Molina-Guzmán, I. 2006. Mediating Frida: Negotiating discourses of Latina/o authenticity in global media representations of ethnic identity. *Critical Studies in Media Communication*, 23(3), pp. 232–251.

Molina-Guzmán, I. 2013. Commodifying black Latinidad in US film and television. *Popular Communication*, 11(3), pp. 211–226.

Morley, D. 2006. Unanswered questions in audience research. *The Communication Review*, 9(2), pp. 101–121.

Mosco, V. 1996. *The political economy of communication: Rethinking and renewal.* London: Sage.

Moten, F. 2014. *The little edges.* Middletown, CT: Wesleyan University Press.

Mukherjee, R. 2011. Bling fling: Commodity consumption and the politics of the 'post-racial'. In M. G. Lacy and K. A. Ono, eds., *Critical rhetorics of race.* New York: New York University Press, pp. 178–196.

Mukherjee, R. 2020. Of experts and tokens: Mapping a critical race archaeology of communication. *Communication, Culture and Critique*, 13(2), pp. 152–167.

Murji, K. and Solomos, J. 2005. Racialization in theory and practice. In K. Murji and J. Solomos, eds., *Racialization: Studies in theory and practice*. Oxford: Oxford University Press, pp. 1–28.

Murphy, M. 2012. *Multiculturalism: A critical introduction*. Abingdon, UK, and New York: Routledge.

Murthy, D. 2010. Muslim punks online: A diasporic Pakistani music subculture on the Internet. *South Asian Popular Culture*, 8(2), pp. 181–194.

Murthy, D. and Sharma, S. 2019. Visualizing YouTube's comment space: Online hostility as a networked phenomenon. *New Media & Society*, 21(1), pp. 191–213.

Nakamura, L. 2008. *Digitizing race: Visual cultures of the Internet*. Minneapolis, MN: University of Minnesota Press.

Nakamura, L. 2013 [2002]. *Cybertypes: Race, ethnicity, and identity on the internet*. London: Routledge.

Nakamura, L. and Chow-White, P. 2012. Introduction – race and digital technology: Code, the color line, and the information society. In L. Nakamura and P. Chow-White, eds., *Race after the internet*. London: Routledge, pp. 1–19.

Negus, K. 1997. The production of culture. In P. Du Gay, ed., *Production of culture/cultures of production*. London and Thousand Oaks, CA: Sage in association with the Open University, pp. 67–118.

Ng, E., White, K.C. and Saha, A. 2020. #CommunicationSoWhite: Race and power in the academy and beyond. *Communication, Culture and Critique*, 13(2), pp. 143–151.

Nikunen, K. 2018. *Media Solidarities: Emotions, Power and Justice in the Digital Age*. London: Sage.

Noble, S.U. 2013. Google search: Hyper-visibility as a means of rendering black women and girls invisible. *InVisible Culture*, (19).

Noble, S.U. 2018. *Algorithms of oppression: How search engines reinforce racism*. New York: New York University Press.

Nwonka, C.J. 2015. Diversity pie: Rethinking social exclusion and diversity policy in the British film industry. *Journal of Media Practice*, 16(1), pp. 73–90.

Nwonka, C.J. and Malik, S. 2018. Cultural discourses and practices of institutionalised diversity in the UK film sector: 'Just get something black made'. *The Sociological Review*, 66(6), pp. 1111–1127.

O'Brien, D., Allen, K., Friedman, S. and Saha, A. 2017. *Producing and consuming inequality: A cultural sociology of the cultural industries*. London: Sage.

O'Brien, D., Laurison, D., Miles, A. and Friedman, S. 2016. Are the creative industries meritocratic? An analysis of the 2014 British Labour Force Survey. *Cultural Trends*, 25(2), pp. 116–131.

O'Connor, J. 2016. After the creative industries: Why we need a cultural economy. *Platform Papers*, 47, pp. 1–60.

Oakley, K. and O'Brien, D. 2016. Learning to labour unequally: Understanding the relationship between cultural production, cultural consumption and inequality. *Social Identities*, 22(5), pp. 471–486.

Olesen, T. 2018. Memetic protest and the dramatic diffusion of Alan Kurdi. *Media, Culture & Society*, 40(5), pp. 656–672.

Omi, M. and Winant, H. 2002. Racial formation. In P. J. M. Essed and D. T. Goldberg, eds., *Race critical theories: Text and context*. Malden, MA: Blackwell.

Parameswaran, R.E. 2006. Resuscitating feminist audience studies. In A.N. Valdivia, ed., *Media Studies*. Oxford: Wiley Blackwell, pp. 311–336.

Park, M.-J. and Curran, J. eds. 2000. *De-Westernizing media studies*. London: Routledge.

Petersen, K. 2017. Hollywood Muslims in Iraq. *Journal of Religion and Popular Culture*, 29(2), pp. 87–103.

Petersen, K. 2019. Intersectional Islamophobia: The case of a Black Ahmadi Muslim celebrity. *Journal of Africana Religions*, 7(1), pp.139–151.

Petey, J. 2006. Still no redress from the PCC. In E. Poole and J.E. Richardson, eds., *Muslims and the news media*. London: I.B. Tauris, pp. 53–62.

Pitcher, B. 2012. Race and capitalism redux. *Patterns of Prejudice*, 46(1), pp. 1–15.

Pitcher, B. 2014. *Consuming race*. London: Routledge.

Ponzanesi, S. and Leurs, K. 2014. On digital crossings in Europe. *Crossings: Journal of Migration & Culture*, 5(1), pp. 3–22.

Poole, E. 2002. *Reporting Islam: Media representations and British Muslims*. London and New York: I.B. Tauris.

Poole, E. 2011. Change and continuity in the representation of British Muslims before and after 9/11: The UK context. *Global Media Journal*, 4(2), pp. 49–62.

Poole, E. and Richardson, J.E. eds. 2006. *Muslims and the news media*. London: I.B. Tauris.

Prashad, V. 2008. *The darker nations: A people's history of the Third World*. New York: The New Press.

Prashad, V. 2013. *The poorer nations: A possible history of the Global South*. London: Verso.

Quinn, E. 2013a. Black talent and conglomerate Hollywood: Will Smith, Tyler Perry, and the continuing significance of race. *Popular Communication*, 11(3), pp. 196–210.

Quinn, E. 2013b. *Nuthin' but a' G' thang: The culture and commerce of gangsta rap*. Chichester, UK: Columbia University Press.

Rashid, N. 2016. *Veiled threats: Representing the Muslim woman in public policy discourses*. Bristol: Policy Press.

Rattansi, A. 2005. The uses of racialization: The time-spaces and subject-objects of the raced body. In K. Murji and J. Solomos, eds., *Racialization: Studies in theory and practice*. Oxford: Oxford University Press, pp. 271–301.

Renton, J. and Gidley, B. 2017. Introduction: The shared story of the history of the Muslim and Jew – a dichronic framework. In J. Renton and B. Gidley, eds., *Antisemitism and Islamophobia in Europe: A shared story?* London: Palgrave Macmillan.

Riley, K.M. 2009. How to accumulate national capital: The case of the 'good' Muslim. *Global Media Journal*, 2(2), pp. 57–71.

Robinson, C.J. 2000 [1983]. *Black Marxism: The making of the Black radical tradition* (2000 edn). Chapel Hill, NC, and London: University of North Carolina Press.

Rose, T. 1994. *Black noise: Rap music and black culture in contemporary America*. Middletown, CT: Wesleyan Press.

Ross, A. 1998. *Real love: In pursuit of cultural justice*. London: Routledge.

Ross, K. 1995. *Black and white media: Black images in popular film and television*. Cambridge, UK: Polity Press.

Saeed, A. 2007. Media, racism and Islamophobia: The representation of Islam and Muslims in the media. *Sociology Compass*, 1(2), pp. 443–462.

Saeed, A. 2016. Islam and Muslims in the media: Industry challenges and identity responses. *Muslim Perspectives*, 1(1), pp. 26–53.

Saha, A. 2012. 'Beards, scarves, halal meat, terrorists, forced marriage': Television industries and the production of 'race'. *Media, Culture & Society*, 34(4), pp. 424–438.

Saha, A. 2013. Citizen Smith more than Citizen Kane? Genres-in-progress and the cultural politics of difference. *South Asian Popular Culture*, 11(1), pp. 97–102.

Saha, A. 2016. The rationalizing/racializing logic of capital in cultural production. *Media Industries*, 3(1).

Saha, A. 2018. *Race and the cultural industries*. Cambridge: Polity Press.

Said, E. 1981. *Covering Islam: How the media and the experts determine how we see the rest of the world*. New York: Pantheon Books.

Said, E. 1991 [1978]. *Orientalism*. London: Penguin Books.

Said, E. 1993. *Culture and imperialism*. New York: Vintage.

Said, E.W. 2004. *Power, politics, and culture: Interviews with Edward W. Said*. London: Bloomsbury.

Sharma, A. 1996. Sounds oriental: The (im)possibility of theorizing Asian musical cultures. In S. Sharma, J. Hutnyk and A. Sharma, eds., *Dis-orienting rhythms: The politics of the new Asian dance music*. London: Zed Books, pp. 15–31.

Sharma, S. 1996. Noisy Asians or 'Asian noise'? In S. Sharma, J. Hutnyk and A. Sharma, eds., *Dis-orienting rhythms: The politics of the new Asian dance music*. London: Zed Books, pp. 15–31.

Sharma, S. 2013. Black Twitter? Racial hashtags, networks and contagion. *new formations: a journal of culture/theory/politics*, 78(1), pp. 46–64.

Sharma, S., Hutnyk, J. and Sharma, A. eds. 1996. *Dis-orienting rhythms: The politics of the new Asian dance music*. London: Zed Books.

Shaw, A. 2012. Do you identify as a gamer? Gender, race, sexuality, and gamer identity. *New Media & Society*, 14(1), pp. 28–44.

Shohat, E. 1992. Notes on the 'post-colonial'. *Social Text*, (31/32), pp. 99–113.

Shohat, E. and Stam, R. 2003. Introduction. In E. Shohat and R. Stam, eds., *Multiculturalism, postcoloniality, and transnational media*. New Brunswick, NJ, and London: Rutgers University Press.

Shohat, E. and Stam, R. 2014. *Unthinking Eurocentrism: Multiculturalism and the media*. London: Routledge.

Shome, R. and Hedge, R. 2002. Postcolonial approaches to communication: Charting the terrain, engaging the intersections. *Communication Theory*, 12(3), pp. 249–270.

Siapera, E. 2010. *Cultural diversity and global media: The mediation of difference*. Oxford: John Wiley & Sons.

Sivanandan, A. 1990. *Communities of resistance: Writings on black struggles for socialism*. London and New York: Verso.

Smith, D. and Deacon, D. 2018. Immigration and the British news media: Continuity or change? *Sociology Compass*, 12(9), pp. 1–13.

Sobande, F. 2017. Watching me watching you: Black women in Britain on YouTube. *European Journal of Cultural Studies*, 20(6), pp. 655–671.

Sobande, F. 2020. *The Digital Lives of Black Women in Britain*. Basingstoke: Palgrave Macmillan.

Sobande, F., Fearfull, A. and Brownlie, D. 2019. Resisting media marginalisation: Black women's digital content and collectivity. *Consumption Markets & Culture*, 23(5), pp. 413–428.

Solomos, J., Findlay, B., Jones, S. and Gilroy, P. 1982. The organic crisis of British capitalism and race: The experience of the seventies. In Centre for Contemporary Cultural Studies, ed., *Empire Strikes Back: Race and racism in 70s Britain*. London: Centre for Contemporary Cultural Studies and Hutchinson, pp. 9–46.

Spillers, H.J. 1987. Mama's baby, Papa's maybe: An American grammar book. *Diacritics*, 17(2), pp. 65–81.

Spivak, G. 1993. Foundations and cultural studies. In S. Bordo, M. Moussa and H. J. Silverman, eds., *Questioning foundations: Truth/subjectivity/culture*. New York: Routledge, pp. 153–277.

Spivak, G.C. 1999. *A critique of postcolonial reason*. Cambridge, MA, and London: Harvard University Press.

Spoonley, P. and Butcher, A. 2009. Reporting superdiversity. The mass media and immigration in New Zealand. *Journal of Intercultural Studies*, 30(4), pp. 355–372.

Stevenson, N. 2002. *Understanding media cultures: Social theory and mass communication* (2nd edn). London and Thousand Oaks, CA: Sage.

Street, J. 2012. *Music and politics*. Cambridge: Polity Press.

Taylor, C. 1994. *Multiculturalism: Examining the politics of recognition*. Princeton, NJ: Princeton University Press.

Titley, G. 2014. After the end of multiculturalism: Public service media and integrationist imaginaries for the governance of difference. *Global Media and Communication*, 10(3), pp. 247–260.

Titley, G. 2019. *Racism and media*. London: Sage.

Titley, G., Freedman, D., Khiabany, G. and Mondon, A. eds. 2017. *After Charlie Hebdo: Terror, racism and free speech*. London: Zed Books Ltd.

Uchida, A. 1998. The orientalization of Asian women in America. In *Women's Studies International Forum*. Oxford: Elsevier, pp. 161–174.

Valluvan, S. 2017. Defining and challenging the new nationalism. *Juncture*, 23(4), pp. 232–239.

Valluvan, S. 2019. *The clamour of nationalism: Race and nation in twenty-first-century Britain*. Manchester: Manchester University Press.

Van Dijk, T.A. 1988. Semantics of a press panic: The Tamil 'invasion'. *European Journal of Communication*, 3(2), pp. 167–187.

Van Dijk, T.A. 1991. *Racism and the press*. London: Routledge.

Vargas, L. 2009. *Latina teens, migration, and popular culture*. New York: Peter Lang.

Venn, C. 1999. Occidentalism and its discontents. In P. Cohen, ed., *New ethnicities, old racisms?* London and New York: Zed Books, pp. 37–62.

Virdee, S. 2019. Racialized capitalism: An account of its contested origins and consolidation. *The Sociological Review*, 67(1), pp. 3–27.

Vrikki, P. and Malik, S. 2019. Voicing lived-experience and anti-racism: Podcasting as a space at the margins for subaltern counterpublics. *Popular Communication*, 17(4), pp. 273–287.

Vukov, T. 2003. Imagining communities through immigration policies: Governmental regulation, media spectacles and the affective politics of national borders. *International Journal of Cultural Studies*, 6(3), pp. 335–353.

Waring, O. 2016. John Boyega 'really sorry' for comments on diversity during Screen Nation Awards acceptance speech. *The Metro*. [Online]. Available from: https://metro.co.uk/2016/03/20/john-boyega-really-sorry-for-comments-on-diversity-during-screen-nation-awards-acceptance-speech-5763880/?ito=cbshare [accessed 27 May 2020].

Warner, K.J. 2015a. *The cultural politics of colorblind TV casting*. New York: Routledge.

Warner, K.J. 2015b. The racial logic of *Grey's Anatomy*: Shonda Rhimes and her 'post-civil rights, post-feminist' series. *Television & New Media*, 16(7), pp. 631–647.

Willems, W. and Mano, W. eds. 2017. *Everyday media culture in Africa: Audiences and users*. New York: Routledge.

Williams, R. 1973. Base and superstructure in Marxist cultural theory. *New Left Review*, (82), pp. 3–16.

Williams, R. 2011 [1958]. Culture is ordinary. In I. Szeman and T. Kaposey, eds., *Cultural theory: An anthology*. Oxford: John Wiley & Sons, pp. 53–59.

Williamson, M. and Khiabany, G. 2010. UK: The veil and the politics of racism. *Race & Class*, 52(2), pp. 85–96.

Young, I.M. 2011. *Justice and the politics of difference*. Woodstock, UK, and Princeton, NJ: Princeton University Press.

Young, L. 1996a. *Fear of the dark: 'Race', gender and sexuality in the cinema*. London: Routledge.

Young, L. 1996b. 'Jacqueline Bobo, Black women as cultural readers; Marie Gillespie, television, ethnicity and cultural change' book reviews. *Screen*, 37(4), pp. 400–408.

Young, R.J.C. 1995. *Colonial desire: Hybridity in theory, culture and race*. London: Routledge.

Zhao, Y. and Chakravartty, P. 2007. *Global communications: Toward a transcultural political economy*. Lanham, MD: Rowman & Littlefield.

Žižek, S. 1997. Multiculturalism, or, the cultural logic of multinational capitalism. *New Left Review*, 1(225), pp. 28–51.

Zuberi, N. 2017. Listening while Muslim. *Popular Music*, 36(1), pp. 33–42.

Index

Adjepong, A., 141
affects, 22
African American studies, 152
Africana Studies, 152
After Empire (Gilroy), 75, 81
agency
  audiences and, 24, 86, 113, 173
  blackness and, 146–147
  commodification of race and, 59
  Islamophobia and, 130
  media power and, 92, 96
  postcolonial studies and, 49–50
Alexander, C., 7, 124
algorithms, 159–160
Ali, M., 134
Alsultany, E., 22, 82, 121, 132–133
alternative public spheres, 160
Althusser, L., 8, 17, 49
Anderson, B., 70, 71–72
anti-essentialism
  blackness and, 139, 143
  diaspora and, 43, 74–75
  media power and, 91
  multiculturalism and, 74–75
  new ethnicities and, 6–7, 17, 143, 152
  politics of recognition and, 10–11
  race-making and, 175–176
anti-racialism, 63
anti-racist movements
  blackness and, 138
  'bling' culture and, 67
  capitalism and, 90
  digital media and, 160–161, 164, 165
  diversity and, 64
  Marxist theory and, 98
  racial capitalism and, 54
  social justice and, 10

antisemitism, 135–136
Appadurai, A., 80, 94
Arab Council of Australia, 130
asylum seekers, 106, 158. *See also* migrants
audiences and audience studies
  overview of, 20–25, 29
  agency and, 86, 113, 173
  blackness and, 141, 146–148,
    151, 152
  digital media and, 160
  Islamophobia and, 130, 133–134
  media power and, 83–84, 88–89
  postcolonial studies and, 47, 51
  race-making and, 91–92
Augoustinos, M., 111
Austin, J., 46

Back, L., 110, 118, 168
Bailey, O., 112–113
banal nationalism, 81–82
Banet-Weiser, S., 67
Banks, M., 11–12
Barthes, R., 8
Bechdel Test, 130
Beck, U., 73
Benjamin, R., 154, 157, 159–160,
  167, 168
Bennett, S., 112
Beyoncé, 58, 141
Bhabha, H., 21, 39, 43, 51, 72, 139
Bhambra, G., 39
Bhattacharyya, G., 66
big data, 158–159
Billig, M., 81–82
biometric techniques, 158
biopolitical governance, 110
Birchall, J., 126

Hall, S.
  profile of, 17
  on audiences, 23
  on blackness, 140–141
  on capitalism and race, 62
  on culture, 19
  on English nationalism, 71
  on folk devils, 120
  Foucault and, 21
  on globalisation, 73, 96
  on hegemony and power, 13–14, 15
  on media power, 88
  on multiculturalism, 81
  on new ethnicities, 6–7, 17, 152
  on politics of representation, 21–22, 24,
    25, 29, 174–175
  on postcolonialism, 39–40
  on postmodernism, 45–46
  on primary definers, 106–107
  on race, 9, 109–110
  on race-making, 30
  on representation, 72
  on 'spectacle of the Other,' 155–156
  on stereotyping, 139
  on use of 'Black,' 138
  See also *Policing the Crisis* (Hall et al.)
Hardy, J., 97
Harindranath, R., 69, 91, 112–113
Hasinoff, A., 64
hauntology, 118
Havens, T., 146–147
Hedge, R., 41, 47–48, 51, 162, 165
hegemony, 13–14
Hesmondhalgh, D., 44, 49–50, 87, 97
Hesse, B., 14, 64
heteropatriarchy, 141
Holohan, S., 124
homophobia, 156
hooks, b., 58, 142, 156
'hostile environment' policy, 82, 107, 108
Hunt, D., 151
Husband, C., 6, 18n2, 105, 106, 117
hybrid media systems, 115
hybridity, 75

hyper-masculinity, 140–141
hypervisibility, 63, 79, 127, 145–146, 150

identity politics, 10
imaginative geography, 21, 42
imagined communities, 70
imperialism, 39, 110–112. *See also*
    colonialism
indigenisation, 80, 94
internet. *See* digital media
intersectional television, 164–165
intersectionality, 11, 139
Iraq, 124
Islamophobia
  antisemitism and, 135–136
  case study: simplified complex portray-
    als of Muslims, 132–133
  concept of, 120–121
  contestation of, 129–132
  media representations of Muslims and,
    124–129, 133–134
  Orientalism and, 49–50, 121–124,
    127–128
  postcolonial cultural economy approach
    and, 97
  postcolonial studies and, 49–50
  race and, 120–121, 123–124
  recommended and further reading
    on, 134

Jackson, P., 59–60
Jackson, S.J., 161
Jakubowicz, A., 79
James, M., 47, 168
Jhally, S., 24–25
Jong, J. de, 77

Kaepernick, C., 67
Kapoor, N., 65, 66
Keeling, K., 140, 141
Khiabany, G., 110, 123, 125, 127
Kim, H., 47
Klein, B., 108, 134
Kuo, R., 52

Made in the USA
Middletown, DE
19 April 2021